GLOBAL
FORTUNE

GLOBAL FORTUNE

THE STUMBLE AND RISE OF WORLD CAPITALISM

EDITED BY
IAN VÁSQUEZ

CATO
INSTITUTE
Washington, D.C.

A slightly different version of chapter 5 of the present work appears as "A Century of Unrivaled Prosperity," in *Keys to Prosperity: Free Markets, Sound Money, and a Bit of Luck* by Rudiger Dornbusch. Copyright © 2000 by MIT Press. Reprinted by permission. The Cato Institute thanks *Perfiles* and the Friedrich Naumann Stiftung for permission to translate and publish chapter 1 of the present work.

Library of Congress Cataloging-in-Publication Data

Global fortune: the stumble and rise of world capitalism / edited by Ian Vásquez.
    p. cm.
Includes bibliographical references and index.
ISBN 1-882577-89-2—ISBN 1-882577-90-6
    1. International finance. 2. Free enterprise 3. Capitalism. 4. Economic history—1990–. 5. Globalization. I. Vásquez, Ian. II. Cato Institute.

HG3881.G57537 2000
303.12'—dc21   00-031530

Cover design by Elise Rivera.

Printed in the United States of America.

CATO INSTITUTE
1000 Massachusetts Ave., N.W.
Washington, D.C. 20001

Contents

Acknowledgments

The publication of this book would not have been possible without the collaboration and support of a number of individuals. I owe a debt of gratitude to Cato Institute president Edward H. Crane and executive vice president David Boaz for recognizing the importance of this project and backing it with enthusiasm. As has been the case with all my work as director of the Institute's Project on Global Economic Liberty, I have been able to rely on Ted Galen Carpenter, vice president for defense and foreign policy studies at the Institute, as an invaluable source of advice and encouragement. Jacobo Rodríguez, assistant director of the Project on Global Economic Liberty, deserves special thanks for helping to organize "The Crisis in Global Interventionism," the June 1999 Cato conference at which many of the chapters in this book were first presented.

Other friends and colleagues whom I would like to thank include David Lampo, Cato's director of publications, who tried hard to keep me to the production schedule; Pat Bullock and Megan Brumleve for incorporating revisions to the manuscripts at various stages of production; Dolores Morrissy and Bill Kloman, the copyeditors who improved the quality of the book; Elise Rivera for designing an attractive cover that conveys the theme of this book; and Pablo García Albano for spending hours checking sources. I am most especially grateful to the authors of this volume for contributing to the understanding of a topic that will concern us all for a long time to come.

Introduction: The Return to a Global Economy

Ian Vásquez

After two world wars, the Great Depression, and experiments with socialism interrupted the liberal economic order that began in the 19th century, the world economy has now returned to the level of globalization that it previously enjoyed. By the 1970s, trade as a share of world economic output had already reached its pre–World War I height.[1] During the past 20 years, international integration has continued to increase with the subsequent liberalization of capital controls, reduction of trade barriers, revolutionary technological advances, and the dramatic collapse of central planning.

Compared with the 1950s and 1960s, when most of the world's population lived in economically unfree countries and only 20 percent of the world's population lived in countries with open economies,[2] the current era of global capitalism seems unprecedented. Yet John Maynard Keynes's description of the world before 1914 vividly reminds us that there was a thriving global economy during that time.

> The inhabitant of London could order by telephone, sipping his morning tea in bed, the various products of the whole earth, in such quantity as he might see fit, and reasonably expect their early delivery upon his doorstep; he could at the same moment and by the same means adventure his wealth in the natural resources and new enterprises of any quarter of the world, and share, without exertion or even trouble, in their prospective fruits and advantages. . . . He could secure forthwith, if he wished it, cheap and comfortable means of transit to any country or climate without passport or other formality, could despatch his servant to the neighboring office of a bank for such supply of the precious metals as might seem convenient, and could then proceed abroad to foreign quarters, without knowledge of their religion, language, or customs, bearing coined wealth upon his person,

and would consider himself greatly aggrieved and much
surprised at the least interference. But, most important of
all, he regarded this state of affairs as normal, certain, and
permanent, except in the direction of further improvement,
and any deviation from it as aberrant, scandalous, and
avoidable.[3]

Significant differences between the two eras of global capitalism
have resulted from the growth of government during the 20th century. For example, central banks, fiat currencies, and various
exchange-rate regimes have replaced the gold standard. Rich countries now impose extensive restrictions on immigration—a result,
as Deepak Lal explains in his chapter, of the rise of the welfare state,
which has created property rights in citizenship. Nevertheless, the
world is by most measures more integrated today than it was 100
years ago.[4] The volume of trade is greater, gross capital flows (now
at some $1.5 trillion per day) are far larger, cross-border lending is
more diversified, and international production is more complex.
Traditionally poor Latin American and Asian nations, moreover, are
experiencing high and self-sustaining growth rates, a sign that the
West's dramatic escape from poverty is an experience that can be
replicated.[5]

But the return to a global economy has been accompanied by
financial turmoil in Asia and elsewhere, prompting a range of critics
to fault markets for spreading instability and poverty. When the
Russian ruble fell in August 1998, financier George Soros asserted
that "right now, market fundamentalism is a greater threat to open
society than any totalitarianism."[6] President Clinton's call to "put a
human face on the global economy"[7] and the International Monetary
Fund's bailouts of Brazil, Russia, and Asian countries—ostensibly
intended to bolster the free market—contributed to the notion that
capitalism had somehow failed. "The proposition that utterly unregulated markets rule society more wisely than sovereign governments," journalist William Greider declared, "is being smashed
by reality."[8]

The purpose of this book is to assess such bold claims and to take
stock of the ways in which the spread of capitalism has contributed
to human progress. The contributors document how the countries
that have succumbed to economic crises in recent years, far from
having experienced an excess of market reforms, have in fact suffered

from perverse forms of state interventionism. Indeed, beginning with Mexico in 1994, all of the crisis countries maintained some combination of the following flawed policies: pegged exchange rates, state-protected banks, irresponsible monetary and fiscal policy, government-directed credit, and implicit or explicit government guarantees to domestic firms and industries. Countries with sound economies, on the other hand, did not become victims of so-called contagion. Thus it is difficult to speak of a truly international economic crisis, much less a crisis of capitalism.

The real crisis of the 20th century was otherwise. Indeed, one of the clearest lessons of the past 100 years has been that inward-looking economic policies of import substitution, development planning, capital controls, and state-owned production have impoverished both the Third World and socialist nations. One of the lessons of the 1990s was that an incoherent mix of market and interventionist policies—such as maintaining pegged exchange rates after liberalizing capital flows—is a recipe for disaster. The challenge for both the developed and developing world is to keep the process of globalization going and not to lose sight of the tremendous blessings of a liberal world economy.

The Spread of Capitalism

Mario Vargas Llosa explains in his chapter that "it is liberalism—more than any other doctrine—that symbolizes the extraordinary advances that liberty has made in the long course of human civilization." Even though classical liberalism has won the great battle of ideas over various forms of totalitarianism, Vargas Llosa warns us not to become complacent. In his view, stereotypes and caricatures are today being used to undermine economic and political freedom. A prominent part of that strategy has been the frequent use of the derisive term "neoliberal" to explain nearly every social and economic ill in society.[9]

To Vargas Llosa, who has met many liberals but no neoliberals, the term is a straw man and is emblematic of much of the misguided criticism aimed at globalization. For example, in response to the oft-heard accusation that multinational corporations behave with impunity, Vargas Llosa stresses the need to establish the proper institutional framework for a free society: "If in many developing

3

countries the behavior of multinationals is reprehensible, the ultimate responsibility rests on those who fix the rules of the game in economic, social, and political life." Thus, Vargas Llosa urges the capitalist democracies to do as much as they can to promote the rule of law and economic and political pluralism in the developing world.

Deepak Lal cautions both developed and developing countries that there is no third way between the free market and socialism. In contrast with Vargas Llosa, however, Lal finds no necessary connection between democracy and development. According to Lal, developing nations can modernize without Westernizing. People in poor countries can easily adapt to, and are eager to attain, economic freedom, but "cosmological beliefs" take longer to evolve and may not be consistent with many values the West wishes to advance.

Thus Lal warns against "the West's growing attempt to legislate its 'habits of the heart' worldwide." The West's efforts to promote labor, environmental, and other standards and its insistence on majoritarian democracy remind Lal of 19th-century imperialism, which helped unravel that era's liberal economic order. That is particularly unfortunate, since other major factors that led to the breakdown of the first era of globalization are absent today. "If the West ties its moral crusade too closely to the emerging processes of globalization," Lal concludes, "there is a danger that there will also be a backlash against the process of globalization."

In the struggle for global capitalism, the liberal cause nevertheless has the long-term advantage, Brink Lindsey contends. He analyzes the arguments of those who claim that recent financial crises have been the result of unrestrained capitalism and finds that the arguments "are illuminating in their almost perfect inversion of the truth."

The world is not seeing an overreliance on markets, a phenomenon that supposedly led to the cataclysms of the 20th century. Lindsey catalogues the anti-market forces that have created bouts of economic instability and notes the dynamics that have changed the world economy. The global economy that existed 100 years ago came to an end because of the rise of economic nationalism and a pervasive loss of faith in markets. Today, by contrast, "although globalization is charged with undermining the state, the more powerful flows of historical causation have actually been in the opposite direction: it is the retreat of the state that has allowed international market

relationships to regain a foothold." Lindsey predicts that liberalization will continue, but because of the widespread presence of statist
distortions to the market economy, that process will occur through
fits and starts in a pattern of reform, crisis, and reform.

The rewards of liberalization are amply demonstrated by the
United States, one of the consistently freest economies in the world.
Stephen Moore and the late Julian Simon document 25 U.S. trends
to show that "there has been more improvement in the human
condition for people living in the United States in the 20th century
than for all people in all previous centuries of human history combined." In the past 100 years, nearly every indicator of health, safety,
environmental quality, and affordability of consumer goods and
services has shown rapid and dramatic progress. For example, U.S.
life expectancy at birth has risen from 47 to 77 years, agricultural
productivity has increased 5- to 10-fold, diseases that used to kill
thousands of Americans per year have been extinguished, and per
capita annual income has grown from $5,000 to $30,000. Moore and
Simon believe that the gains of the 20th century are part of a long-
term trend. Those gains are virtually irreversible because they are
based primarily on advances in knowledge, which, in the information age, are difficult to erase or suppress.

As Rudiger Dornbusch notes in his chapter, the 20th century was
a time of unrivaled prosperity not only for rich countries but also
for mankind in general. That was particularly true of the past three
decades, during which developing nations began to enjoy sustained
high growth rates. By most measures, "1900 was the stone age
compared with where we stand today," Dornbusch observes. The
world wars and the Great Depression turned out to be tragic but were
momentary setbacks on the path to the most rapid improvements in
living standards on record. To keep the world economy on the right
track, Dornbusch advises that it adopt "a heavy dose of prosperity
policies," including deregulation in Europe and more expansionary
monetary policy in Japan.

Asia, Latin America, and Russia

When currency and financial crises erupted in Thailand, South
Korea, and Indonesia in 1997, many observers concluded that the
"Asian miracle" was a fraud. Bill McGurn explains that, despite the
turmoil, East Asian countries have achieved remarkable progress in

pulling millions of people out of poverty in the past few decades. He notes, however, that, although detractors of globalization have exaggerated Asia's failures, some proponents of globalization have overstated Asia's successes. Many of the region's countries, after all, maintained highly inefficient systems of capital allocation. Those countries that relied most heavily on government-directed credit and protection of politically favored industries suffered the most during the crisis (e.g., Korea and Indonesia); those that intervened less fared much better (Hong Kong and Singapore). Thus, the varied Asian policy landscape gives clues about the solution to the region's problems: the troubled nations must move away from Asian-style corporatism and toward liberalization.

Tomas Larsson's account of the causes of the Asian debacle concurs with McGurn's observations. Close ties between government and business led to massive malinvestments that were politically, rather than market, determined. Once the crisis broke out, the IMF made matters worse by helping to bail out clearly bankrupt institutions and by creating uncertainty in the region with its drawn-out, bureaucratic negotiation process. Larsson observes that the region's recent economic recovery is due mostly to lower exchange rates and interest-rate cuts but that fundamental structural reform has yet to take place. He believes that globalization will promote those reforms and finds it ironic that so many Western proponents of "globalization with a human face" advocate such measures as capital controls, which the region's dictators have so effectively used before to repress their populations.

Byeong-Ho Gong describes the "Korean sickness" that led to the country's financial crisis and reports that the crisis itself compelled Korea to introduce extensive reforms in its labor, industrial, financial, and government sectors. The economy has rapidly improved, but, according to Gong, it would be misleading "to conclude that the government's economic reforms have strengthened the fundamentals of the Korean economy." Korea still needs a paradigm shift. Instead of letting a market-based financial system determine the restructuring of the *chaebol* (large conglomerates) through a process of creative destruction, the government has nationalized the banks and instructed the chaebol to engage in certain business activities. Gong categorizes that newly emerging industrial policy as destructive reform and worries that it is the same kind of government-business relationship that got the country into trouble in the first place.

6

In his chapter, Martín Krause relates how Latin America emerged in the 1990s, after successive cycles of populism and IMF-led adjustment programs, to introduce far-ranging market reforms. Those changes were not imposed from outside; rather, they resulted from a Latin American consensus based on the region's dismal experience with state-led development planning. Yet the fall of the Mexican peso and the Brazilian real and the collapse of the Ecuadoran and Venezuelan economies show that the region's free-market revolution remains unfinished.

According to Krause, the remaining agenda includes fiscal reform (both tax rates and tax evasion remain high), institutional reform (the separation of powers is still nonexistent in many countries), and deregulation (bureaucratic obstacles hamper entrepreneurial activity and harm small and medium businesses). Likewise, Latin American governments have not reformed social services, though they have devoted more resources to them with few or no results. Krause concludes that failure to complete such reforms may lead to periodic eruptions of social and economic turmoil.

In Russia, nine years of "reforms" have barely moved the country from the plan to the market, according to Andrei Illarionov. Indeed, Russia is still among the least economically free countries in the world. The 1998 financial crisis, which was "the culmination of years of misguided policy," wiped out the country's few successes—namely, low inflation and exchange-rate stability. Illarionov describes a country in which a corruption-plagued government has increasingly interfered in the economy and in which "domestic economic liberalization effectively stopped in mid-1992." The real struggle over the past eight years in Russia has been not between liberal reformers and old-line statists but rather over who or whose team would win control over the state institutions in charge of distributing economic resources.

Unfortunately, the IMF and other lending institutions have helped sustain that situation by providing Russia with more than $25 billion in credits. Because Moscow has for years been uninterested in reform, Illarionov asserts that IMF credits have actually "postponed the implementation of a coherent economic strategy . . . and have reduced the willingness of national authorities to make painful, but necessary changes in economic policies." The most perverse and discouraging legacy of the "transition" period, however, is that, in the minds of many Russians, the free market itself has been discredited.

The International Financial System

The increasing frequency and severity of financial crises, accompanied by more than $180 billion in IMF-led bailout packages since 1997, have forced a reexamination of the "global financial architecture." The instability has also caused many observers to look back fondly to the golden era of Bretton Woods, when the IMF managed the international system of pegged exchange rates. British prime minister Tony Blair, for example, called for "a new Bretton Woods for the next millennium."[10] Francis Gavin questions whether the Bretton Woods system ever did really function.

In Gavin's view, the system was doomed to failure because its reliance on pegged exchange rates and independent monetary policies made it prone to instability once currency convertibility began to be introduced in the late 1950s. In the absence of a reliable adjustment mechanism, the system went from crisis to crisis as countries suddenly and massively changed their exchange-rate parities without the IMF's approval. The current nostalgia for Bretton Woods is even more unfounded now that the world's major countries have moved to flexible exchange rates.

A more liberal world economy requires that borrowers and creditors be more responsible for their investment decisions. That is one reason Onno de Beaufort Wijnholds and Arend Kapteyn oppose proposals to turn the IMF into an international lender of last resort. Not only would such a function be unfeasible—unlike domestic central banks, the IMF has no ability to print its own money or effectively monitor the solvency of the entities to which it provides liquidity—it would also be undesirable because it would increase the moral hazard that has been part of recent IMF financial packages. Wijnholds and Kapteyn believe that the IMF should still play a role as an indispensable lender but that, with large-scale financing, "there is a danger that the IMF could be shifting in the wrong direction."

In the following two chapters, Larry White and I go much further. White agrees that the fund should not become an international lender of last resort and argues that developing countries would be better off without the IMF. In a world of national fiat currencies, a laissez-faire alternative to the current international financial system would be characterized by the only two exchange-rate regimes compatible with free markets: free-floating rates and fully fixed rates.

The lack of an official lender of last resort under fixed exchange rates (as in the case of dollarization and currency boards), however, does not mean that there would be no lenders of last resort; private lenders can fulfill and have fulfilled that function. The disadvantage of floating rates is that the presence of domestic central banks increases the risk of exchange-rate swings. The historical record shows that, in those banking systems closest to laissez faire, contagion effects have been virtually absent. IMF lending, by contrast, contributes to contagion by subsidizing risky investment behavior. Ending IMF interventions would substantially reduce such moral hazard.

In the final chapter, I describe how the IMF has been at the center of a crisis-generating system in the international economy. Indeed, over the past 20 years, a dysfunctional relationship between lenders and borrowers has become more acute, as evidenced by financial crises in the 1990s. Through official lending and mediation, usually led by the IMF, authorities have reduced the possibility of sovereign default in an effort to stop the spread of financial turmoil. But that strategy has shielded investors and debtors from economic reality.

The historical experience suggests that direct two-party bargaining between creditors and debtors is a less traumatic way of handling financial crises than is the current approach, in which the IMF has become a burdensome third party. Indeed, private investors in the 19th and 20th centuries regularly solved collective-action problems and provided so-called public goods that official lending agencies today intend to provide. Default, or the real possibility of default, led to renegotiations of debt conditioned on reforms in the debtor country.

IMF interventions, on the other hand, have not been characterized by fundamental reforms based on credible conditionality, as recent experiences in Russia, Brazil, and East Asia demonstrate. The Third World debt crisis of the 1980s also showed how the fund's lending created among all parties a stalemate that postponed recovery for years. Thus, I advocate closing the IMF, because its interventions are disruptive of an increasingly liberal world economy. In a world without the IMF, economic decisions would be more decentralized and market institutions in insurance, credit, and surveillance would do much more to stabilize the international financial system than would continued interventions.

Global Fortune

The welfare of humanity is in large part tied to the fortune of capitalism itself. We must not again allow globalization to "stumble" because of a loss of faith in liberal institutions. The consequences of doing so would be devastating to world prosperity and peace. That is why it is important to dispel erroneous notions about global capitalism before they become enduring myths that influence policymakers and the public at large.

This book attempts to contribute to that effort. Drawing lessons from a century that began and ended with globalization, the authors in this volume take a generally optimistic view of the prospects of the new era of global capitalism. Their sentiments are summed up by Vargas Llosa, who writes, "We should celebrate the achievements of liberalism with joy and serenity, but without triumphalist hubris. . . . That which remains to be done is more important still."

Notes

1. International Monetary Fund, *World Economic Outlook* (Washington: IMF, May 1997), p. 112.

2. Jeffrey D. Sachs and Andrew Warner, "Economic Reform and the Process of Global Integration," Development Discussion Paper no. 552, Harvard Institute of International Development, September 1996, p. 12.

3. John Maynard Keynes, *The Economic Consequences of the Peace* (New York: Harcourt, Brace and Howe, 1920), pp. 11–12.

4. See Michael D. Bordo, Barry Eichengreen, and Douglas Irwin, "Is Globalization Today Really Different Than Globalization a Hundred Years Ago?" in *Brookings Trade Forum 1999*, ed. Susan M. Collins and Robert Z. Lawrence (Washington: Brookings Institution Press, 1999), pp. 1–72.

5. Andrea Boltho and Gianni Toniolo, "The Assessment: The Twentieth Century—Achievements, Failures, Lessons," *Oxford Review of Economic Policy* 15, no. 4 (1999): 4.

6. Quoted in David E. Sanger, "Clinton Appeals for Joint Attack in Economic Crisis," *New York Times*, October 6, 1998, p. A12. *Business Week* also declared that "the first and biggest task is to tame the anarchy of markets that globalization has unleashed." See Michael J. Mandel and Dean Foust, "How to Reshape the World Financial System," *Business Week*, October 12, 1998, p. 113.

7. William Jefferson Clinton, "State of the Union Address," January 19, 1999.

8. William Greider, "Breakdown of Free-Market Orthodoxy," *Washington Post*, October 7, 1998, p. A21.

9. That tendency was especially evident in Mexico after its peso crashed in 1994. Ironically, few people recalled Milton Friedman's visit to Mexico in 1992, when he emphatically urged the country to move away from its pegged exchange rate system

because of its inflationary and destabilizing potential. See Hiram Ordóñez Morales, "Necesario Liberar la Paridad Cambiaria del Peso Frente al Dólar: Friedman" (Friedman: It's Necessary to Liberalize the Peso-Dollar Exchange Rate) *El Economista* (Mexico City), May 20, 1992. At the time, that suggestion met with severe criticism by prominent members of the business community, the ruling party, the press, and the far left. One headline in an edition of *El Financiero*, the leading financial newspaper, typified the sentiment: "Friedman Does Not Have the Most Minimum Understanding of Mexican History, Say the PRI and PRD" (May 26, 1992).

    10. Quoted in David Wighton, "Blair Urges Big IMF Overhaul," *Financial Times*, September 28, 1998, p. 4.

PART I

THE SECOND ERA OF GLOBAL CAPITALISM

1. Liberalism in the New Millennium

Mario Vargas Llosa

A short time ago, the town council of El Borge, a tiny town in the Spanish province of Málaga, held a plebiscite of its thousand inhabitants. The citizens were asked to decide between two alterna-tives: humanity or neoliberalism. The result of the poll was 515 votes for humanity and 4 votes for neoliberalism. Since that time, I have not been able to chase those four votes from my thoughts. In the face of such a dramatic dilemma, those four musketeers did not hesitate to charge against humanity in the name of the macabre scarecrow of neoliberalism. Were they four clowns or four sages? Was this a "Borgean" joke or was it the only sign of sense in the entire farcical plebiscite?

Not long after, in Chiapas, an International Congress against Neo-liberalism was convened by Subcomandante Marcos, the latest hero of the frivolous, media-driven politics of the West. Among the atten-dees were numerous Hollywood luminaries, a belated Gaullist (my friend Regis Debray), and Danielle Mitterrand, the incessant widow of President François Mitterrand, who gave her socialist benediction to the event.

Those are quaint episodes, but it would be a grave error to write them off as the insignificant fluttering of human idiocy. In truth, they are but the tense and explosive extremes of a vast political and ideological movement, solidly rooted in sectors of the left, center, and right, and united in a tenacious distrust of liberty as an instrument for the solution to the problems of humanity. They have built up their fears into a new phantom and called it "neoliberalism." In the mumbo jumbo of sociologists and political scientists, it is also known as the "only thought," a scapegoat on which to hang both present calamities and those of the past in world history.

Brainy professors from the universities of Paris, Harvard, and Mexico pull their hair out trying to show that free markets serve for little more than making the rich richer and the poor poorer. They

15

tell us that internationalization and globalization only benefit the giant multinationals, allowing them to squeeze developing countries to the point of asphyxiation and entirely devastate the planetary ecology. So it should not surprise us that the uninformed citizens of El Borge or Chiapas believe that the true enemy of mankind— guilty of all evil, suffering, poverty, exploitation, discrimination, abuses, and crimes against human rights committed on five continents against millions of human beings—is that terrifying, destructive entelechy known as neoliberalism. It is not the first time in history that what Karl Marx called a "fetish"—an artificial construction, but at the service of very concrete interests—acquired consistency and began to provoke such great disruptions in life, like the genie who was imprudently catapulted into existence when Aladdin rubbed the magic lamp.

I consider myself a liberal. I know many people who are liberals, and many more who are not. But, throughout a career that is beginning to be a long one, I have not known a single neoliberal. What does a neoliberal stand for? What is a neoliberal against? In contrast with Marxism, or the various kinds of fascism, true liberalism does not constitute a dogma, a closed and self-sufficient ideology with prefabricated responses to all social problems. Rather, liberalism is a doctrine that, beyond a relatively simple and clear combination of basic principles structured around a defense of political and economic liberty (that is, of democracy and the free market), welcomes a great variety of tendencies and hues. What it has not included until now, nor will include in the future, is that caricature furnished by its enemies with the nickname neoliberal.

A "neo" is someone who pretends to be something, someone who is at the same time inside and outside of something; it is an elusive hybrid, a straw man set up without ever identifying a specific value, idea, regime, or doctrine. To say "neoliberal" is the same as saying "semiliberal" or "pseudoliberal." It is pure nonsense. Either one is in favor of liberty or against it, but one cannot be semi-in-favor or pseudo-in-favor of liberty, just as one cannot be "semipregnant," "semiliving," or "semidead." The term has not been invented to express a conceptual reality, but rather, as a corrosive weapon of derision, it has been designed to semantically devalue the doctrine of liberalism. And, as we enter the new millennium, it is liberalism— more than any other doctrine—that symbolizes the extraordinary advances that liberty has made in the long course of human civilization.

We should celebrate the achievements of liberalism with joy and serenity, but without triumphalist hubris. We must be clear in understanding that although the achievements of liberalism are notable, that which remains to be done is more important still. Moreover, as nothing in human history is fated or permanent, the progress obtained in these last decades by the culture of liberty is not irreversible. Unless we know how to defend it, the culture of liberty can become stagnant and the free world will lose ground to the forces of authoritarian collectivism and tribalism. Donning the new masks of nationalism and religious fanaticism, those forces have replaced communism as the most battle-hardened adversaries of democracy.

For a liberal, the most important thing to occur in this century was the defeat of the great totalitarian offensives against the culture of liberty. Fascism and communism, each in its moment, came to threaten the survival of democracy. Now they belong to the past, to the dark history of violence and unspeakable crimes against human rights and rationality, and there is no indication that they will rise from their ashes in the immediate future. Of course, reminiscences of fascism linger in the world. At times, ultra-nationalist and xenophobic parties, much like Jean Marie Le Pen's National Front in France or Jörg Haider's Liberal Party in Austria, attract a dangerously high level of electoral support. Also, there exist anachronistic vestiges of the vast Marxist archipelago, represented today by the flagging specters of Cuba and North Korea. Even so, those fascist and communist offshoots do not constitute a serious alternative— less still a considerable threat—to the democratic option.

Dictatorships still abound, true enough, but in contrast to the great totalitarian empires, they lack messianic aura and ecumenical pretensions; many of them, like China, are now trying to combine the monolithic politics of the single-party state with free-market economics and private enterprise. In vast regions of Africa and Asia, above all in Islamic societies, fundamentalist dictatorships have arisen that have returned those countries to a state of barbaric primitivism in matters concerning women, education, information, and basic civic and moral rights. Still, whatever the horror represented by countries like Libya, Afghanistan, Sudan, or Iran, they are not challenges that the culture of liberty needs to take seriously: the backwardness of the ideology they profess condemns those regimes to fall ever farther behind in the race of modernity—a swift race, in which the free countries have already taken a decisive lead.

Despite the gloomy geography of persistent dictatorships, liberals have much to celebrate in these last decades. The culture of liberty has made overwhelming advances in vast regions of Central and Western Europe, Southeast Asia, and Latin America. In Latin America, for the first time in history, civilian governments—born of more or less free elections—are in power in nearly every country. (The exceptions are Cuba, an explicit dictatorship, and Peru, a subtle dictatorship.) Even more notably, those democracies are now applying—sometimes with more gritting of teeth than enthusiasm, sometimes with more clumsiness than skill—market policies, or at least policies that are closer to a free economy than to the interventionist and nationalizing populism that traditionally characterized the governments of the continent.

Perhaps the most significant thing about that change in Latin America is not the quantity, but the quality. Although it is still common to hear intellectuals who have been thrown out of work by the collapse of collectivist ideology howling at neoliberalism, their howls are like those of wolves to the moon. From one end of Latin America to the other, at least for now, a solid consensus exists in favor of the democratic system and against dictatorial regimes and collectivist utopias. Although that consensus is more restricted with regard to economic policy, Latin American governments are also bowing to liberal economic doctrine. Some governments are embarrassed to confess that, and others—including some real Tartuffes—cover their bases by spewing out volleys of rhetoric against neoliberalism. Nevertheless, they have no other recourse than to privatize businesses, liberalize prices, open markets, attempt to control inflation, and try to integrate their economies into international markets. They have come to learn—the hard way—that in today's economic environment, the country that does not follow those guidelines commits suicide. Or, in less terrifying terms—that country condemns itself to poverty, decay, and even disintegration. Many sectors of the Latin American left have evolved from being bitter enemies of economic liberty to embracing the wise confession of Václav Havel: "Though my heart may be left of centre, I have always known that the only economic system that works is a market economy. . . . This is the only natural economy, the only kind that makes sense, the only one that can lead to prosperity, because it is the only one that reflects the nature of life itself."[1]

Those signs of progress are important and give historical validity to liberal theses. By no means, however, do they justify complacency, since one of the most refined (and rare) certainties of liberalism is that historical determinism does not exist. History has not been written so as to negate any further appeal. History is the work of men, and just as men can act rightly with measures that push history in the direction of progress and civilization, they can also err, and by conviction, apathy, or cowardice, allow history to slide into anarchy, impoverishment, obscurantism, and barbarism. The culture of democracy can gain new ground and consolidate the advances it has achieved. Or, it can watch its dominions shrink into nothingness, like Balzac's *peau de chagrin*. The future depends on us—on our ideas, our votes, and the decisions of those we put into power.

For liberals, the war for the progress of liberty in history is, above all else, an intellectual struggle, a battle of ideas. The Allies won the war against the Axis, but that military victory did little more than confirm the superiority of a vision of man and society that is broad, horizontal, pluralist, tolerant, and democratic over a vision that was narrow-minded, truncated, racist, discriminatory, and vertical. The disintegration of the Soviet empire before the democratic West validated the arguments of Adam Smith, Alexis de Tocqueville, Karl Popper, and Isaiah Berlin concerning the open society and the free economy, and invalidated the fatal arrogance of ideologues like Karl Marx, V. I. Lenin, and Mao Zedong, who were convinced that they had unraveled the inflexible laws of history and interpreted them correctly with their proletarian dictatorships and economic centralism. We should also remember that the West achieved its victory over communism at a time when its societies were full of inferiority complexes: ordinary democracy offered scant "sex appeal" next to the fireworks of the supposedly classless societies of the communist world.

The present battle is perhaps less arduous for liberals than the one that our teachers fought. In that battle, central planners, police states, single-party regimes, and state-controlled economies had on their side an empire that was armed to the teeth, as well as a formidable public relations campaign, conducted in the heart of democracy by a fifth column of intellectuals seduced by socialist ideas. Today, the battle that we must join is not against great totalitarian thinkers, like Marx, or intelligent social democrats like John Maynard Keynes but, rather, against stereotypes and caricatures that attempt to introduce doubt and confusion in the democratic camp; hence the multiple offensive launched from various trenches against the monster nicknamed neoliberalism. The battle is also against the apocalyptics, a new species of skeptical thinker. Instead of opposing the culture of democracy, as did Georg Lukacs, Antonio Gramsci, or Jean-Paul Sartre, the apocalyptics are content to deny it, assuring us that democracy does not really exist and that we are dealing with a fiction, behind which lurks the ominous shadow of despotism.

Of that species, I would like to single out an emblematic case: that of Robert D. Kaplan. In a provocative essay,[2] he maintains that, contrary to the optimistic expectations about the future of democracy heralded by the death of Marxism in Eastern Europe, humanity is actually headed toward a world dominated by authoritarianism. In some cases, this authoritarianism is undisguised; in others, it is masked by institutions of civil and liberal appearance. For Kaplan those institutions are mere decorations. The real power is—or will soon be—in the hands of giant international corporations, the owners of technology and capital that, thanks to their ubiquity and extraterritoriality, enjoy almost total impunity in their actions.

"I submit that the democracy we are encouraging in many poor parts of the world is an integral part of a transformation toward new forms of authoritarianism; that democracy in the United States is at greater risk than ever before, and from obscure sources; and that many future regimes, ours especially, could resemble the oligarchies of ancient Athens and Greece more than they do the current government in Washington."[3]

His analysis is particularly negative with regard to the possibility that democracy may be able to find root in the developing world.

According to Kaplan, all Western efforts to impose democracy in countries that lack a democratic tradition have resulted in terrible failures. Some of those failures have been very costly, as in Cambodia, where $2 billion invested by the international community have not advanced legality or liberty even a single millimeter in the ancient kingdom of Angkor. The result of those efforts in places like Sudan, Algeria, Afghanistan, Bosnia, Sierra Leone, Congo, Mali,

Russia, Albania, or Haiti have created chaos, civil wars, terrorism, and the resurgence of ferocious tyrannies that apply ethnic cleansing or commit genocide against religious minorities.

Kaplan looks with similar disdain upon the Latin American process of democratization. The exceptions are Chile and Peru. The fact that the first experienced the explicit dictatorship of Augusto Pinochet and the second is going through the oblique dictatorship of Alberto Fujimori and the armed forces guarantees, in his view, stability to those countries. By comparison, the so-called rule of law is incapable of preserving that stability in Colombia, Venezuela, Argentina, or Brazil where, in his judgment, the weakness of civil institutions, the excesses of corruption, and the astronomical inequalities are pushing "a backlash from millions of badly educated and newly urbanized dwellers in teeming slums, who see few palpable benefits to Western parliamentary systems."[4]

Kaplan wastes no time in circumlocutions. He says what he thinks with clarity, and what he thinks is that democracy and the developing world are incompatible: "Social stability results from the establishment of a middle class. Not democracies but authoritarian systems, including monarchies, create middle classes."[5] He cites the examples of the Asian Pacific Basin (his prime exponent is the Singapore of Lee Kuan Yew) and Pinochet's Chile. Although he does not mention it, he could have also cited Francisco Franco's Spain. The present-day authoritarian regimes he sees creating middle classes and making democracy possible are the China of "market socialism" and Fujimori's Peru (a military dictatorship with a civilian puppet as figurehead). Those are the models of development that he sees as forging "prosperity from abject poverty."[6] For Kaplan the choice in the developing world is not "between dictators and democrats" but between "bad dictatorships and slightly better ones."[7] In his opinion, "Russia may be failing in part because it is a democracy and China may be succeeding in part because it is not."[8]

I have taken the space to review these arguments because Kaplan has the merit of saying out loud what others—many others—think but do not dare to say, or only say in whispers. Kaplan's pessimism with respect to the developing world is great; but it is not less than that inspired in him by the developed world. Once the efficient dictatorships have developed the poor countries and the new middle classes seek to gain access to Western-style democracy, they will only be chasing a mirage. Western democracy will have been supplanted by a system (similar to those of Athens and Sparta) in which oligarchies—the multinational corporations, operating on the five continents—will have snatched from governments the power to make significant decisions for society and the individual. The oligarchies will exercise that power without accountability, because power comes to the giant corporations not by electoral mandate but through their technological and economic strength. In case the reader is unaware of the statistics, Kaplan reminds us that out of the top 100 economies in the world, 51 are not countries, but businesses, and that the 500 most powerful companies alone represent 70 percent of world commerce.

Those arguments are a good point of departure for comparison with the liberal vision of the state of things in the world here on the cusp of the new millennium. In the liberal vision, the human creation of liberty, even with the abundant disorder it has caused, is the source of the most extraordinary advances in the fields of science, human rights, technical progress, and the fight against despotism and exploitation.

The most outlandish of Kaplan's arguments is that only dictatorships create middle classes and bring stability to countries. If that were so, the paradise of the middle classes would not be the United States, Western Europe, Canada, Australia, and New Zealand, but Mexico, Bolivia, or Paraguay. Latin American history is a veritable zoo of petty tyrants, strongmen, and maximum leaders. Juan Domingo Perón—to give but one example—nearly destroyed the middle class of Argentina—a middle class that until his rise to power was vast, prosperous, and had developed its country at a faster pace than most of the European countries. Forty years of dictatorship have not brought Cuba the least prosperity, but have reduced it to the status of an international beggar; to keep from starving, Cubans have been condemned to eat grass and flowers, while their women prostitute themselves to capitalist tourists.

Of course, Kaplan can say that he is not talking about all dictatorships, but only the efficient ones like those of Pacific Asia and those of Pinochet and Fujimori. I read his essay—coincidentally enough—just when the supposedly efficient autocracy of Indonesia was crumbling, General Suharto was renouncing his office under pressure, and the Indonesian economy was collapsing. Shortly before that, the ex-autocracies of Korea and Thailand had collapsed and the famous Asian Tigers had begun to vanish into smoke, like something out of a Hollywood super-thriller. Apparently, those market dictatorships were not as successful as Kaplan thought. They are now gathered on their knees before the International Monetary Fund, the World Bank, the United States, Japan, and Western Europe, asking to be saved from total ruin.

From the economic point of view, the dictatorship of General Pinochet was successful, and up to a certain point (that is, if efficiency is measured only in terms of the rate of inflation, the fiscal deficit, official reserves, and the growth rate of gross domestic product), so is Fujimori's dictatorship. Even so, we are talking about a very relative efficiency. When we leave the comfortable security of an open society (the United States, in Kaplan's case) and examine those regimes from the perspective of those who have suffered the crimes and outrages of dictatorship, that relative efficiency vanishes. In contrast with Kaplan, we liberals do not believe that ending economic populism—or snapping the neck of inflation—constitutes the slightest progress for a society if, at the same time that prices are freed, public spending is cut, and the public sector is privatized, a government causes its citizens to live in abject fear. Progress does not run roughshod over the rights of citizens. Progress does not deprive citizens of a free press or deny them recourse to an independent judiciary when they are abused or defrauded. Progress does not permit that citizens be tortured, expropriated, disappeared, or killed, according to the whim of a country's ruling gang. Under liberal doctrine, progress is simultaneously economic, political, and cultural. Or, simply, it is not progress. That is for practical as well as moral reasons. Open societies, in which information circulates without impediment and in which the rule of law governs, are better defended against crises than satraps. That was demonstrated by the Mexican PRI (Institutional Revolutionary Party) regime several years ago and more recently by General Suharto in Indonesia. The role performed by the lack of genuine legality in the authoritarian countries of the Pacific Basin has not been sufficiently underlined in the current crisis.

How many efficient dictatorships have there been? And how many inefficient ones? How many dictatorships have sunk their countries into prerational savagery, as is happening today in Algeria and Afghanistan? The great majority of dictatorships are of the inefficient variety; efficient ones are the exception. Is it not reckless to opt for the recipe of dictatorship to achieve development—to hope that such a regime will be efficient, decent, and transitory— and not the contrary? Are there not less risky and cruel paths to economic progress? Indeed, there are, but people like Kaplan do not wish to see them.

In countries in which democracy flourishes, the culture of liberty is not necessarily a longstanding tradition. It was not a tradition in any of the current democracies until, after many setbacks and trials, those societies chose that culture and moved forward, perfecting it along the way, until they made that culture their own. International pressure and aid can be a factor of the first order in a society's adoption of democratic culture, as demonstrated by the examples of Germany and Japan, two countries as lacking in democratic tradition as any in Latin America. In the short time since the end of World War II, they have joined the advanced democracies of the world. Why, then, would developing countries (or Russia) be unable to free themselves from the authoritarian tradition? Why would they be unable to do as the Japanese and Germans did, and make the culture of liberty theirs?

Contrary to the pessimistic conclusions that Kaplan reaches, globalization opens up a first-class opportunity for the democratic countries of the world—and especially for the advanced democracies of America and Europe—to contribute to expanding tolerance, pluralism, legality, and liberty. Many countries are still slaves to the authoritarian tradition, but we should remember that authoritarianism once held sway over all of humanity. The expansion of the culture of liberty is possible as long as the following occur:

(a) We have a clear belief in the superiority of this culture over those that legitimize fanaticism, intolerance, and racism, and that legitimize religious, ethnic, political, or sexual discrimination.

(b) We adopt coherent economic and foreign policies, orienting them in such a way that at the same time as they encourage democratic tendencies in the developing world, they penalize and discriminate automatically against those regimes that, like China's or the civilian-military crony-state of Peru's, promote liberal policies in the economic field but are dictatorial in their politics.

Unfortunately, contrary to Kaplan's position, the kind of discrimination in favor of democracy that brought so many benefits to countries like Germany, Italy, and Japan a half century ago has not been applied by the democratic countries of today to the rest of the world. When it has been applied, it has been done in a partial and hypocritical manner, as in the case of Cuba.

With the advent of the new millennium, however, the advanced democracies of the world have a stronger incentive to act with firm and principled conviction in favor of democracy. That incentive comes from the existence of a new danger, a danger that Kaplan mentions in his essay. In apocalyptic terms, Kaplan prophesies the emergence of a future nondemocratic world government composed of powerful multinational corporations that operate without restraint in all corners of the globe. That catastrophic vision points to the real danger of which we are conscious. The disappearance of economic borders and the proliferation of world markets stimulate fusion and alliance between businesses as they attempt to compete more effectively in all areas of production.

The formation of giant corporations does not constitute in and of itself a danger to democracy as long as democracy is a reality, that is to say, as long as there are just laws and strong governments. (For a liberal, "strong" means "small and effective," rather than "big.") In a market economy that is open to competition, a big corporation benefits the consumer because its scale enables it to reduce prices and multiply services. It is not in the size of a business in which danger lies; the danger lies in monopoly, which is always a source of inefficiency and corruption. As long as there are democratic governments that command respect for the law—governments that will even prosecute Bill Gates if he transgresses that law—there is no danger. As long as democratic governments maintain markets that are open to competition and are free of monopolies, then there is nothing to fear from giant corporations, which frequently serve society by spearheading scientific and technological progress.

The capitalist firm has the nature of a chameleon. In a democratic country, it is a beneficent institution of development and progress. However, in countries in which there is no rule of law, no free markets, and in which everything is resolved by the absolute will of a leader or a ruling clique, the capitalist firm can be a source of catastrophe. Corporations are amoral, and they adapt with ease to the rules of the game in the environment in which they operate. If in many developing countries the behavior of multinationals is reprehensible, the ultimate responsibility rests on those who fix the rules of the game in economic, social, and political life. We cannot blame firms for following those rules in their quest for profits.

From that reality, Kaplan extracts this pessimistic conclusion: the future of democracy is gloomy because in the coming millennium the giant corporations will act in the United States and Western Europe with the same impunity that they currently do in, say, the Nigeria of the late Colonel Abacha.

In truth, there is no historical or conceptual reason for such an extrapolation. Instead, we should reach the following conclusion: it is imperative that all countries today under dictatorship evolve quickly toward democracy and develop the kind of free legal order that can demand of corporations that they act decently and equitably, as they are required to do in the advanced democracies. Without the globalization of legality and liberty, economic globalization presents a serious danger for the future of civilization—and, above all, for the planetary ecology. The great powers have a moral obligation to promote democratic processes in the developing world. They also have a practical obligation. With the evaporation of borders, the greatest guarantee that economic forces will benefit all people is to ensure that throughout the world economic life flows within the limits of liberty and competition, and is guided by the incentives, rights, and restraints imposed by democratic society.

None of that will be easy, and none of it will be achieved in a short time. For liberals, however, it is a great incentive to know that we are working toward an attainable goal. The idea of a world united around a culture of liberty is not a utopia but a beautiful and achievable reality that justifies our efforts. As Karl Popper, one of our greatest teachers, said,

"Optimism is a duty. The future is open. It is not predetermined. No one can predict it, except by chance. We all contribute to determining it by what we do. We are all equally responsible for its success."

Notes

This essay was translated by Tom Jenney.

1. Václav Havel, *Summer Meditations* (Toronto: Vintage Books, 1992), p. 62.

2. Robert D. Kaplan, "Was Democracy Just a Moment?" *Atlantic Monthly*, December 1997, pp. 55–80.
3. Ibid., pp. 55–56.
4. Ibid., p. 58.
5. Ibid., p. 61.
6. Ibid., p. 68.
7. Ibid., p. 58.
8. Ibid., p. 61.

2. The Challenge of Globalization: There Is No Third Way

Deepak Lal

In thinking about globalization, I like to imagine a Rip Van Winkle who had gone to sleep in about 1870, and has just awakened. He would find that little has changed in the world economy. He would note the various technological advances in transportation and communications (aircraft, telephones, and computers). These advances have further reduced the costs of international trade and commerce and led to the progressive integration of the world economy, which was well under way—after the first Great Age of Reform—when he went to sleep.

He would not have known of the terrible events of this century: two world wars, the Great Depression, and the battles against two illiberal creeds—fascism and communism—that led to the breakdown of the first liberal international economic order (LIEO) created under British leadership after the repeal of the Corn Laws. Nor would the various and varying fads in economic policy—both national and international—during this century make any sense, including, for example, exchange controls, the use of quotas rather than tariffs as instruments of protection, centralized planning and its associated controls on production and distribution, as well as restrictions on the free flow of capital.

He would be surprised by two features of the current world economy. Unlike the 19th century, when there was free movement of goods, money, and people, today there are relatively free flows of goods and money but there is no free movement of labor. This is related to the second surprising feature he would soon observe: the welfare states to be found in most advanced countries have created property rights in citizenship. This necessarily leads to restrictions on immigration because immigration creates new citizens with an automatic right of access to the purses of existing citizens through the transfer state.

He would also not be surprised that, as more and more developing countries, particularly India and China with their vast pools of relatively cheap labor, are brought into an integrated world economy, a new international division of labor is emerging, with developed countries mainly providing services and developing ones manufactures. With this spatial division between the "head" and the "body" of economic activity, trade is becoming essential for the well-being of all countries.

Being of a curious mind he would read about the events that took place during the time he was asleep, and find a world gone mad. He would recognize that many of these events resulted in part from a backlash against those very processes of globalization that had promised an unending age of peace and prosperity when he went to sleep. He would recognize that the welfare state he found so surprising was created in part as a result of this backlash, and he would wonder if it was still needed to prevent backsliding in the new globalized economy. Reading about the worries expressed by many seemingly eminent observers about the processes of globalization, he would be puzzled by what many of them describe as a Third Way.

To find out, he would refer to a book written by Anthony Giddens, a sociologist who was U.K. Prime Minister Tony Blair's guru and also director of the prestigious London School of Economics.[1] He would find the book unreadable. But he would be comforted by reading in a British newspaper (*The Sunday Telegraph*) that Giddens is noted among his colleagues for "pretentious waffle ... an airy and vapid mixture of the obvious and the obviously false, all of it smeared in unintelligible jargon. There isn't anything in his writing which sustains serious scrutiny."[2] He would pass the same judgment on the ruminations on globalization of French sociologist Pierre Bourdieu and of British philosopher John Gray.[3] But even if their twaddle was unimpressive, he would still wonder if the "social question"[4] that seemingly had led to the unraveling of his 19th-century globalizing world would undo the new one. He would look inquiringly at the statement by some boffins who hold conferences on a mountaintop in the Alps that says, "We need to devise a way to address the social impact of globalization, which is neither the mechanical expansion of welfare programs nor the fatalistic acceptance that the divide will grow wider between the beneficiaries of globalization and those unable to muster the skills and meet the requirements of integration in the global system."[5] So he would wonder if they had found a Third Way. What he would find is merely more hot air, a prescription for " 'compassionate government' that some political leaders are now advocating as an alternative to the old dichotomy between right and left."[6] This would seem merely a commendation of window dressing of the inescapable processes of globalization by that new breed called spin doctors: a plea for "mutton dressed as lamb."

He would also have heard of the Asian financial crisis that removed the stripes from so many of the tigers in the region. Having read of the disastrous dirigiste policies of the Third World, he would wonder if their recent conversion to global capitalism would last, or whether they too would find some elusive Third Way.

But he would wonder if (1) these fears of a backlash against globalization in both the developed and developing world were rational, (2) if there was any Third Way, and (3) if there were any other lurking dangers that might reverse globalization that happened while he was asleep. I will try to answer these three questions on Rip's behalf.

Developing Country Fears

The developing countries' main fear is that globalization will lead to greater volatility in their national incomes and, as the recent Asian crisis has shown, to serious instability, causing years of progress to be wiped out.

This is an ancient worry of the Third World, earlier expressed as the purported adverse effects on growth of the export instability engendered by integrating primary-product exporting countries in the world economy. In the 25-country study covering the period since World War II, development economist H. Myint and I[7] could find no statistical evidence that volatility of growth rates affected long-run growth performance—a conclusion consonant with the numerous studies of the effects of export instability on growth. Thus, Hong Kong has had one of the most volatile growth rates among developing countries, while India one of the most stable—but the long-run growth performance of Hong Kong puts the Indian one to shame. Although there may undeniably be greater volatility in national incomes of countries integrating with the world economy, this need not damage their long-run growth rates.

Does the Asian crisis portend the beginning of the end of the decade-old trend of economic liberalization in the Third World aimed at integrating it into the world economy? To answer this question we need to briefly outline the causes of this crisis. These are threefold: (1) the exchange rate regime, (2) the moral hazard in the domestic banking systems caused by the "Asian model," and (3) the international moral hazard created by the actions of the International Monetary Fund (IMF).

The first cause of the Asian crisis was the quasi-fixed exchange rate regimes in many of the countries. It is becoming increasingly clear that in a world with a globalized capital market only two exchange regimes are viable: a fully floating exchange rate or a rigidly fixed rate as in the currency board of Hong Kong. The reason is that these are the only ones that allow automatic adjustment to external and internal shocks without need for any discretionary action by the authorities.[8] This lesson has now been learned by many countries in the Third World.

The second cause of the Asian crisis was a systemic flaw in the "Asian model" of development. A central feature of this model— as seen most clearly in Korea but presaged by the development of Japan—is a close linkage between the domestic banking system, industrial enterprises (particularly the biggest), and the government.[9] The fatal danger of this model is that by making the banking system the creature of the government's will, a tremendous moral hazard is created in the domestic banking system. With the banks' having no incentive to assess the creditworthiness of their borrowers or the quality of the investments their loans are financing, they know that no matter how risky and overextended their lending, they will always be bailed out by the government. This can lead in time to a mountain of bad paper and the de facto insolvency of a major part of the banking system, as has happened in both Korea and Japan— not to mention the corruption that is inevitably involved in this type of development.

But, as the example of the U.S. savings and loan crisis shows, this mess in the banking system can ultimately be cleared up if there is the political will. Korea does have the will, and is already bouncing back. By contrast, Japan, which inherited a political system based on institutionalizing political paralysis from the Meiji oligarchs, shows no sign as yet of grasping this nettle, and its prospects must therefore remain a cause for continuing concern.

The problem of moral hazard for the domestic banking system created by this Asian model has been aggravated by the actions of the IMF and the entrance of foreign bankers as lenders in the newly liberalized capital markets. Of the three types of capital flows that can be distinguished—direct foreign investment, portfolio investment, and bank lending—the income and foreign currency risk of the first two types is shared by both the lender and the borrower, as the investments are denominated in domestic currency. By contrast foreign bank loans are usually denominated in dollars and the interest rate is linked to the London Interbank Offered Rate (LIBOR). This means that, if faced by a shock that requires a devaluation, the domestic currency burden of the foreign bank debt rises pari passu with the changing exchange rate. If the debt is incurred by the private sector, this rising debt burden need pose no problem for the country because, if the relevant foreign banks run, the borrowers can always default on their debts.

But now enter the IMF. Ever since the 1980s debt crisis, the foreign banks faced by a default on their Third World debt have argued that such a possibility poses a systemic risk to the world's financial system, and asked in effect for an international bailout to prevent a catastrophe. The IMF has been more than willing to oblige. For since the era of the Bretton Woods adjustable peg exchange rate regime—which the IMF was set up to manage—ended with President Nixon's closing of the gold window in the early 1970s, the IMF has been like a character in Luigi Pirandello's play *Six Characters in Search of an Author*. The debt crisis of the 1980s provided it one such play, another was the rocky transition of the Second World from plan to market, and a third was the Mexican and Asian crises. The IMF has increasingly become the international debt collector for foreign money center banks, as well as an important tool of U.S. foreign policy. It should be shut down.

With regard to the Asian model, it is dead. Countries are increasingly recognizing that the derisively labeled Anglo-Saxon model of capitalism is the only viable one in the long run. It alone can deliver the prosperity that a globalized economy offers in an unprecedented manner to all of its participants. Thus, most of the countries involved in the crisis are now moving to adopt its institutional bases: transparent financial systems and deeper financial markets that allow hedging of foreign currency risk, and either a floating or a rigidly fixed exchange rate regime as in a currency board or a monetary union. Those bucking the trend, like Mahathir's Malaysia, are about to learn the costs in terms of the future prosperity of their citizens.

Fears of Developed Countries

Developed countries perceive that the major threat from globalization that would result from trade with the Third World is to the living standards of their poorest and least skilled workers. The resulting protectionist response would be a serious threat to the developing countries' growth prospects. There is a continuing and unsettled debate about the causes of the stagnation in the wages of low-skilled workers in the West (or historically high unemployment rates—which is the other side of the same coin—as in Europe). Whether low-skilled wages are now set by those of Chinese and Indian coolies (à la Stolper-Samuelson) or are stagnant because of technological changes in the West is unlikely in my view to be resolved because of a massive structural change taking place in the global economy, which is as momentous as the first Industrial Revolution. The late Sir John Hicks had characterized the dominant feature of the latter as the substitution of fixed for circulating capital in the processes of production—as the "factory" replaced the "putting out" system. The current structural revolution can be characterized as the replacement of human for fixed capital as epitomized by the communications revolution in the West.

Unlike heavy industry—in which many of the larger Third World countries increasingly have a comparative advantage—much of industry's supplying consumer goods seems to be going "bespoke." This means that instead of mass-produced consumer goods relying on long production lines—called "Fordism" by some in recognition of the revolution in standardized mass production of consumer durables achieved by Henry Ford—the current tendency is to produce differentiated versions of the same good more closely tailored to differing individual tastes. Variety rather than standardization is the name of the game, in this "designer" world of commodities in the affluent West. Shifts in its variegated tastes are increasingly reflected in changes in differentiated products to meet this volatile demand. A new international division of labor, based on "outsourcing" and "just-in-time production," reminiscent of the old national "putting out" systems, is emerging in which the "design" and "sales" capacities that are human-capital-intensive are located in "rich" countries. They then have "virtual factories," with their production bases spread across the world, which, using modern telecommunications, convert these "designs" into the differentiated "bespoke" consumer goods increasingly demanded by consumers in the West.

Both trade and technology will thus put a premium on skills in the West. A signal for the acquisition of these skills will be a widening of skill differentials—as is evident in the United States—and the stagnation of the wages of the unskilled (or if these are artificially kept high, as in Europe, rising unemployment). But, as a result of these incentives to skill acquisition, once the necessary accumulation of human capital takes place, the standards of living of even those on the lowest rung of the current income distribution should rise. But this process will take time—witness the still unsettled debate about living standards in the 19th century in the United Kingdom when the previous major structural change was taking place. It appears that these living standards took a long time to rise as, for instance, the handloom weavers of the old "putting out" system were converted into the factory workers of the modern age.

The Social Question

It was precisely this so-called "social question" that in part led to the unraveling of the 19th-century LIEO, as the redistributive and egalitarian politics arising from the rise of demos undermined that belief in classical liberalism that formed the intellectual underpinnings of the LIEO. With globalization picking up where it left off before this "socialist impulse" undermined the LIEO, the implicit philosophy behind the so-called "Washington consensus" on economic policy is underpinned by classical liberalism. In this sense, globalization has put an end to what might be called the Age of Keynes.

One of the consequences of the breakdown of the 19th-century LIEO was that convertibility of currencies and free mobility of capital were greatly attenuated and in many countries snuffed out by exchange controls—which were only abolished in the United Kingdom with the accession of the first Margaret Thatcher government.

The bottling up of capital was essential for the Keynesian system to work. This was explicitly recognized in its international expression—the so-called gold exchange standard established at Bretton Woods—which required controls on what were deemed to be short-term capital flows to allow the adjustable peg exchange rate system to work—free from the speculative attacks that plague such systems.

The domestic consequence of bottling up mobile capital was that Keynesian remedies that required taxing capital to subsidize labor would not work if capital were free to move and escape these arbitrary and exorbitant imposts. This is not the place to relate the story of how the world moved to free mobility of capital, but once it did, dirigiste states found it increasingly difficult to claim that they were able to promote national prosperity and welfare through fiscal policies to maintain "full employment" and increases in redistributive taxation. Globalized capital markets, by allowing the prey to exit, have diminished the power of the predatory state to maintain, let alone increase, its take. Even those imbued by the "socialist impulse" now recognize that their political prospects rely on the two Clintonian slogans: "It's the economy, stupid!" and "It's the bond market, stupid!"

There is also less danger today that the "social question" posed by the current phase of globalization will undermine the new LIEO as it did its 19th-century predecessor. This is because of the different nature of the "losers" in the North in the two cases and the mitigating actions they can take to preserve their prosperity.

The rise of the factory system in the 19th century meant that the economic integration of the Atlantic economy by the LIEO led to relative declines or stagnation in the real incomes of the factors of production in each region that were relatively scarce, and a rise in the incomes of the more abundant factors.[10] This meant that in the United States, which was labor scarce and natural resource-cum-land abundant, the distribution of income moved against labor. This led to the growth of populist politics and creeping protectionism on grounds first propounded by Alexander Hamilton. In Europe, which was labor abundant and land scarce, this 19th-century globalization led to landowners' losing out relatively. This then led to political coalitions such as the famous one between "rye and steel" in Germany and growing protectionism justified by the "infant industry" arguments of Friedrich List.[11] The United Kingdom alone stood by its free trade creed. That was largely because the country had fought off the "landed interest" at the time of the repeal of the Corn Laws and had been the first industrial nation. Thus, the prosperity of both its industrial capitalists and workers was enhanced by the cheap grain flowing across the Atlantic as a result of the LIEO.

Although political action by threatened interest groups seemed inevitable in order to deal with the distributive consequences of globalization at the end of the 19th century, the situation is much more benign in the current phase of globalization. In the earlier phase the losers—the industrial workers in the United States or the landowners in Germany, for instance—could not acquire the means to prevent their relative decline, whereas this is not so in the current situation in the North. The main losers are the unskilled, but unlike the industrial factory workers of the 19th century who could not acquire the physical or financial capital to stem their relative decline in incomes, today's unskilled can acquire the necessary human capital to share in the immense gains from globalization of their skilled compatriots in the North.

Second, and equally important, with most Northern economies becoming primarily service economies, many more workers will be working in areas in which the products produced are "non-traded," that is, sheltered from foreign competition. Hairdressers in South Central Los Angeles are not going to see their rates cut by competition from barbers in Bangkok. But, many of these personal services require not just skills but also personal attributes like tidiness, punctuality, politeness, and trustworthiness. Mothers are hardly likely to employ a member of the so-called "underclass" as a baby sitter or housekeeper even if they were willing to accept the wages of a maid in India. The undermining of the Victorian personal virtues in the underclass created by Western welfare states provides yet another reason why their reform is so important for helping the potential "losers" from the current processes of globalization.

The Threat: A New Ethical Imperialism

A more potent threat to the new emerging global economy is posed by the West's growing attempt to legislate its "habits of the heart" worldwide, in the name of universal human rights. This bears an uncanny resemblance to the 19th-century imperialism that was in part responsible for the breakdown of the 19th-century LIEO.

This imperialism was in part motivated by the civilizing mission embodied in the white man's burden. Something similar is afoot today: the calls for ethical trading, ethical foreign policies, the insistence that everyone embrace the West's political system of majoritarian democracy are symptomatic of these trends.

There are dangerous pressures in the West to use multilateral institutions overseeing the emerging global economy to legislate their "habits of the heart" worldwide. The various proposals to introduce labor and environmental standards in the World Trade Organization and to tie issues of "human rights" to trade and investment under the rubric of "ethical trading" are of this ilk. They have neither logic nor ethics on their side.[12] Even if these "protectionist" attacks on the LIEO are beaten back, they can in the meantime lead to increasing international friction that could slowly unravel the new LIEO. They, moreover, tend to aggravate the suspicion of many developing countries that the newly emerging globalized economy will lead to a form of cultural imperialism that will undermine their ancient and cherished ways of life.

Cultural Fears of the Rest

These cultural fears from globalization concern not only the cultural pollution supposedly coming over the airwaves with the communications revolution but also the effects on ancient cultures of modernization that globalization will inevitably produce. This reflects an old debate in development studies: whether modernization will lead to Westernization.[13]

It is useful to distinguish between what I label the material and cosmological beliefs of different cultures and civilizations. The former relate to ways of making a living, the latter to, in Plato's words, "how one should live." There is considerable cross-cultural evidence to show that material beliefs are fairly malleable, altering rapidly with changes in the material environment. There is greater hysterics in cosmological beliefs—how people view their lives: its purpose, meaning, and relationship to others. The cross-cultural evidence shows that it is the *language group* rather than the environment that influences these world views.

The great Eurasian agrarian civilizations had more similarities than differences in their material and cosmological beliefs. They can broadly be described as "communalist." I have argued in *Unintended*

Consequences that the rise of the West was due to its breaking away from this agrarian past as a result of the twin revolutions of Pope Gregory the Great in the 6th century and Pope Gregory VII in the 11th century. The former created a "family revolution" that broke with the cosmological beliefs of its fellow agrarian civilizations in the domestic domain by essentially promoting "individualism" and the independence of the young.

The second Papal Revolution of Pope Gregory VII brought the Church into the world with his proclamation that from then on the City of God was to be placed above Caesar, and its will was to be enforced through the powerful sanction of excommunication. This led the Church-state to create all the legal and commercial infrastructure for a market economy.[14] This provided the essential institutional infrastructure for the Western dynamic that led to the European miracle.

Though the twin Papal revolutions, which changed the cosmological and material beliefs of the West, were historically conjoined, they no longer have to be. With the universal victory of the market over the plan, all cultures and civilizations are willing to accept the institutional revolution of Pope Gregory VII that promotes the modernization leading to the material prosperity sought worldwide. But, as the example of a modernized but non-Westernized Japan shows, there is no need for the non-Western world to accept the cosmology promoted by Pope Gregory the Great's family revolution. The "Rest" can modernize without losing their souls.

Legislating Western "Habits of the Heart"

If the cultural fears of globalization of the non-Western world are therefore exaggerated, the same cannot be said of the current Western moral crusade to legislate its own cosmological beliefs worldwide. Its claim that it is thereby promoting universal values is unjustified.

There is an important difference between the cosmological beliefs of what became the Christian West and the other ancient agrarian civilizations of Eurasia. Christianity has a number of distinctive features that it shares with its Semitic cousin Islam, but not entirely with its parent Judaism, and that are not found in any of the other great Eurasian religions. The most important feature is Chistianity's universality. Neither the Jews, nor the Hindu or Sinic civilizations, had religions claiming to be universal. You could not choose to be a Hindu, a Chinese, or a Jew; you were born as one. This also meant that unlike Christianity and Islam, those religions did not proselytize. Third, only the Semitic religions, being monotheistic, have also been egalitarian. Nearly all of the other Eurasian religions believed in some form of hierarchical social order. By contrast alone among the Eurasian civilizations, the Semitic ones (though least so the Jewish) emphasized the equality of men's souls in the eyes of their monotheistic deities. Louis Dumont has rightly characterized the resulting profound divide between the societies of *Homo Aequalis* that believe all men are born equal (as the philosophes and the U.S. Constitution proclaim) and those of *Homo Hierarchicus* that believe no such thing.[15] The so-called universal values being promoted by the West are no more than the culture-specific proselytizing ethic of what remains at heart Western Christendom.

Nor is there a necessary connection as the West claims between democracy and development.[16] If democracy is to be preferred as a form of government, it is not because of its instrumental value in promoting prosperity—at times it may well not—but because it promotes a different Western value, namely liberty. Again, many civilizations have placed social order above this value and, again, it would be imperialistic for the West to ask them to change their ways.

If no universal claims for cherished Western cosmological beliefs are valid, it is unlikely that they will be found acceptable by the Rest. If the West ties its moral crusade too closely to the emerging processes of globalization, there is a danger that there will also be a backlash against the process of globalization. This potential cultural imperialism poses a greater danger to the acceptance of the new LIEO in developing countries than the unfounded fears of their cultural nationalists that the modernization promoted by globalization will lead to the erosion of cherished cosmological beliefs.

Conclusion

In sum, there is no Third Way. Departing from the so-called Anglo-Saxon model of capitalism leads to a dirigisme, which undermines prosperity. Nor, unlike the 19th century, is there a danger of the "social question" undermining the newly emerging LIEO. It is threatened instead by the likely resistance in the Rest to the West's current moral crusade to legislate its "habits of the heart," which could undermine the Rest's acceptance of globalization. It would be best for the West to remember Queen Elizabeth's sage injunction during the religious turmoil of her reign that she would not seek to "make windows into men's souls."

Notes

1. Anthony Giddens, *The Third Way: The Renewal of Social Democracy* (Malden, Mass.: Polity Press, 1999).

2. "The Third Man: This Year's Reith Lecturer May Advise Mr. Blair, But He Bewilders Many Others," *Sunday Telegraph* (London), March 28, 1999, p. 41.

3. Pierre Bourdieu, *Acts of Resistance: Against the Tyranny of the Market* (Cambridge: Polity Press, 1998); and John Gray, *False Dawn: The Delusions of Global Capitalism* (New York: New Press, 1999).

4. Tony Judt, "The Social Question Redivivus," *Foreign Affairs* 75, no. 5 (September / October 1997): 95–117.

5. Klaus Schwab and Claude Smadja, "Globalization Needs a Human Face," *International Herald Tribune*, January 28, 1999, p. 8.

6. Ibid.

7. Deepak Lal and H. Myint, *The Political Economy of Poverty, Equity and Growth* (Oxford: Clarendon Press, 1996).

8. Ibid.

9. For an explanation based on the "agency" problems of semi-industrialized countries for this "model" see ibid, pp. 94–99.

10. This is called the Stolper-Samuelson theorem in international economics. There is an ongoing and unsettled debate among economists about whether the current wage trends in the United States and other developed countries are due to the growing economic integration promoted by the current LIEO, in particular of the low-wage and abundant labor countries of Asia, or due to technological changes. See Robert Feenstra, "Integration of Trade and Disintegration of Production in the Global Economy," *Journal of Economic Perspectives* 12, no. 4: 31–50 (1998). In my judgment it is likely to be a bit of each, with it being very difficult empirically to assign the relative shares to these two increasingly complementary forces. For the empirical evidence on the effects of the income distribution effects of the 19th-century LIEO, see Jeffrey G. Williamson, "Globalization, Labor Markets and Policy Backlash in the Past," *Journal of Economic Perspectives* 14, no. 4 (1998): 51–72.

11. For this "factor-price" explanation of changing trade policies in the 19th century, see Ronald Rogowski, *Commerce and Coalitions* (Princeton, N.J.: Princeton University Press, 1989).

12. Deepak Lal, "Social Standards and Social Dumping," in *Merits and Limits of Markets*, ed. Herbert Giersch (Berlin: Springer-Verlag, 1998).

13. Deepak Lal, *Unintended Consequences: The Impact of Factor Endowments, Culture, and Politics on Long-Run Economic Performance* (Cambridge, Mass.: MIT Press, 1998).

14. Harold J. Berman, *Law and Revolution* (Cambridge, Mass.: Harvard University Press, 1983).

15. Louis Dumont, *Homo Hierarchicus: The Caste System and Its Implications* (London: Weidenfeld and Nicholson, 1970).

16. See Lal and Myint.

3. The Invisible Hand vs. the Dead Hand

Brink Lindsey

In the world economy today there are signs of struggle: financial crises in Asia, Russia, and Latin America; chronic double-digit unemployment in Europe; slowing growth in China; and slow-motion collapse in Japan. But what is the nature of the struggle?

Critics of economic liberalization believe that the world is in the grip of unrestrained market forces, and that those forces must be subdued if order is to be restored. They are profoundly wrong. It is not the invisible hand of market competition that the world is straining against, but the dead hand of a failed statist past—a past whose animating spirit is gone but whose malignant influence continues to weigh down on us.

Polanyi's Disciples

To understand the historical context of the present situation, it is useful to review the arguments of those who claim that the present struggle represents a crisis of unrestrained capitalism. These arguments are illuminating in their almost perfect inversion of the truth.

In recent years critics of free markets from across the ideological spectrum have charged that "globalization"—the growing internationalization of market relations—is out of control. They claim that the various currency crashes of this decade bear witness to the inherent instability of markets. Meanwhile, in the rich industrialized countries, the pressures of unrestricted international competition are allegedly causing unemployment, dragging down living standards, and eroding hard-fought social protections. A blind faith in laissez faire is to blame for these troubling developments, they say; governments must reassert control or catastrophe will ensue.

Pat Buchanan typifies this point of view when he denounces the dogmatic attachment to markets that supposedly holds sway at present: "What is wrong with the Global Economy is what is wrong

43

with our politics," he contends; "it is rooted in the myth of Economic Man. It elevates economics above all else."[1]

"To worship the market," Buchanan argues, "is a form of idolatry no less than worshiping the state. The market should be made to work for man, not the other way around. 'What is the market? It is the law of the jungle, the law of nature. And what is civilization? It is the struggle against nature.' So declared France's Prime Minister Edouard Balladur at the close of the GATT negotiations in 1993; he is right."[2]

If it is odd to hear "America Firster" Buchanan make common cause with a Frenchman, it is perhaps even stranger to hear a financier trash the markets in which he has made billions. But that is what George Soros does: "Financial markets are inherently unstable and there are social needs that cannot be met by giving market forces free rein. Unfortunately these defects are not recognized. Instead there is a widespread belief that markets are self-correcting and a global economy can flourish without any need for a global society.... This idea was called laissez faire in the nineteenth century, but ... I have found a better name for it: market fundamentalism."[3]

"[M]arket fundamentalism," Soros concludes in what even he concedes is a "shocking" contention, "is today a greater threat to open society than any totalitarian ideology."[4]

Some of the critics of globalization cite historical parallels with the aborted world economy of the early 20th century. The internationalization of economic life at that time rivaled and in some respects exceeded our present situation, only to be swallowed up by the cataclysms of world war, depression, and totalitarianism. Capitalism self-destructed then allegedly because of its unregulated volatility and brutality; it was saved only when governments tamed its energies to the service of social goals. The utopian faith in self-regulating markets thus supposedly brought ruin in the past, and again threatens ruin today.

Left-wing journalist William Greider adopts this line in his book *One World, Ready or Not.*

> The gravest danger I perceive at this moment is the understandable inclination of people and societies to ... replay the terrible conflicts of the twentieth century....
>
> Assuming that the global economic system is not redirected toward a more moderate course, these weary political

and class conflicts are sure to ripen, leading toward the same stalemate between markets and society in which fascism arose and flourished nearly a hundred years ago.[5]

This last twist represents a revival of the historical analysis of Karl Polanyi, author of the 1944 book *The Great Transformation*. Polanyi argued that the catastrophes of his time could ultimately be traced back to the evils of laissez faire. "[T]he origins of the cataclysm," he wrote, "lay in the utopian endeavor of economic liberalism to set up a self-regulating market system."[6]

Here Polanyi elaborates:

> [T]he idea of a self-adjusting market implied a stark utopia. Such an institution could not exist for any length of time without annihilating the human and natural substance of society; it would have physically destroyed man and transformed his surroundings into a wilderness. Inevitably, society took measures to protect itself, but whatever measures it took impaired the self-regulation of the market, disorganized industrial life, and thus endangered society in yet another way. It was this dilemma which forced the development of the market system into a definite groove and finally disrupted the social organization based upon it.[7]

The conflict between "society" and the market ultimately gave rise, in Polanyi's view, to totalitarianism: "The fascist solution of the *impasse* reached by liberal capitalism can be described as a reform of market economy achieved at the price of the extirpation of all democratic institutions, both in the industrial and the political realm."[8]

Karl Polanyi has been rescued from well-deserved obscurity to become a kind of patron saint of global capitalism's current critics. His influence is cited explicitly by both Greider and Soros; Dani Rodrik of Harvard University and author of *Has Globalization Gone Too Far?* refers to him frequently; as does John Gray, a professor at the London School of Economics who wrote *False Dawn: The Delusions of Global Capitalism*.[9]

The Industrial Counterrevolution

Polanyi's analysis and its reappearance today turn history on its head. The destruction of the first global economy stemmed not from overreliance on markets, but from a pervasive loss of faith in them.

45

The spectacular wealth creation of the Industrial Revolution, made possible by the decentralized trial and error of market competition, was widely misinterpreted at the time and afterward as a triumph of top-down control and central planning. People believed that the new giant industrial enterprises demonstrated the superiority of consolidation and technocratic control over the haphazard wastefulness of market competition. They concluded that the logic of industrialization compelled an extension of the top-down rationality of the factory to the whole of society—in other words, social engineering.[10]

This tragic error gave rise to a social phenomenon that may be described as the Industrial Counterrevolution—an assault on the principles that brought modern technological society into being. This reactionary movement was far broader than any one ideology—it encompassed the "one best way" of "scientific management"; the cartelization of the "associative state"; the welfare state; the developmental "catch-up" state; and at the extreme, the totalitarian state.

The belief in technocratic control—and especially in vesting that control in the state—gained momentum steadily from around 1880 onward. Aside from the damage it wrought within national boundaries, its fundamental incompatibility with the liberal international order that developed during the 19th century meant that one of them had to give way. It was the latter that yielded: as societies closed, so did borders.

The great catastrophe from which the first world economy never recovered was World War I. But the roots of that carnage lay in the rise of economic nationalism and its international projection through imperialism. The free-trade order presided over by Great Britain fell on the defensive as the "newly industrializing countries" of the late 19th century—the United States, Germany, and Russia—were all explicitly protectionist. The spreading belief in zero-sum economic conflict among nations was strengthened by the combination of colonial land-grabs and systems of imperial trade preferences. The arms races and deepening antagonisms of the pre-war period made sense only in a world in which political control over territory was necessary to gain access to its raw materials and markets.[11]

After the war, attempts were made to rebuild the old system; but the economic shock waves of inflation and debt that reverberated after the war, and the new political realities of social democracy and totalitarianism, rendered a return to ante-bellum stability impossible. Finally, the Great Depression and the protectionist spasms it provoked rang the death knell for the old liberal order. Indeed, for a dark time it appeared that any future international order would be totalitarian.

It is utterly preposterous to attribute this collapse, as did Polanyi and do his followers, to excessive faith in market competition. Throughout this period all the intellectual momentum was running in the opposite, collectivist direction. Polanyi's bogeyman—the minimal-state ideal of laissez faire—was so defunct as to be virtually without prominent adherents, much less practical influence over the course of events.

Twilight of the Idols

In the years after World War II there was a partial move back toward a liberal international order through the Bretton Woods system and tariff reductions under the General Agreement on Tariffs and Trade. But much of the world remained outside this reborn international economy: the Communist nations and most of the so-called Third World pursued economic policies of autarky and isolation. For the bulk of the world's population, the ascendancy of the Industrial Counterrevolution continued to squelch any significant participation in an international division of labor.

Only in the past couple of decades has the counterrevolutionary momentum exhausted itself in failure and collapse.[12] And as overweening state control has receded—with the opening of China, the dissolution of the Soviet bloc, and the abandonment by many developing countries of "import substitution"—market connections have been reestablished. So although globalization is charged with undermining the state, the more powerful flows of historical causation have actually been in the opposite direction: it is the retreat of the state that has allowed international market relationships to regain a foothold.

This is a point that bears some emphasis. The unprecedented degree of international economic integration that the world enjoys today is certainly attributable in part to steadily falling transportation costs, and a spectacular fall in the costs of processing and communicating information. But there would be no *global* economy today except that large parts of the globe decided to abandon economic policies of self-imposed isolation from international commerce. And this policy shift has been part of a much broader movement away

47

from centralized state control in favor of the decentralized experimentation of the liberal market system.

In other words, the reunited world economy must be understood fundamentally as a *political* event: in particular, as a consequence of the death and repudiation of the old counterrevolutionary ideal of top-down planning. Critics of globalization portray the spread of markets as the impingement of blind economic forces upon otherwise functional policies. In fact, the dramatic changes in economic policy that have swept through the communist and Third Worlds over the past 20 years, of which one important element has been reintegration into the international economy, have been driven primarily by the recognition on the part of national political leaders that their state-dominated systems had failed—failed in absolute terms as billions of people remained mired in grinding poverty, and failed in relative terms by comparison with the prosperous West and the relatively open and thriving Pacific Rim.

Meanwhile, over the same period, the failures of interventionism have prompted a wave of economic reforms in the industrialized democracies as well. Tax cuts, privatizations, elimination of price and entry controls, and perhaps, most important, the repudiation of inflationary monetary policy—these steps in the direction of liberalization became politically possible only after the stagflation of the 1970s discredited the "mixed economy" and macroeconomic "fine tuning."

Thus, the reemergence of a global economy occurred at the same time as, and as one consequence of, a global disillusionment with top-down control and central planning. The critics of globalization thus get the temper of the times all wrong when they condemn the present era as one of market "idolatry" and dogmatic enthusiasm. This is a time of idol-smashing, not of setting up new gods.

Yes, Ronald Reagan and Margaret Thatcher were vigorous and eloquent spokespersons for free markets and limited government, though their rhetoric far outdistanced their accomplishments. But as ideological reformers they stand more or less alone. Nobody has done more to liberate more people than Deng Xiaoping—an ardent communist and veteran of the Long March. Mikhail Gorbachev, a loyal Leninist, inadvertently toppled the Soviet Empire. Argentina has rediscovered liberalism under Carlos Menem, a Peronist. New Zealand went from one of the most protectionist to one of the most open economies in the world under a Labor government. And so on and so on—around-the-world pragmatism, not ideological zeal, has been the guiding spirit of liberalization.

Global Battle Lines

But this pragmatic process of unraveling state controls still has a long, long way to go. Although the belief in central planning has lost its utopian fire, its effects are still very much with us. Both friends and enemies of globalization have made breathless pronouncements about the unrestrained ascendancy of market forces in today's world economy, but such hype cannot bear scrutiny. The Industrial Counterrevolution may have expired as a living faith, but the dead hand of its accumulated institutions, mindsets, and vested interests still imposes a heavy and disfiguring burden.

Our present world situation, then, is far removed from the unchallenged triumph of markets that Buchanan, Soros, Greider et al. complain about. Rather, we live in the midst of an ongoing and uncertain struggle between the revitalization of markets on the one hand and the dead hand of top-down control on the other. Call it the invisible hand versus the dead hand. That struggle strains and distorts market and social development, and gives rise to occasional, crippling instability. Globalization is as a consequence an uncertain and uneven process, and subject to sudden and traumatic reverses and dislocations. Critics of globalization blame the distortions and volatility on free markets run amok; in fact, however, these problems are overwhelmingly due to the continuing bulking presence of anti-market policies and institutions.

Please note that this struggle cannot be reduced to a conflict between government *per se* and markets; it is not simply an issue of governments doing too much or too little. The problem is that governments are simultaneously doing too much *and* too little. By diverting so much of their attention to preempting and controlling voluntary, private activity, governments have often failed to do the necessary work of building and fostering the institutions within which voluntary, private activity can flourish.

The exact nature of the conflict between markets and the dead hand differs from country to country. Still, it is possible to identify certain broad battle lines. Together, they define the critical challenges facing the emerging world economy today.

(1) The Monetary Trilemma. Critics of free markets blame the recent financial crises in Asia and Latin America on unregulated capital movements. This charge is partly true, in that the crises could not have occurred if capital flows had not been liberalized. But the whole story is that currency crashes happen when governments abuse their access to international capital markets by pursuing unsustainable monetary policies.

There are three desiderata of international monetary policy: free currency convertibility to ensure full access to global investment capital and opportunities; flexibility to respond to macroeconomic shocks; and stable exchange value to promote certainty and transparency in international transactions. Unfortunately, no monetary regime can pursue more than two out of three of these worthy objectives at any given time. Free capital flows and monetary flexibility come at the expense of exchange rate stability; free capital flows and exchange rate stability come at the expense of monetary flexibility; exchange rate stability and monetary flexibility come at the expense of free capital flows. In short, a country must either let its currency float, or fix it and abandon independent monetary policy, or else withdraw from full integration into the international economy.[13]

Currency crises happen when monetary authorities try to have their cake and eat it too—by pegging their rates but still pursuing an independent monetary policy. These currency crises have been wreaking havoc in the world economy over the past few years—up and down the Pacific Rim, in Russia, and then in Brazil. Each and every time, the explosion occurred because of an unsustainable over-burdening of monetary policy.

(2) Economic Gangrene. Commercial failure is an essential if unpleasant part of the market process. It allows poorly used resources to be redirected to more productive pursuits, and it signals to other enterprises what mistakes to avoid. When economic institutions do not recognize and respond to failure, growth and vitality can be undermined by a buildup of rot in the system. Specifically, unresolved bad debts and chronically loss-making state-owned enterprises plague today's world economy and threaten traumatic collapse and dislocation when the burden of necrosis becomes unbearable. For example, bad debt is at the root of Japan's economic malaise, while a wealth-destroying state-owned sector imperils China's continued rapid growth.

(3) Hollow Capitalism. At the core of the capitalist market order are the institutions that direct the flow of capital from savers to investors. Around the world, those institutions are to a greater or lesser extent characterized by overcentralization and perverse incentives. Direct state intervention and politicized banking industries too often dominate capital allocation, while the legal structures that allow decentralized access to capital through bond and equity markets are underdeveloped or suppressed.

The problem is especially acute in the post-communist and developing world; in particular, even the most successful developing countries have achieved at most a kind of hollow capitalism, where state-directed mimicry of Western industrial development substitutes poorly for market-signaled investment. Anti-market policies afflict the financial systems of advanced countries as well—witness the U.S. savings and loan disaster and the flagging returns on capital in the bank-dominated systems of Europe and Japan. Wherever market-driven finance is frustrated, malinvestment and underperformance are the universal result.

(4) The Rule of Lawlessness. An even more fundamental deformity in developing and transition economies is the failure of governments to provide reliable security for property and contract rights. This failure stems partially from corruption, partially from sheer fecklessness. Without stability and congruence in expectations regarding the present and future disposition of property, the ability to make long-term investments and construct intricate divisions of labor is seriously undermined. In addition to throttling domestic entrepreneurial initiative and discouraging foreign investment, the absence of a reliable rule of law can lead to horrendous environmental despoliation as resources of uncertain ownership are ruthlessly plundered.

(5) Strangulation by Safety Net. However well-intentioned, policies to protect individuals from economic hardship too often backfire because of the perverse incentives they create. Nowhere is this more evident today than in Europe, where rigidities in the labor market and overindulgent welfare policies have resulted in chronic double-digit unemployment. In the United States, welfare policies have fostered the social pathologies of the inner cities, although now reform efforts give some cause for hope of improvement. Around the world, pay-as-you-go public pension systems rob the world of

51

a massive pool of savings, while over the longer term their demographic inviability threatens fiscal breakdown.

Liberalization by Fits and Starts

What is the outlook for the ongoing struggle between the invisible hand and the dead hand? Will liberalization continue to gain ground? Or have the past couple of decades of worldwide reform been a kind of Prague spring, to be crushed sooner or later by a reassertion of anti-market policies—in the form of capital controls, protectionism, renationalizations, and the like?

By characterizing the anti-market forces as the dead hand, I have already given some clue as to my answer: I believe that the long-term advantage lies with the liberal cause. Since the collectivist, top-down ideal is moribund, there is at present only one viable model of economic development—the liberal model of markets and competition. Consequently, the ongoing struggle is not one between rival ideologies, but between what *is* and what *works*. Those terms of battle consign defenders of the dead hand to a perpetual rear-guard action.

Vested interests and sheer inertia will render existing dirigiste policies difficult to dislodge—there will be few easy victories. But as dysfunctional controls and restrictions cause acute crises and breakdowns or chronic underperformance relative to more open countries, national political leaders will find themselves recurrently under extreme pressure to act. When such points are reached, they must move either toward liberalization or toward ever more heavy-handed interventionism. The current intellectual climate strongly favors the former alternative.

The economic crises of the past couple of years illustrate this dynamic. For the most part economic collapse has accelerated the process of pro-market reform. There have been exceptions—Russia, certainly, and to a lesser extent Malaysia—but by and large the dominant political response in the crisis-affected countries has been in a liberal direction. What real choice is there?

There is little cause, however, for liberal triumphalism. So-called reforms will all too often turn out to be weak half-measures, debilitated by political compromise. At the same time, the sheer poverty and backwardness of most of the world affords enormous opportunities for higher-than-Western "catch-up" growth rates even when public policies are far from optimal. The ongoing availability of catch-up growth, and the legitimacy it confers upon even deeply flawed policies, will weaken the incentives for thoroughgoing reform.

Liberalization's advances, then, will come in fits and starts. Crisis, reform, euphoria, disillusionment, and crisis and reform again—such is the dialectic of the invisible hand against the dead hand.

Notes

1. Patrick J. Buchanan, *The Great Betrayal: How American Sovereignty and Social Justice Are Being Sacrificed to the Gods of the Global Economy* (Boston: Little, Brown and Company, 1998), p. 287.

2. Buchanan, p. 288.

3. George Soros, *The Crisis of Global Capitalism* (New York: Public Affairs, 1998), p. xx.

4. Soros, p. xxi.

5. William Greider, *One World, Ready or Not: The Manic Logic of Global Capitalism* (New York: Simon & Schuster, 1997), p. 309.

6. Karl Polanyi, *The Great Transformation: The Political and Economic Origins of Our Time* (Boston: Beacon Press, 1957), p. 29.

7. Ibid., p. 3.

8. Ibid., p. 237.

9. Dani Rodrik, *Has Globalization Gone Too Far?* (Washington: Institute for International Economics, 1997); and John Gray, *False Dawn: The Delusions of Global Capitalism* (New York: The New Press, 1998).

10. For an interesting examination of the rise of this idea in American history, see John M. Jordan, *Machine-Age Ideology: Social Engineering and American Liberalism 1911–1939* (Chapel Hill: The University of North Carolina Press, 1994).

11. "While under free trade and freedom of migration no individual is concerned about the territorial size of his country, under the protective measures of economic nationalism nearly every citizen has a substantial interest in these territorial issues. The enlargement of the territory subject to the sovereignty of his own government means material improvement for him or at least relief from restrictions which a foreign government has imposed upon his well-being." Ludwig von Mises, *Human Action* (Chicago: Contemporary Books, 1949), p. 824.

12. A number of recent books do a good job of narrating the worldwide sputtering of the Industrial Counterrevolution. See, for example, Robert Skidelsky, *The Road from Serfdom: The Economic and Political Consequences of the End of Communism* (New York: Penguin Books, 1995); Daniel Yergin and Joseph Stanislaw, *The Commanding Heights: The Battle between Government and the Market That Is Remaking the Modern World* (New York: Simon & Schuster, 1998); David Henderson, *The Changing Fortunes of Economic Liberalism: Yesterday, Today and Tomorrow* (London: The Institute of Economic Affairs, 1998).

13. See, for example, Paul Krugman, "The Eternal Triangle," http://web.mit.edu/krugman/www/triangle.html.

4. Twenty-Five Miraculous U.S. Trends of the Past 100 Years

Stephen Moore and Julian L. Simon

We step upon the threshold of 1900 . . . facing a brighter dawn of civilization.

—*New York Times*, January 1, 1900

There has been more improvement in the human condition for people living in the United States in the 20th century than for all people in all previous centuries of human history combined. Gigantic strides have been made in living standards in most other parts of the world as well, but not all. The European Jews, the Russians, and the Chinese experienced dreadful episodes of tyranny under Adolf Hitler, Joseph Stalin, and Mao Zedong.

When one considers the age of the planet, the 20th century has been a momentary flash in time. Yet the documentable improvement in the quality of human life in this brief period has been nothing short of miraculous. Although the leap forward in human progress began in the 19th century with the Industrial Revolution, the greatest strides took place in the 20th century. Virtually every statistic presented in the pages that follow confirms that we have just completed what the 1933 World's Fair in Chicago aptly called "the Century of Progress."

The roughly sixfold rise in the living standards of Americans in the 20th century is particularly impressive when we consider that for thousands of years human progress occurred at a glacial pace. For the thousand years before the Industrial Revolution, incomes were virtually flat, growing by about 0.5 percent per year. Life expectancy was not much greater in 1700 than it was at the time of

Figure 4.1
LIFE EXPECTANCY AT BIRTH, PAST MILLENNIUM

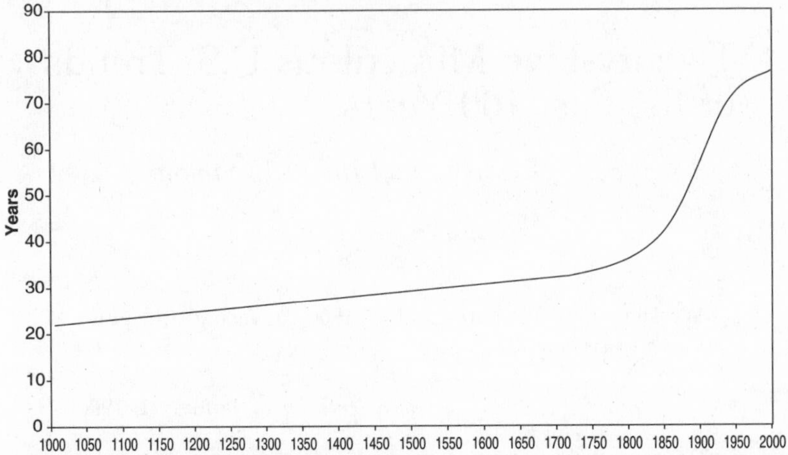

SOURCES: For 1000–1850 (Europe), Julian L. Simon, *The Ultimate Resource 2*, rev. ed. (Princeton: Princeton University Press, 1996), p. 319; for 1990–96 (United States), Centers for Disease Control, National Center for Health Statistics, *Monthly Vital Statistics Report 47*, no. 45, Table 16; and U.S. Bureau of the Census, *Historical Statistics of the United States: Colonial Times to 1970* (Washington: Government Printing Office, 1975), Series B 107.

the Greek and Roman Empires (Figure 4.1). Throughout most of human history, life was, as Thomas Hobbes famously put it, "nasty, brutish, and short."

One way to appreciate the improvements in quality of life over the course of the century is to mentally travel back 100 years. What was life really like? The latter part of the 19th century was an era of tuberculosis, typhoid, sanitariums, child labor, child death, horses, horse manure, candles, 12-hour workdays, Jim Crow laws, tenements, slaughterhouses, and outhouses. Lynchings—not just of blacks—were common. (In the South 11 Italians were lynched in one month.)[1] To live to 50 was to count one's blessings. For a mother to have all four of her children live to adulthood was to beat the odds of nature. One in 10 children died before his or her first birthday. One hundred years ago parents lived in eternal fear of a child's dying; nowadays, many parents live in eternal fear of their child's not making the county select soccer team.

Industrial cities were typically enveloped in clouds of black soot and smoke. At that stage of the Industrial Revolution, factories belching poisons into the air were regarded as a sign of prosperity and progress. Streets were smelly and filled with garbage before modern sewerage systems and plumbing were put in place. Leading killers of the day included pneumonia, tuberculosis, diarrhea, and violence. In 1918 pneumonia killed 675,000 Americans. In the first two decades of the 20th century, before the era of acid rain and global warming, pollution killed people—lots and lots of people. Deadly diseases were carried by milk and what then qualified as "drinking water." Cancer was not one of the primary causes of death as it is today, because most Americans succumbed to infectious diseases and occasional epidemics before their bodies had time to contract cancer.

Medical care was astonishingly primitive by today's standards. Abraham Flexner, writing in the famous Flexner report on medical education in 1910, commented that until then, a random patient consulting a random physician had only a 50-50 chance of benefiting from the encounter.[2] Health historian Theodore Dalrymple notes that until the late 19th century it was often considered "beneath a physician's dignity to actually examine a patient."[3] Most of the drugs used throughout the ages, including arsenic, which was still used through the early 1900s, were useless and in many cases poisonous. Oliver Wendell Holmes was reported to have declared that if all of the drugs in his time were tossed into the ocean it would be better for mankind and worse for the fish.[4]

So why did mankind experience such a burst of progress all of a sudden at the start of the 20th century? And why did so much of that progress originate in the United States? The shorthand answer to the second question is this: Freedom works. The unique American formula of individual liberty and free enterprise has encouraged risk taking, experimentation, innovation, and scientific exploration of a magnitude that is unprecedented in human history.

Economic freedom and freedom from government repression, in particular, are necessary ingredients for human progress. In the United States the government has, for the most part, set down a reasonable rule of law and then gotten out of the way. The tragedy of the past century is that mankind has had to relearn the lesson of history again and again—most recently in the former Soviet Union, where life expectancies have tragically fallen, and in China, where

Figure 4.2
LIFE EXPECTANCY AND ECONOMIC FREEDOM

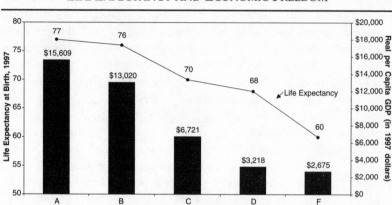

SOURCES: Calculations by DKT International based on James D. Gwartney and Robert L. Lawson, *Economic Freedom of the World: 1997 Annual Report* (Vancouver: Fraser Institute, 1997); and Population Reference Bureau, World Population Data Sheet 1999, http://www.prb.org/pubs/wpds99/wpds99_2.htm.

tens of millions of Chinese starved to death under collectivist agricultural policies—that repression by government short-circuits the human spirit and produces sustained periods of stagnation and even anti-progress. Figure 4.2 shows that there is a strong positive relationship between economic freedom and life expectancy across countries.

The United States also enjoys a unique advantage over other nations because it is a nation that remakes itself through the new blood of immigrants. The tens of millions of new Americans who came through Ellis Island or the Golden Gate or across the Rio Grande have been some of the brightest and most ambitious people in the world. Americans are a people who are self-selected problem solvers and progress seekers. Historian Paul Johnson states this point in his book, *A History of the American People*, when he describes Americans as "the first, best hope for the human race."[5]

The answer to the first question, why was all this progress compressed into the historical nanosecond of the 20th century, is not so straightforward. We believe, however, that three relatively modern developments have revolutionized human life:

58

The *first* was modern medicine and vaccines. Scientists generally attribute up to half the increase in life expectancy in the 20th century to improved drugs, vaccines, and other medical treatment breakthroughs.

The *second* development was the harnessing of electrical power. Although generating electrical power was possible by the late 19th century, electricity started to become widely available in homes and factories only in the early decades of the 20th century. The magic of electrical power not only literally brought us out of the darkness but also launched thousands of inventions, all of which have allowed mankind to begin to harness the forces of nature, thus improving nearly every aspect of our daily lives.

The *third* transforming development was the invention of the microchip. As the brains of the computer, the semiconductor has been mankind's passport to a whole new universe of knowledge. The average American worker with a $799 Pentium-chip laptop computer has more computing power at his fingertips than was contained in all of the computers in the entire world during World War II. One hundred years ago, all of the greatest mathematicians in the world together did not have the problem-solving resources of today's fourth grader with a $19.95 Texas Instruments pocket calculator.

An Unprecedented Era of Progress

Americans have a tendency to believe that things used to be better than they are now. This inclination typically impels us to look to government to make things better. The nostalgia that many Americans express for the 1950s is a notable example. However, as the comedian Jackie Gleason once noted, "The past remembers better than it lived." For the vast majority of Americans—particularly minorities and women—life was not better in the 1950s than it is today. We are healthier; we live longer; we are richer; we can afford to purchase far more; we have more time and money for recreation; we have bigger and better homes; we are at much less risk of catastrophic accidents; and we breathe cleaner air and drink safer water. The list could go on and on. It is impossible, of course, to measure Americans' spiritual well-being, but there can be little argument that our material well-being has never been better.

The doubters will wonder whether our present glorious age in America is just another blip in history, like the Egyptian, Persian, and Roman Empires and the Golden Age of Greece. Skeptics moan that either the progress we experienced in the 20th century will be reversed or, as some environmentalists fear, we will be done in by growth mania itself. We may simply be living through another episode of dynastic glory that will soon falter.

We doubt it. The advance of civilization that we are now living through is different from previous advances. Ours is the first age in which affluence has been enjoyed by more than just a tiny fraction of the population. In previous times, even in the great empires, at least 90 percent of the populace remained at a Malthusian level of subsistence. Never before have improvements in the quality of life been spread to virtually every segment of the population as they were in the United States and the developed world in the 20th century.

Perhaps the best way to dramatize this point is to compare the living conditions of the poor today with those of well-to-do citizens 100 years ago. As we close the books on the 20th century, most Americans who are considered "poor" today have routine access to a quality of food, health care, consumer products, entertainment, communications, and transportation that even the Vanderbilts, the Carnegies, the Rockefellers, and 19th-century European royalty, with all their combined wealth, could not have afforded. No mountain of gold 100 years ago could have purchased the basics of everyday life that we take for granted today: a television set, a stereo with the first music ever recorded, a cellular telephone, a car, a vaccination against polio, a Häagen Dazs ice cream bar, a sinus tablet, contact lenses (to say nothing of laser surgery), or the thrill of seeing Michael Jordan majestically soar through the air as if defying gravity while dunking a basketball. Today, almost all Americans can afford these things.

We are also optimistic because, unlike previous eras of progress, the gains that were made in the 20th century are truly irreversible since they are primarily the result of the wondrous advances of human knowledge that accumulated in the past century. That knowledge can never be erased, even if barbarians or Luddites were to burn every library to the ground. Encyclopedias can now be stored on a six-inch, $10 computer disk. If, God forbid, a bomb were to destroy all the physical capital and infrastructure of the United

States, those structures could be rebuilt in a generation, provided there were still people around to do the rebuilding. (Consider how quickly Germany was resurrected after World War II.) Moreover, the information age makes it almost futile for repressive governments, like that of the former Soviet Union, to try to restrain freedom through military might, as they did in previous eras.

Finally, we are convinced that the progress of the 20th century is not a mere historical blip but rather the start of a long-term trend of improved life on earth, because almost every measure of human material welfare has shown gains. This is the first time in human history that has happened.

Indeed, we are hard-pressed to find more than a small handful of trends that worsened in the 20th century. Taxes are higher and government is a lot bigger and more intrusive than 100 years ago in the United States. (We believe that big government may be a consequence, but surely not the cause, of prosperity.) The good news is that, at this moment in history, for most inhabitants of the planet, freedom is marching forward and is not in retreat. Even in the United States, federal spending as a percentage of gross domestic product has now dipped to its lowest level in 25 years—suggesting that perhaps Bill Clinton was right that "the era of big government is over."

Some social trends, of course, indicate deterioration not improvement over the past 30 to 40 years, as William Bennett and Robert Bork have emphasized. There have been worrisome increases in family breakups, abortions, illegitimate births, and teen suicides, for example. Violent crime rates have drifted upward—in the 1920s, 1960s, 1970s, and 1980s—and downward—in the 1930s and 1990s—not long enough to confirm long-term improvement. However, there are glimmers of good news. In recent years, most of these troubling trends of social decay have been abating, and for almost all the other social problems, the arrow points to improvement on a grand scale.

Winston Churchill once said that "the further back you look, the further ahead in the future you can see."[6] The declinists are wrong when they say that mankind is on a collision course with doomsday. For Americans, the 20th century was not mostly an era of world war, environmental degradation, catastrophic global warming, capitalist exploitation, overpopulation, and a deep divide between the haves and the have-nots. (As John Tierney of the *New York Times* lamented

61

Figure 4.3
U.S. LIFE EXPECTANCY AT BIRTH, 20TH CENTURY

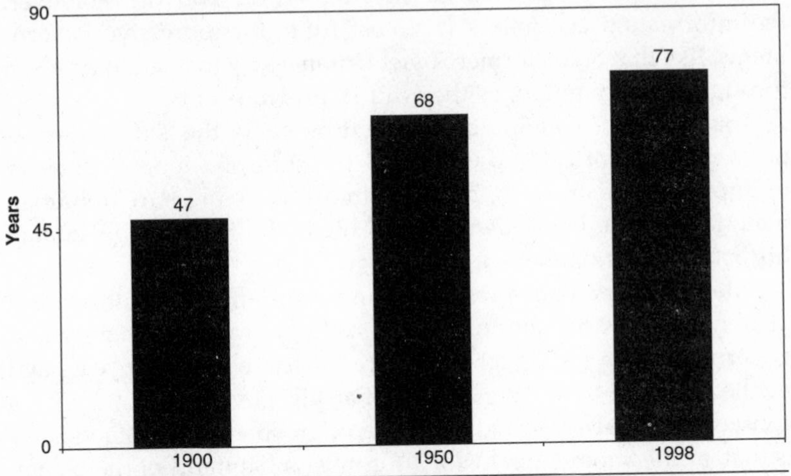

SOURCES: *Historical Statistics of the United States,* Series B 107; and *Monthly Vital Statistics Report 47,* no. 45, Table 16.

not long ago: "No matter how much healthier and wealthier everyone becomes, we always read about a gap between one group or another. . . . As more babies survive, we focus on endangered species of beetles."[7]) It is imperative that we understand and appreciate the advances of our recent history so we can use our resources wisely for solving real societal problems, not make-believe ones.

So the purpose of this chapter is in part to set the historical record straight; it is a plea that the history books and the media try to get the story right. We hope that the 25 great trends presented in the following pages and in Table 4.1 will convince people that the 20th century was the greatest century that ever was. It should also convince even the zealous skeptics that the past 100 years truly have been the American century.

Human Life Span

The most amazing demographic fact of the past century, and the greatest human achievement in history in our view, is that humanity has almost won the battle against early death. We are not alone in this assessment. Several years ago the *New York Times* described the

Figure 4.4
INFANT AND MATERNAL MORTALITY RATES

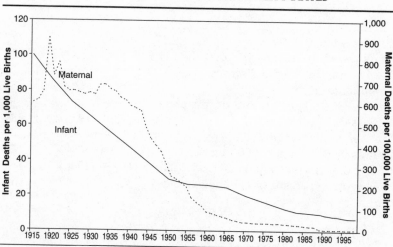

SOURCES: Centers for Disease Control, National Center for Health Statistics, *Health, United States, 1999* (Hyattsville, Md.: NCHS, 1999), Tables 22, 44; *National Vital Statistics Report 47*, no. 45, Table D; and *Historical Statistics of the United States*, Series B 136, B 145.

doubling of life expectancy since the start of the Industrial Revolution as "the greatest miracle in the history of our species."[8] Throughout most of human history, death came at an early age—often 25 to 35 years was a typical life span. In the United States over the past 100 years, life expectancy has increased to 77 years (Figure 4.3)— triple the life span of our ancient ancestors and three decades longer than our great-grandparents could expect to live at the turn of the century. Incredibly, the life expectancy of black Americans has almost doubled in this century.

Death Rate of Children and Mothers

Dear to the hearts of all parents is the safety of their children. Any parent who has experienced the joy of bringing a healthy baby into the world can imagine the agony that parents suffer when they lose a child at birth. In the early part of the 20th century, more than 1 child in 10 died before his or her first birthday. In some areas of the country, infant mortality was as high as 1 in 4. Today, only 1 in about 150 babies dies within the first year. The probability of a

Table 4.1
25 WONDERFUL TRENDS OF THE 20TH CENTURY

Trend	1900–1920[a]	1995–98[b]
Life expectancy (years)	47	77
Infant mortality (deaths per 1,000 live births)	100	7
Deaths from infectious diseases (per 100,000 population)	700	50
Heart disease (age-adjusted deaths per 100,000 population)	307 (1950)	126
Per capita GDP (1998 dollars)	$4,800	$31,500
Manufacturing wage (1998 dollars)	$3.40	$12.50
Household assets (trillions of 1998 dollars)	$6 (1945)	$41
Poverty rate (percent of U.S. households)	40	13
Length of workweek (hours)	50	35
Agricultural workers (percent of workforce)	35	2.5
TV ownership (percent of U.S. households)	0	98
Homeownership (percent of U.S. households)	46	66
Electrification (percent of U.S. households)	8	99
Telephone calls (annual per capita calls)	40	2,300
Cars for transportation (percent of U.S. households)	1	91
Patents granted	25,000	150,000
High school completion (percent of adults)	22	88
Accidental deaths (per 100,000 population)	88	34
Wheat price (per bushel in hours of work)	4.1	0.2
Bachelor's degrees awarded to women (percent of degrees)	34	55
Black income (annual per capita, 1997 dollars)	$1,200	$12,400
Resident U.S. population (millions)	76	265
Air pollution (lead, micrograms per 100 cubic meters of air)	135 (1977)	4
Computer speed (millions of instructions per second)	0.02 (1976)	700
Computer ownership (percent of U.S. households)	1 (1980)	44

[a] Values are for earliest year for which data are available.
[b] Values are for latest year for which data are available.

Figure 4.5
INCIDENCE OF SELECTED DISEASES IN THE UNITED STATES

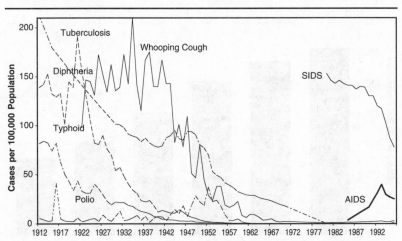

SOURCES: *Historical Statistics of the United States*, Series B 149, B 291, B 295, B 299–300, B 303; *Health, United States, 1999*, Table 53; and American SIDS Institute, www.sids.org/rsearch/webrate/sld001.htm.

NOTE: SIDS rate is per 100,000 live births. AIDS definition was substantially expanded in 1985, 1987, and 1993. TB rate before 1930 is estimated as 1.3 times the mortality rate.

child's dying before the age of 5 is now 50 times lower than it was at the beginning of the past century (Figure 4.4). Most impressive of all has been the decline in the maternal death rate. One hundred years ago a mother was 100 times more likely to die giving birth than she is today—now there are fewer than 8 maternal deaths per 100,000 births.

Infectious Diseases

One of the greatest success stories of the 20th century is that we have extinguished almost all of the major diseases that have killed billions of people throughout human history. Because of vaccines and better public health measures, we no longer even worry about the scourges of typhoid fever, cholera, typhus, plague, polio, small-pox, and the other terrifying killers of humankind. Throughout most of history plagues and epidemics could wipe out a fourth to a half

65

Figure 4.6
HEART DISEASE MORTALITY

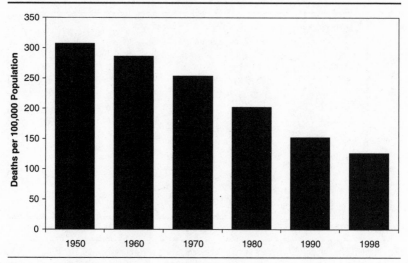

SOURCE: *Health, United States, 1999,* Table 37.

of a country's population in the course of a decade. Even as recently as the beginning of the 20th century, the death toll from infectious diseases was about 700 per 100,000 Americans per year.[9] Today infectious diseases kill only about 50 per 100,000—a stunning 14-fold reduction in deaths from disease in one century. The number of cases of those diseases has fallen even more rapidly. Although sudden infant death syndrome and AIDS are not diseases per se, the number of cases of those ailments has also decreased (Figure 4.5).

Cancer and Heart Disease

The eradication of the most horrible and deadly infectious diseases, which often afflicted children, has meant that more Americans die from chronic and degenerative diseases associated with growing old—most notably, cancer and heart disease. Although we have not yet found complete cures for those two diseases, modern medicine and treatments have made spectacular strides in both cases. The age-adjusted death rate from heart attacks has fallen between two- and threefold in just the last 50 years (Figure 4.6), and the survival rate of cancer victims has nearly doubled in the past 40 years

Figure 4.7
FIVE-YEAR RELATIVE CANCER SURVIVAL RATES

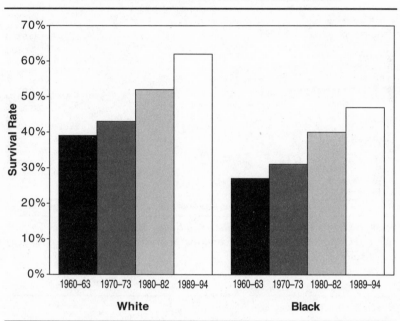

SOURCE: *Health, United States, 1999,* Table 58.

(Figure 4.7). For whites, the rate of cancer survival went from 38 percent in 1960–63 to 62 percent in 1994. For blacks the probability of survival has risen from roughly 1 in 4 in the early 1960s to 1 in 2 today.

National Output

The broadest measure of a nation's overall economic performance is the rise in its national output, or what is now commonly called gross domestic product (GDP). The real GDP of the United States mushroomed from roughly $0.5 trillion in 1900 to about $8.5 trillion in 1998 (in constant dollars). The average annual per person output in the United States has grown from $5,000 to $30,000 (Figure 4.8). This rapid growth contrasts with the economic performance of the world over the last 1,000 years when, according to the late Harvard economic historian Simon Kuznets, economic growth was "virtually nonexistent." "We Americans are so used to sustained economic growth in per-capita product that we tend to take it for granted—

Figure 4.8
GROSS DOMESTIC PRODUCT

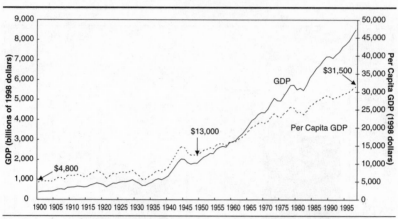

SOURCES: *Historical Statistics of the United States*, Series F 1; and U.S. Department of Commerce, Bureau of Economic Analysis, www.bea.doc.gov/bea/dn/gdplev.htm.

Figure 4.9
WORKER COMPENSATION

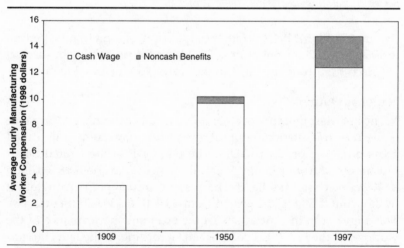

SOURCES: *Historical Statistics of the United States*, Series D 802; and U.S. Bureau of the Census, *Statistical Abstract of the United States: 1998* (Washington: Government Printing Office, 1998), Table 867.

not realizing how exceptional growth of this magnitude is on the scale of human history," Kuznets concluded.

Wages

We often hear nostalgic talk of the good old days of the 1950s when it took only one parent's income to raise a family. Dad went to the office or factory. There was enough income for Mom to stay home and take care of the kids. Good jobs were available at good wages. Nowadays, we are told, families struggle on two incomes just to make ends meet. The century-long wage data tell a different story. The hourly manufacturing wage in the United States at the start of the 20th century (in today's dollars) was $3.43, or less than the minimum wage today. By 1950 that wage rate had risen to $9.70. Today, the average manufacturing wage is $12.47 an hour (Figure 4.9). It appears from the data that wages have stagnated in recent decades, but that is a statistical illusion. When the value of fringe benefits—such as employer-provided medical insurance, retirement packages, stock options, increased vacation time, and unemployment insurance—is taken into account, average real hourly worker compensation has risen by about 50 percent since 1950.

Wealth

It is amazing but true that more financial wealth has been generated in the United States over the past 50 years than was created in all the rest of the world in all the centuries before 1950. Fifty years ago, real financial wealth was about $5 trillion in 1998 dollars. By 1970 that financial wealth had doubled to roughly $10 trillion. Since then the value of Americans' financial wealth has tripled to $30 trillion. When we combine this burst in financial assets with the sevenfold real increase in housing equity owned by Americans, we discover that the nation's assets have risen from about $6 trillion to more than $40 trillion in real terms in the past half century (Figure 4.10). Not all of this wealth is captured by the richest Americans. Median household wealth more than doubled from 1965 to 1995. Although we hear complaints about Americans' indebtedness, asset values have risen at a much faster rate than has debt.

Poverty

In the United States today, a smaller percentage of the population suffers from material deprivation than at any previous time in history. And people classified as "poor" in the United States have

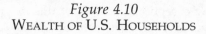

Figure 4.10
WEALTH OF U.S. HOUSEHOLDS

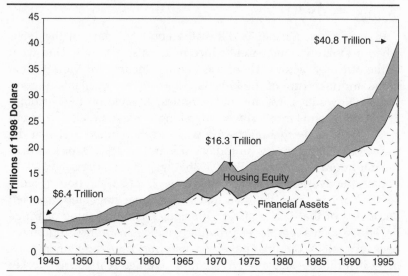

SOURCE: Federal Reserve Board, "Flow of Funds Accounts of the United States," www.federalreserve.gov/releases/z1/Current/data.htm.

incomes that exceed the average income of most nations. Our success in reducing poverty is not a result of government welfare programs.[10] Rather, it appears that the continuing rising tide of America's free-market economy is lifting almost all boats. Some 30 million Americans, or between 10 and 15 percent of the population, are still officially classified as poor. At the previous turn of the century, between 40 and 50 percent of American households had income levels that would have classified them as poor if judged by today's standards. The number of "poor" senior citizens, children, and blacks is half of what it was in 1950 (Figure 4.11).

The Workweek

The typical American works substantially less nowadays and has substantially more leisure time than his counterpart did 100 years ago. Because workers are so much more productive on the job today than in earlier times, we can afford to work fewer hours and still receive higher pay and maintain a high-quality lifestyle. The average workweek has shrunk from about 66 hours in 1850, to 50 hours in

Figure 4.11
U.S. POPULATION BELOW OFFICIAL POVERTY LEVEL

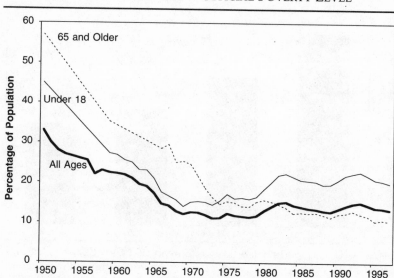

SOURCE: *Statistical Abstract of the United States: 1998*, Tables 764, 765.

1909, to 35 hours today (Figure 4.12). And, because Americans have more holidays, vacation time, sick leave, and so on, the average number of hours worked in a year is now half of what it was in the latter part of the 19th century. We Americans now complain that we don't have enough time to get everything done—work, family responsibilities, household chores, exercise, and other must-do activities—in just 24 hours a day. The fact is that our ancestors were more overworked than we are.

Farm Productivity

A defining characteristic of a modern, wealth-generating economy is ever-increasing output with ever-decreasing input. This is the essence of what we mean when we talk about productivity: getting more of what we want for less human toil. Nowhere has productivity been more impressive than on the farm (Figure 4.13). Throughout most of human history, at least half of the workers in most societies were employed in agriculture. Today, only 2 to 3 percent of Americans work on farms. But those farmers produce enough food for the

71

Figure 4.12
LENGTH OF THE WORKWEEK

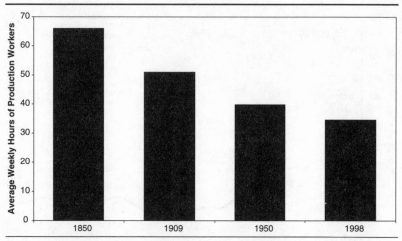

SOURCES: U.S. Department of Labor, Bureau of Labor Statistics, http://146.142.4.24/cgi-bin/surveymost?ee. Hours for 1850 estimated from nonagricultural data in Julian L. Simon, ed., *The State of Humanity* (Cambridge, Mass.: Blackwell, 1995), p. 295.

Figure 4.13
U.S. FARM LABOR PRODUCTIVITY

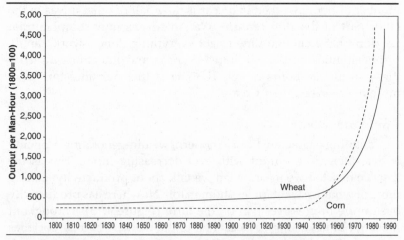

SOURCE: Authors' calculations from data in I. Welfeld, *Where We Live* (New York: Simon and Schuster, 1988).

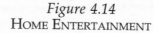

Figure 4.14
HOME ENTERTAINMENT

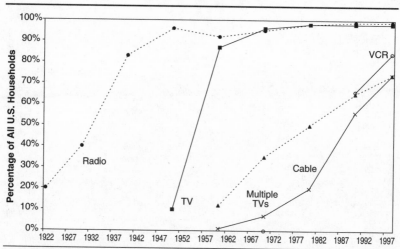

SOURCES: Stanley Lebergott, *The American Economy: Income, Wealth, and Want* (Princeton: Princeton University Press, 1976), pp. 281, 286–88, 290, 355; and U.S. Bureau of the Census, *American Housing Survey for the United States in 1997* (Washington: Government Printing Office, 1998).

entire nation and then enough more to make America the world's breadbasket. Productivity and innovation on the farm have translated into a 5- to 10-fold increase in farm output per man-hour worked in the 20th century—one of the greatest success stories in human history. Modern technologies—for farm equipment, pesticides, fertilizers, irrigation techniques, and bioengineering—account for this surge in agricultural output. The result: American farmers now feed at least three times as many people with one-half as many total man-hours on one-third less farmland than they did in 1900.

Entertainment

Motion pictures were perhaps the first form of modern entertainment. The motion picture industry was launched at the turn of the century and was so instantly popular that by 1930 Hollywood sold three tickets per week per household—an all-time high. In the 1960s, 1970s, and 1980s, movie ticket sales dropped dramatically. Why? Television. Just before the midpoint of the century, 1946, there were

Figure 4.15
IMPROVEMENT IN U.S. HOUSING

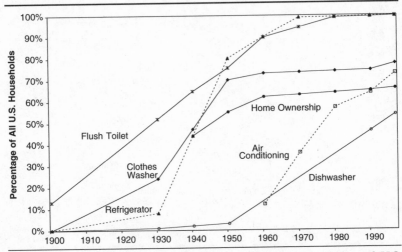

SOURCES: *American Housing Survey for the United States in 1997;* and U.S. Bureau of the Census, "Housing Then and Now," www.census.gov/hhes/ www/housing/census/histcensushsg.html.

about 17,000 TV sets in the country. By 1960 there were more than 40 million TV sets in use. Those Zenith and Motorola TV sets were black-and-white and full of static. Today, 98 percent of American households own a color TV, 67 percent own two color TVs, 40 percent own three TVs, 74 percent have cable TV, 40 percent get pay cable stations, 84 percent have a VCR, 32 percent have at least two VCRs, and 93 percent have a remote control with their TV (Figure 4.14). The diffusion of stereos and CD players into American homes has also been remarkably rapid.

Housing

In 1890 Jacob Riis published his famous book, *How the Other Half Lives,* which describes the horrid and unsanitary conditions of tenement slums.[11] Families with three or four children were crowded into single rooms. The dilapidated housing units typically lacked hot water and toilet facilities and were often infested with rats. Today's homes are far superior to those squalid and cramped living quarters. The average home today has two to three times as many

74

Figure 4.16
˙ELECTRIFICATION OF U.S. HOMES

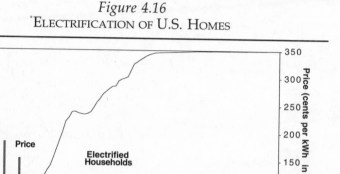

SOURCES: *Historical Statistics of the United States,* Series S 109, S 116; and *Statistical Abstract of the United States: 1998,* Table 959.

rooms per resident as was the case at the turn of the century. In 1900 only about 1 in 100 homes had a toilet or central heating. Even in 1950 air conditioning was rare. Today, at least 97 percent of homes have electricity, central heating, and modern plumbing (Figure 4.15). The rate of home ownership in America has risen from less than 50 percent in 1945 to an all-time high of 67 percent today.

Electrification

Electricity modernized almost every aspect of American industry and home life in the 20th century. Electricity replaced water and steam as a much more powerful and efficient source of energy for industrial production. And, of course, the electrification of American homes first brought light and then made possible the massive revolution in household appliances: radios, TVs, refrigerators, vacuum cleaners, and washing machines. In 1900, 2 percent of homes had electricity. In 1950 about 80 percent did. By 1955 about 99 percent of American homes had electricity. Electric bills are much lower today than in the past. In 1900 the wage-indexed price of electricity

75

Figure 4.17
MODERN COMMUNICATION

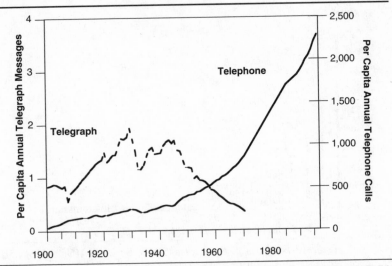

SOURCES: *Historical Statistics of the United States,* Series R 9-12, R 48, R 56; and *Statistical Abstract of the United States: 1998,* Table 915.

was six times above its current level. Residential electricity costs were nearly 10 times higher than today (Figure 4.16).

Communications

A little more than 100 years ago, Americans sent more telegrams than they made telephone calls (Figure 4.17). In the 20th century we went from 5 percent to 99 percent telephone ownership. Today, Americans do not have phones just in their homes. We increasingly have phones in our briefcases, purses, and cars. The corded phone is fast becoming obsolete because it does not travel well and is inconvenient. Sales of corded phones were relatively flat in the 1990s. But sales of cordless and cellular phones have risen sharply (Figure 4.18).In 1997, for the first time ever, Americans bought more cordless than corded phones. Phone calls are not just more convenient, they are substantially cheaper than they used to be. A 10-minute coast-to-coast phone call in 1915 cost about $65.00 in today's dollars.[12]

Transportation

Henry Ford's assembly line brought the price of an automobile—ideal for the wide-open frontiers of a spacious country—within

Figure 4.18
CUTTING THE CORD

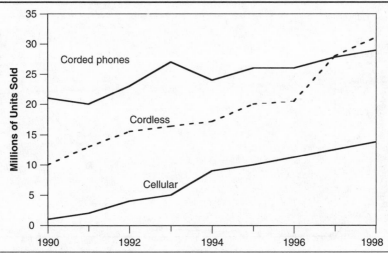

SOURCE: Consumer Electronics Association, cited in *Time,* March 23, 1998, p. 38.
NOTE: Cellular includes digital wireless phones.

Figure 4.19
GROUND TRAVEL: HORSES TO HORSEPOWER

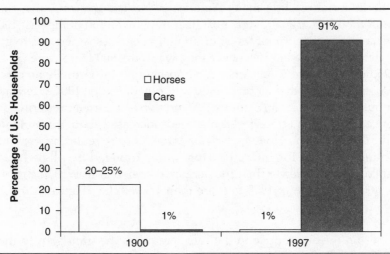

SOURCES: Stanley Lebergott, *The Americans: An Economic Record* (New York: W. W. Norton, 1984); and *American Housing Survey for the United States in 1997,* Table 2-7.

77

Figure 4.20
AIR TRAVEL

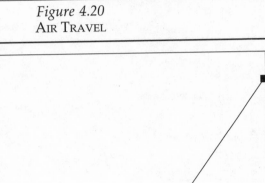

SOURCES: *Historical Statistics of the United States*, Series Q 4; and *Statistical Abstract of the United States: 1998*, Table 1016.

the financial reach of many Americans. Next to the computer, the automobile is arguably the most liberating invention of the past 100 years—a rapid form of transportation that enables Americans to go wherever they want whenever they want. In 1900 there were 20 to 25 horses for every 100 American households and virtually no cars. At the end of the century about 91 out of every 100 American households had a car (Figure 4.19), and horses are used primarily for pleasure. Ground transportation speeds increased about threefold in the 20th century. Nonetheless, air travel is now replacing ground transportation for intercity trips. Miles traveled by plane have increased from fewer than 100 per person per year in 1950 to almost 1,000 per person in 1978 to more than 1,500 today (Figure 4.20).

Inventions

From the automobile to the refrigerator, to the transistor, to the laser, to fiber optics, to modern medicines, the inventiveness and genius of Americans have been a principal driving force behind the rise in the U.S. standard of living over the past 100 years. Probably

Figure 4.21
PATENTS GRANTED BY THE UNITED STATES

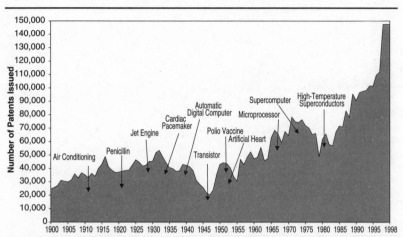

SOURCES: U.S. Patent and Trademark Office, *U.S. Patent Activity, 1790–1998* (Washington: Government Printing Office, 1999); and Louisiana State University, Important Historical Inventions and Inventors, www.lib.lsu.edu/sci/chem/patent/srs136.html.

the greatest inventor in history was Thomas A. Edison (1850–1931), whose light bulb, motion picture projector, phonograph, tape recorder, and roughly 1,000 other patents propelled the United States into the electronic age. But Edison's giant footsteps have been followed by thousands of less well-known American scientists and inventors whose brilliance and creativity are improving the quality of life on earth with every passing year. In 1900 roughly 25,000 patents were issued. By 1950 that number had risen modestly to 43,000. But after 1950 the number of patents tripled to nearly 150,000 in 1997 (Figure 4.21). In the 20th century the number of patents issued grew at twice the pace of the U.S. population.

The Information Age

Texas Instruments introduced the first computer chip to the world in 1958. Since then the semiconductor has been doubling in capacity and speed (Figure 4.22) almost every 18 months (Moore's law)—a geometric growth rate that makes all notions of "limits to growth" obsolete. Today the microchip contained in a single laptop computer

Figure 4.22
MEGABYTE PRICES AND MICROPROCESSOR SPEEDS

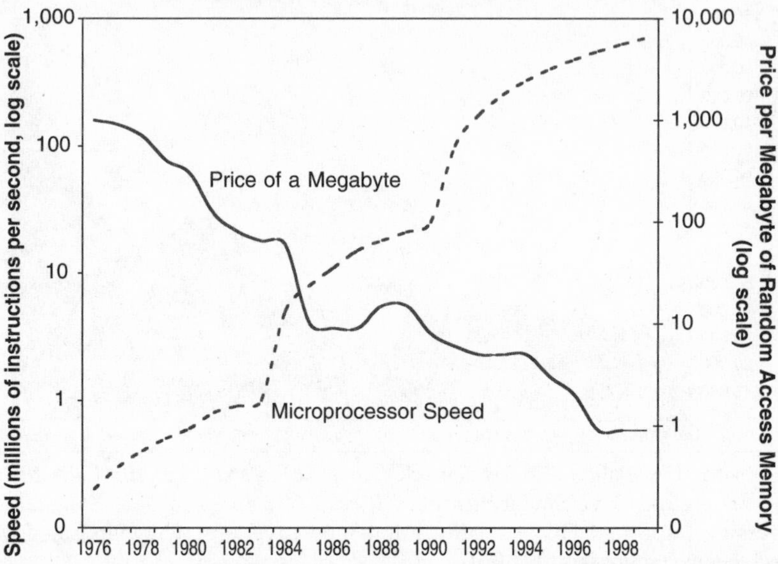

SOURCES: Intel Corporation, www.intel.com; and World Semiconductor Trade Statistics, www.wsts.org.

has more computing power than all the computers used in all the universities across the country in 1950. The cost of processing information and data that once might have been hundreds of thousands, if not millions, of dollars is rapidly falling to zero. The IBM-370-168 mainframe (circa 1975) sold for $3.4 million; today a personal computer with an Intel Pentium chip retails for about $1,500 and is nearly 1,000 times faster. According to an analysis by Microsoft, if automobile and aerospace technology had exploded at the same pace as computer and information technology, a new car would cost about $2 and go 600 miles on a thimble of gas, and you could buy a Boeing 747 for the cost of a pizza.[13]

Computers and the Internet

In 1943 Thomas Watson, chairman of IBM, declared: "I think there is a world market for about five computers." In 1949 *Popular Mechanics* prophesied that "where a calculator on the ENIAC computer is equipped with 18,000 vacuum tubes and weighs 30 tons,

Figure 4.23
AMERICAN HOUSEHOLDS IN THE INFORMATION AGE

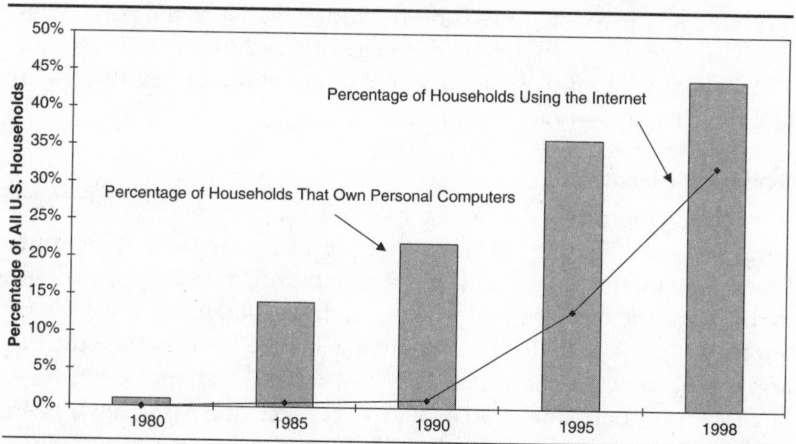

SOURCES: CEMA Research Center, cited in the *Washington Post*, April 26, 1999; and Forrester Research, cited in *USA Today*, June 22, 1999.

computers in the future may have only 1,000 vacuum tubes and perhaps only weigh 1 1/2 tons." Steve Jobs, the founder of Apple Computer, was asked by Xerox executives in the mid-1970s: "Why would anyone ever need a computer in their home?" Thanks to the rapid decline in price of the personal computer, today almost half of all U.S. homes have personal computers. Home computers are rapidly connecting every American to an information source far greater than the Library of Congress: the Internet (Figure 4.23). Eric Schmidt, chairman and CEO of Novell, predicts: "At the current rate of growth of the Internet, every man, woman, and child in the United States will be connected to the Internet by 2007."[14]

Education

Today, the United States has the most highly schooled workforce in the history of the world. The quantity (though perhaps not the quality) of schooling received by Americans rose in almost every decade of the 20th century. Today, the percentage of Americans graduating from college (28 percent) is higher than the percentage of Americans graduating from high school in 1920 (22 percent). Average years of schooling have increased from 8 to 12 for whites and from 6 to 12 for blacks. The percentage of American adults with

81

a high school diploma has risen from about 4 in 10 in 1940 to more than 8 in 10 today. Meanwhile, the percentage of Americans receiving advanced degrees is higher today than was the percentage receiving a college degree at the start of the 20th century (Figure 4.24). The increased years of schooling very closely track the rise in lifetime earnings of our workforce.

Accidental Deaths

Anyone who reads the newspaper headlines or watches the evening news on TV must believe that we live in mighty dangerous times. It sometimes seems that the number of murders, shootings, thefts, airplane crashes, hurricanes, highway fatalities, and acts of terrorism has soared to unprecedented levels. Here is the surprisingly good news: As Figure 4.25 shows, the accidental death rate has fallen by half since 1903–12. The biggest decreases have been in the rate of accidental deaths of infants (down 88 percent since 1900) and of seniors (down 67 percent). The accidental death rate on the job has also plummeted. In 1930 about 38 of every 100,000 workers died at the workplace, versus about 4 per 100,000 today. This sevenfold reduction in job-related deaths is due to several factors: First, fewer Americans work in risky places, such as unsafe factories and coal mines; second, safety measures are vastly improved for those who do work in risky occupations; and finally, improved medical care saves the lives of more people who are injured.

Environmental Quality

There is almost certainly no other issue about which Americans' general preconceptions are so contrary to objective reality as they are about the environment. Most Americans believe that, because of industrialization, population growth, and our mass-consumption society, the quality of our air and water is deteriorating and that our natural resources will soon run dry. The scientific evidence tells us precisely the opposite: Between 1977 and 1997, levels of six major air pollutants decreased significantly: sulfur dioxide levels decreased 58 percent, nitrogen oxides decreased 27 percent, ozone decreased 30 percent, carbon monoxide decreased 61 percent, and lead decreased an overwhelming 97 percent (Figure 4.26). The quality of

Figure 4.24
PERCENTAGE OF ADULTS AGES 20–29 WHO COMPLETED HIGH SCHOOL OR COLLEGE

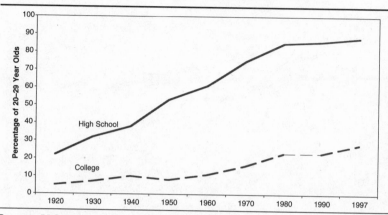

SOURCE: U.S. Department of Education, National Center for Education Statistics, *Digest of Education Statistics 1998* (Washington: Government Printing Office, 1999), Table 8.

Figure 4.25
ACCIDENTAL DEATH RATES BY AGE
(1903–12 AND 1998, WITH PERCENT CHANGE)

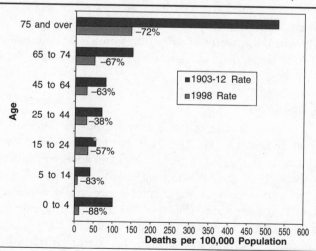

SOURCE: National Safety Council, *Accident Facts* (Washington: NSC, various years).

83

Figure 4.26
NATIONAL AMBIENT AIR QUALITY

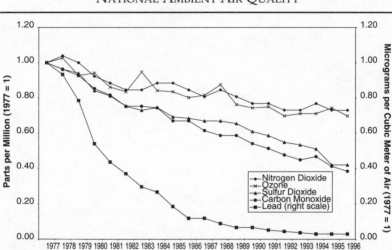

SOURCE: Environmental Protection Agency, Office of Air Quality, Planning and Standards, *National Air Quality and Emissions Trends Report* (Research Triangle Park, N.C.: EPA, 1997).

our water has also improved: The percentage of American households served by modern wastewater treatment plants, which improve environmental water quality, has doubled in the past 40 years. Our drinking water is safer; the number of Americans who contract waterborne diseases has fallen between 5- and 10-fold since the end of the 19th century.

Natural Resources

Anxiety about running out of natural resources dates at least to the time of ancient Greece. The truth is that the price of virtually every commodity—agricultural, mineral, and energy products—fell steadily throughout the 20th century relative to wages. A declining price is an indication of greater abundance, not greater scarcity. Food is so abundant today (Figure 4.27) that the government pays farmers not to grow so much. Of 13 major metals, the only one that has risen in price relative to wages in this century is platinum. The prices of most of the rest have fallen an average of fivefold since 1900. The price of fuel has fallen so sharply since the last OPEC oil

Figure 4.27
WHEAT AND COTTON PRICES RELATIVE TO WAGES

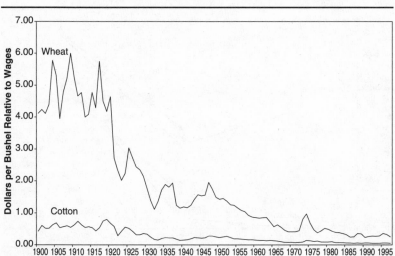

SOURCE: U.S. Department of Agriculture, National Agricultural Statistics Service, www.nass.usda.gov/ipedb.

NOTE: Price of a bushel of each crop was divided by the average wage rate in each respective year.

embargo that "oil is now cheaper than water," according to a 1999 Associated Press bulletin. Fifty years ago the world had about 20 years' worth of known reserves of oil. Thanks to technological innovation, which is outstripping the pace of depletion of reserves, the world now has at least 50 years of reserves.

Sexual Equality

Nearly every positive trend presented in this study—particularly trends of earnings, education, and health—shows greater improvement for women than for men. According to a study by former Congressional Budget Office director June O'Neill, when men and women are similar in all work-relevant characteristics, women now earn 98 cents for every dollar men do, which is close to wage parity.[15] In 1950 only half of American female workers had a high school diploma. Now 90 percent do. More than half of bachelor's and

Figure 4.28
PERCENTAGE OF DEGREES AWARDED TO WOMEN

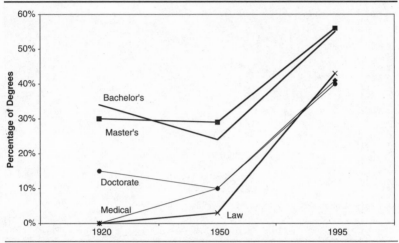

SOURCE: U.S. Department of Education, National Center for Education Statistics, Integrated Postsecondary Education Data System, "Completions" survey, cited in Diana Furchgott-Roth, *Women's Figures* (Washington: American Enterprise Institute, 1998).

master's degrees today are awarded to women (Figure 4.28). Women are more likely than ever to earn advanced degrees in areas once virtually closed to them: law, business management, and medicine, to name a few. One final thought: The proud moment for Americans in 1999 when Mia Hamm and the U.S. women's soccer team won the World Cup against China would not have been possible 50 years ago, when very few women were able to play organized sports.

Racial Equality

Slavery and racism have been two of the greatest stains on American society since our independence—mocking the American claim that "all men are created equal." As recently as 1968 the Kerner Commission on race, appointed after the riots in Los Angeles, Detroit, and other cities, concluded glumly: "Our nation is moving toward two societies, one black, one white—separate and unequal." The commission was wrong. The racial divide in America narrowed, not widened, over the course of the 20th century. African Americans

86

Figure 4.29
BLACK INCOME PER CAPITA AND BLACK/WHITE INCOME RATIO

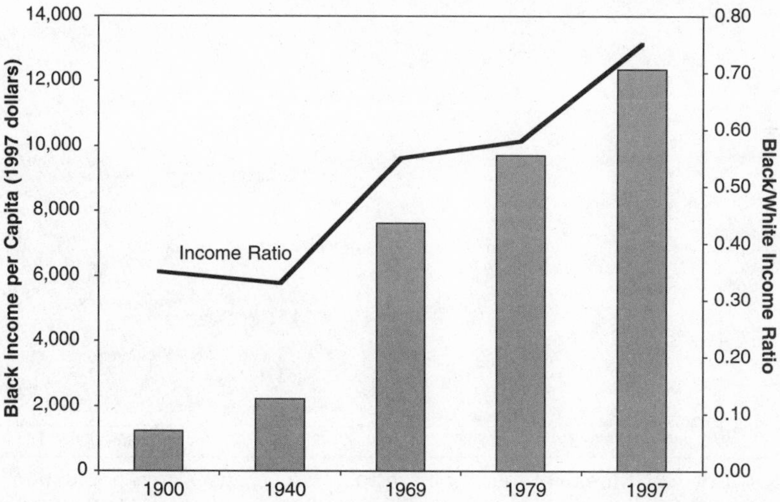

SOURCES: Robert Higgs, *Competition and Coercion: Blacks in the American Economy, 1865–1914* (New York: Cambridge University Press, 1977); and U.S. Bureau of the Census, *Measuring 50 Years of Economic Change* (Washington: Government Printing Office, 1998).

made strong gains in income levels (Figure 4.29), educational attainment, health status, poverty rates, home-ownership rates, and life expectancy in both absolute and relative terms compared with whites. According to economic historians Robert Higgs and Robert Margo, real black per capita income increased "between 1900 and 1940 by 61 percent," and "between 1940 and 1985 by 342 percent."[16] In 1900 black incomes were less than 40 percent of those of whites; in 1979 they were about 58 percent of those of whites; and today they are more than 75 percent of those of whites. The income gap is still too wide, but it was cut in half in the 20th century.

Conclusion: The Greatest Resource

A central message of this study is that the fruits of a free society are prosperity, wealth, and better health. All of the evidence in this analysis documents that, in every material way, life in the United States, with a population of 270 million, is much better today than

Figure 4.30
RESIDENT U.S. POPULATION

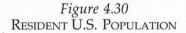

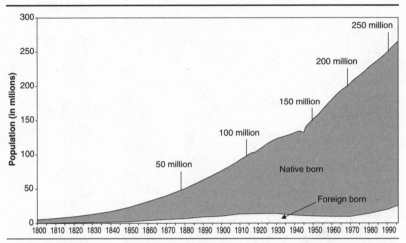

SOURCES: U.S. Bureau of the Census, http://www.census.gov/population/ estimates/nation/popclockest.tst; *Historical Statistics of the United States*, Series A6-8; and U.S. Bureau of the Census, *Profile of Foreign-Born Population in the United States: 1997* (Washington: Government Printing Office, 1999), p. 9.

it was in 1900 when the population was 75 million people. Moreover, the American people are net resource creators, not resource depleters—protectors of the environment, not destroyers. Each generation has left the planet and our continent in better ecological condition for future generations. We have produced more than we have consumed, leaving the savings and wealth to our children and grandchildren. So we consider the happiest social indicator of all in the 20th century to be the rise in the number of Americans (Figure 4.30) who now live in greater affluence than ever before. We hope and predict that millions more people will live long, healthy, happy lives in America in the 21st century.

Notes

Most of the research findings in this chapter come from Julian Simon's lifetime of work showing how life on earth is getting better, not worse. The research assistance of Stephen A. Slivinski and Philip Kerpen is gratefully acknowledged.

1. Henry Allen, "Living in the American Century: 1900–1910," *Washington Post*, September 10, 1999, p. C8.

2. Theodore Dalrymple, "Taking Good Health for Granted," *Wall Street Journal*, March 31, 1999, p. A22.

3. Ibid.

4. Ibid.

5. Paul Johnson, *A History of the American People* (New York: Harper Perennial, 1999), p. 976.

6. Cited in Julian Simon, "Simon Said: Good News!" *Washington Post*, February 22, 1998, p. C1.

7. John Tierney, "The Optimists Are Right," *New York Times Magazine*, September 28, 1996, p. 95.

8. Ibid.

9. American Council on Science and Health, *America's Health: A Century of Progress* (Sumner, N.J.: American Council on Science and Health, 1983), pp. 9–10.

10. See Robert Rector, "The Myth of Widespread American Poverty," Heritage Foundation Backgrounder no. 1221, September 18, 1998.

11. Jacob Riis, *How the Other Half Lives: Studies among the Tenements of New York* (New York: Penguin, 1991).

12. W. Michael Cox and Richard Alm, *The Myths of Rich and Poor* (New York: Basic Books, 1999).

13. See Microsoft's "Open Letter to Ralph Nader Appraising the Nader Conference," PR Newswire, November 13, 1997.

14. Quoted in Gary Dempsey, "The Myth of an Emerging Information Underclass," *The Freeman*, April 1998, p. 217.

15. Diana Furchgott-Roth and Christine Stolba, *Women's Figures* (Washington: American Enterprise Institute, 1998).

16. Robert Higgs and Robert Margo, "Black Americans: Income and Standard of Living from the Days of Slavery to the Present," in *The State of Humanity*, ed. Julian Simon (Cambridge, Mass.: Blackwell, 1995), p. 183.

5. A Century of Unrivaled Prosperity

Rudiger Dornbusch

A world on the verge of deflation, Japan bankrupt and Europe near standstill, emerging markets battered, and the United States entranced by a glorious bubble—are these the culmination of a great century of prosperity? And yet, this has been the best century ever, never mind the Great Depression, a momentary setback from communism and socialism, and two great wars. Mankind today is far ahead of where it has ever been, and the seeds of innovation sprouting from biology to the Internet portend better and richer lives beyond our wildest dreams.

One of the great economists of the 20th century, Joseph Schumpeter—Austria's finance minister in the 1920s and later a Harvard professor—wrote of creative destruction as the dramatic mechanism of economic progress.[1] The past century, in particular its last three decades, witnessed such destruction as the nation-state receded in favor of a global economy, state enterprise and economic repression gave way to free enterprise, and breathtaking innovation and "greedy" capitalism broke down government and corporate bureaucracies. Anyone who says *impossible* finds himself interrupted by someone who just accomplished the seemingly impossible. The process is far from complete: innovation and free enterprise expand the mindset, promote the success and acceptance of this model (to the horror of status-quo politicians), and enhance the exuberance of those willing to embrace a can-do attitude. If the 20th century taught us anything, it is surely this: even daunting setbacks like depression and war are momentary tragedies—buying opportunities, if you like—in a relentless advance of the standard of living and the betterment of human lives.

A Century of Unrivaled Growth

For centuries human progress was limited by low productivity. Estimates of per capita gross domestic product in 1700 (reported in

Figure 5.1
WORLD PER CAPITA GDP

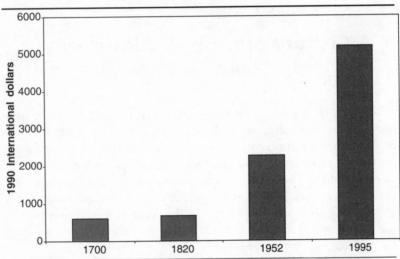

SOURCE: Angus Maddison, *Monitoring the World Economy: 1820–1992* (Paris: Organization for Economic Cooperation and Development, 1995).

the creative work of Angus Maddison) show every region in the world with much the same income per capita and minimal differences between the United States, China, and India. From 1700 to 1820 almost nothing happened to world per capita GDP (see Figure 5.1). True, Europe was somewhat ahead, but by less than 20 percent. A century later, by 1820, the differences had widened to give Europe and the United States twice the income per head enjoyed in China, Japan, or Russia, where near-stagnation had been the rule.[2] Yet, at the time India and China combined accounted for one-half of world GDP! Then a great burst of economic growth tripled Europe's standard of living in the 19th century while quadrupling that in the United States. After centuries of virtually no progress, rapid advances in the standard of living changed both the fact and the perception of what could be achieved. The driving forces were capital accumulation and technical innovation, the division of labor, and the spread of skills and capital around the world.

But what seemed dramatic progress in the 19th century does not begin to compare with the achievements of the 20th century. The

20th century saw the most rapid advance in living standards on record, much of it concentrated in the second half. Just since the 1950s, Japan has increased its standard of living eightfold and China has raised its per capita income more than sevenfold. And emerging-market Asia has done much the same. An opening world economy, high savings almost everywhere (except in the United States), and the implementation of ever-better technologies and economic structures have done much to provide the engine. Moreover, a half century of peace (and superpower competition) has helped not divert attention from economic growth. Whether progress is measured by automobiles and TV sets per head, the decline in the cost of phone calls around the world, the exploding capacity of ever-smaller computers, increasing perfection of a CD recording, or the laser surgery that yields a new life—by any measure, 1900 was the Stone Age compared with where we stand today. Long-distance learning live and on-screen is a far leap from black-and-white still photography.

The record pace of growth in per capita GDP in the second half of the last century naturally invites the question of what is behind it and whether there is a common explanation that is useful everywhere. Economics identifies two elements: first, and obviously, a high pace of saving and capital formation in the world. This equips the labor force with increasing amounts of machinery and structures that make labor more productive. No less obvious is another factor, technological progress, which allows the same amount of labor to produce increasing amounts of output. Technical progress means that over time new ideas and better machinery improve productivity, and so do ways of organizing production and institutions that are more conducive to specialization and productivity. Some highlight creative destruction and others view stable accumulation as the cause. Have war and ideological clashes held back progress compared to what might have occurred without such conflict? Or is it possible, on the contrary, that conflict has driven progress by destroying crusty structures and obsolete technologies? The latter case has been made by those who cite Japan's progress and that of Germany after World War II, putting them far ahead of the rest of the crowd. But then why did similar progress not happen in France?

Economics Nobel laureate Robert Solow was the first to ask how much of growth derives from capital formation and how much from "residual" technical progress—really only a buzzword for everything else. His stunning conclusion gave capital formation credit for

93

just one-third of per capita growth and identified residual technical progress as responsible for the rest. That conclusion remains dramatic because it suggests that the emphasis on saving and investment—popular among economists in Japan and in Europe—is perhaps overdone. After all, the economic game is about consumption, and if it is possible to both consume and get ahead, so much the better. But that is probably the wrong conclusion to draw.

The right conclusion focuses on just what makes up the mysterious concept of technical progress. Is it good financial institutions, is it an economic setting that fosters efficient allocation, is it political stability and property rights? Is it Japanese-style obedience training in schools and on the job? Is it copying other countries' best technologies, or is it the unrelenting pressure of stock markets to extract increasingly better cost performance from CEOs and workers? Disappointingly, the empirical evidence does not give us a short list of factors that enhance technical progress; the evidence remains inconclusive except in a few respects: instability, inflation, mindless bureaucracies, closed and repressed economies. All of these create environments where progress is possible, but only by working and saving extra hard. But when it comes to corporate governance, U.S. style versus Japanese, or labor market characteristics with European long-term relations or U.S.-style high turnover, it is hard to show that one or another has the better influence on how to get ahead. Japanese governance and the German labor market once seemed to hold out the prospect for much better performance; today one is identified with the bankruptcy of Japan and the other with the sclerosis of Europe. The search for lasting good answers continues.

Both the 19th and 20th centuries saw the rapid progress of the advanced countries and there is no surprise in that we identify them with innovation and sustained high rates of capital formation. But the surprise is surely that in just a span of 50 years developing countries have shaken off century-old backwardness. Japan was the first to embark on this path, starting with the reform waves in the last decades of the past century (see Figure 5.2). But it was in particular the last three decades of that century that witnessed the dramatic performance of emerging economies throughout Asia but also, off and on, in other parts of the world. In that period, India nearly tripled its standard of living. From endemic near-starvation it moved far in the direction of sustained rates of per capita GDP growth.

Figure 5.2
ECONOMIC PROGRESS

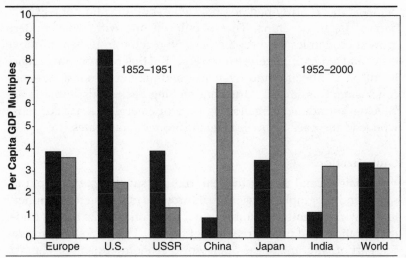

SOURCE: Angus Maddison, *Monitoring the World Economy: 1820–1992* (Paris: Organization for Economic Cooperation and Development, 1995).

Singapore came from nowhere to overtake Great Britain, and China accomplished a phenomenal sixfold increase in living standards starting from a situation in 1950 that was no different from what it had been in 1700! There must be no mistake in reading the Asian performance: it involves very hard work—more hours and more days—and it involves formidable sacrifices of current consumption in favor of capital accumulation and economic advance. Asia has covered the path in just a few decades that elsewhere has taken centuries. But only very authoritarian regimes can accomplish such progress; in open societies sacrificing a few generations is not a viable option.

One is tempted to ask which major country is the great winner of the 20th century. Clearly, Russia is not; it has seen more suffering and deprivation and less progress than almost anywhere else. That was not obvious by the mid-1970s, when Russian per capita GDP peaked, but it is beyond question today and it is increasingly the case. Europe, Japan, the United States, and China are among the finalists; on sheer numbers, Japan is the winner—the Great Depression and a drastic defeat notwithstanding. China is next with its awesome growth of the past three decades. Europe and the United States did well enough by historical standards—quintupling income per head in a century had no precedent—but they did not reach the pace of Japan or China. That is quite in line with what modern growth economics teaches: the ones who come from behind move faster and tend, ultimately, to converge. But that pace of convergence is still very unequal and even its continuation is not a foregone conclusion: Russia and Africa are moving backwards; India is advancing but not at the galloping pace of emerging Asia. For those who lead the pack, growth tapers off to moderate rates.

Globalization

The late second part of the 19th century saw the steamship, railroads, and telegraph as major breakthroughs in joining the periphery to the world's center economies. Globalization was the rule in trade, in migration, and in the free flow of capital. The gold standard was but part of what made the open world economy function. The rich countries wrote the rules. They had gunboats to collect debts, and they had an interest in keeping open the world economy even as they collected colonies, spreading the benefits of free trade. This was the period in which the United States had risen rapidly to prosperity and in which Australia and Argentina came to top rank in the world economy. Migration to the New World, and the migration of capital, rapidly developed the world's periphery. If there were concerns about globalization then, they were too minor to be remembered.

In the 20th century, the Great Depression produced the total collapse of trade flows, belief in open trade, and belief in free-market economics. In a handful of years the lessons of a century were discredited. In just three years, from 1929 to 1932, world trade fell by 70 percent in value terms and 25 percent in real terms. Prices in world trade collapsed, and trade restrictions were mounted around the world, as "beggar-thy-neighbor" policies became the rule. Tariffs were escalated, quantitative restrictions and selected preferences prevailed, and exchange controls soon followed. The open economy had given way to protection of national markets and an overwhelming presumption that economics stops at the border. The periphery responded in kind to the policies at the center. Debt default became common and industrialization behind protective barriers became

A Century of Unrivaled Prosperity

the rule in those countries where commodity collapses no longer afforded a living. Latin America is a case in point.

But already by 1934, driven by the all-important U.S. Reciprocal Trade Agreements, the attempt to reopen world trade got under way. But it would take decades to gradually break down the fortresses. A key part of that reconstruction was the Marshall Plan, which rewarded European restoration of trade. An attempt at a World Trade Organization failed, but the General Agreement on Tariffs and Trade (GATT) became a pragmatic way of negotiating reciprocal, nondiscriminatory opening of trade. At the end of the 1950s exchange controls were gradually dismantled, for trade first and increasingly for all cross-border transactions. But all this was only the case for the advanced countries; the world's periphery and Japan had firmly accepted protection and currency controls as the only way to go. For them, opening up had to wait until the 1980s.

By the 1980s the world was basically back to where it had been before the collapse in the Great Depression. Of course, communications had improved radically, which made for more openness and trade as did dramatic improvements in transport. But at the time, fully in the midst of an open world economy, it was rare to find sharp skepticism of globalization. That seems to be an issue of far more recent vintage, fostered predominantly by five factors.

First, corporations learned to operate globally in the pursuit of markets and cost reductions. The recipe was easy, capital was mobile, and in no time workers anywhere felt the competition from workers everywhere. Second, because of the mobility of capital, more financial accidents occurred, inevitably or not. Their large fallout costs evidently cast a deep suspicion on the globalization that had allowed the money to come in.

The third reason the global economy has a bad name is that competitive pressure forced governments to retreat from their statist policies. That left workers with a reduced sense of protection; standard responses of trade protection were ruled out by international agreements; there was no way to leave the ring. Fourth, with leverage and integrated world capital markets, a disturbance anywhere can immediately become a problem everywhere. With more volatile economies and markets no day passes without reminders of the precariously small control people feel they have over their economic lives.

Last, the sheer pace of change in technology and finance, innovation, products—and in winners and losers—outstripped people's ability to cope: their reaction has often been to opt out simply because things were happening too fast. They predominantly see the threat and very little of the vast benefits. They certainly fail to recognize that when jobs are threatened it is mostly better technology, which in itself is a blessing, rather than cross-border competition that puts people out of their jobs.

Globalization is the great challenge of the turn of the century because, unlike in 1900, the pace of integration of the world economy has become phenomenally rapid. Competitors like China can in a decade or two move from producing entry-level technologies well into the middle level, threatening not only emerging markets but even established industries at the center. Workers believe that globalization is responsible for poor real wages, and governments feel that their ability to control events, or at least give the appearance of doing so, is sharply diminished by the impact of world shocks on the domestic scene. The wish to opt out, or at least limit interdependence, is heard all too often.

The openness and interdependence of the world economy are not going to be sacrificed. But we cannot be sure that the volatility of financial markets will decline or the pace of innovation and implementation of techniques will slow down. Globalization will cease to be a concern in a generation or so when the young who have known no other world and are tuned to less stability come to be representative. But that means globalization will be controversial and will be challenged with a sympathetic hearing for quite a while. It puts the burden on policymakers to keep the world economy open and to deal with unnecessary instability in a sound way.

The Fate of Good Money

Throughout the past century, major changes in the value of money were a prime economic and social issue. As the century closed, the circle was complete: we are back to good money and to institutions that promise to keep it that way. For most of the century we had inflation, interrupted briefly in the interwar period. The post–World War II period in particular saw intolerably high inflation as the

Figure 5.3
PRICE LEVEL IN THE UNITED STATES AND UNITED KINGDOM

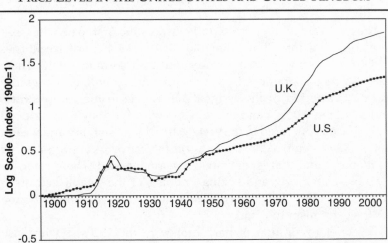

result of irresponsible monetary policy (see Figure 5.3). The price paid for instability has been steep, both while it lasted and in the aftermath, as good money had to be restored.

The century started with the gold standard: Britain had been there for a century, the United States joined after the Civil War and Germany after the Franco-German war; by 1900 every major country from Japan to Europe and Argentina was on gold. Very few countries were on paper standards and even fewer were hanging on to silver. The gold standard meant fixed exchange rates around the world and moderate inflation because gold discoveries were not plentiful and central banks and politicians had not yet discovered the printing press. Public finance was for the most part conservative and economic horizons were long—British perpetuities yielded 3 percent for much of the second part of the 19th century and on to World War I. Pax Britannica was a good monetary regime.

World War I ended all that in the most dramatic fashion. Along with revolution and social upheaval, good money and the emperor all landed in the garbage dump. Governments who could do virtually nothing could do that one thing: print money. And that is what marked the early 1920s: phenomenal money creation and even more extreme inflation throughout central Europe and Eastern Europe,

99

from Germany to Russia, from Austria to Greece. France, to its own surprise, did not go quite as far; Britain and the United States, not at all.

The hyperinflation of the early 1930s was the first to be witnessed in recorded history. True, the gold discoveries in earlier centuries had led to a trend of rising prices, but ever so moderately. There had also been sporadic episodes of paper money inflation in France during the period of the assignats, in Russia in the 19th century, and a little in Austria and in Latin America. But they were after all insignificant compared to the vast destruction of stability and wealth in the 1920s. Lenin said, "if you want to destroy a country, destroy its money," and that is, of course, what happened. There could be no more convincing and lasting undoing of the established order and the middle class. Hyperinflation was surely the prime reason for the extremism to come.

The brief restoration of hard money in the 1920s did not last. Britain, which had championed the return to gold around the world and had in fact returned to it at the pre-war parity, locked itself into a desperately uncompetitive situation. From there it was just a few years to the next bout of instability as, following Britain, country after country went off gold, competitive devaluation became the rule along with exchange controls, and world trade collapsed. But going off gold was neither easy nor obvious. It was a deeply counter-cultural move, going against the grain of everything Britain and the City stood for. In fact, Winston Churchill said at the time, "nobody told me you could do that"—famous last words for the end of Victorian finance. Whereas in the 1920s hyperinflation was the rule, the Great Depression brought deep deflation, which was just as unsettling to stable finance or public confidence. Those who tried to stay on gold did terribly; those who printed more money and debased their currency most aggressively did best. The world had turned upside down. Internationalism and capitalism were discredited; nationalism and ever more pervasive government took their place.

Post-war monetary reconstruction did not come easy. Huge debts, private and public, had been accumulated everywhere and many of the assets, including the tax base, had been devastated. Price controls everywhere held off the confrontation between a vast monetary overhang and a shortage of goods; black markets were the rule, from foreign exchange to sausages. Monetary reform and reconstruction, including drastic write-downs of private claims and public debts, were the rule throughout Europe. Monetary reform paved the way for price liberalization and the extraordinary resumption of economic activity thought by many to be impossible. The audacity of reform in Germany, in particular, stands out: U.S. General Lucius Clay told the great reformer Ludwig Erhard, "Mr. Erhard, my advisers tell me you are making a terrible mistake," and Erhard replied, "General, my advisers say the same."[3] Still, Erhard proved right: without functioning money, economic activity could not possibly start, but with good money it could flourish.

On the domestic front, sound money was restored rapidly almost everywhere. With a brief interruption during the Korean War, inflation was not an issue. But on the external side it took to the end of the 1950s to restore convertibility, and even then it was not general. France had recurrent lapses and Britain got there only in 1980 as one of Margaret Thatcher's first moves in office. Japan got there almost a decade later and increasingly so did the entire world. Among major players, only India and China retain inconvertibility as a vestige of government control.

The 20th century's monetary history would not be complete without one more attack of instability and the fierce reaction to restore hard money at any price. U.S. overexpansion of the 1960s, the oil shocks of the 1970s, and, above all, an unwillingness to confront slow growth or even recession to maintain good money are behind the great inflation of that period. True, by the standards of the 1920s, there was serious inflation, but double-digit rates of price inflation alarmed the electorate and became an even more pressing issue than unemployment. In hindsight, a half century of inflation has shrunk the purchasing power of money drastically in every advanced country. Germany fared best—of a 1950 deutsche mark there is almost 25 percent left in real terms; in France, the United Kingdom, or Italy the value remaining is only around 5 percent (see Figure 5.4). Clearly it is time to return to stable money, and that was the battle of the past decade. The mandate for much better money emerged in a strong fashion and turned central banks deaf to the pleas for accommodation. A new order, dating from the early 1980s, increasingly took hold as inflation was pushed down harder and harder. It took that decade, and another decade, to make it credible and lasting.

Figure 5.4
WHAT IS LEFT OF 1950 PURCHASING POWER?

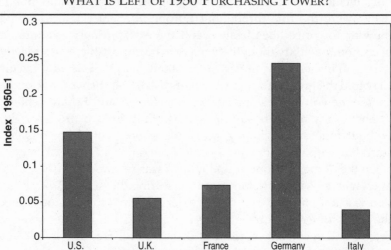

Today the world has no more inflation, and if it comes back it will soon hit a concrete wall. Central banks, in Europe and in the United States, are independent and committed to the idea that inflation needs to be killed at its very inception. Surely that proposition still needs to be tested, surely bond market yields do not quite reflect that lasting regime change quite yet, but skeptics are sure to be proven wrong.

Thus, monetary and financial troubles prevailed basically from World War I to the late 1960s, that is, for half a century. The world we know today is pretty recent, even if it is a return to where we were a century ago. The fight for hard money that has marked the past two decades has brought important changes in finance. Governments had to retreat and formally give up their authority over central banks. In Europe, that has gone furthest with the disarmament of central banks in the soft money belt, from France to Italy and Spain. Debate about whether the European Central Bank (ECB) is a bit too stingy with interest rate cuts must not obscure the central achievement: money has been taken out of the hands of politicians who have mismanaged it for the better part of this century. The ECB is a monument to the proposition that money is too serious to be left to politicians. In these matters there is no such thing as a responsible politician; democratic money thus understood is bad money.

The quest for hard money is also taking over the periphery: country after country has suffered the clash between bad central banking and fixed currencies. In the aftermath of defeat and collapse, a simple lesson is becoming apparent. Countries with poor political and financial institutions cannot afford their own money. They will do far better with unconditional surrender to the ECB or the Federal Reserve. They should adopt the Euro or the U.S. dollar as the national money, get the benefit of sound money and low interest rates, avoid crises, and thus enjoy a better prospect for economic development. Surely, 20 years from now there will be very few currencies left in the world—just as at the beginning of the 20th century. Perhaps there will be Chinese money in Asia, the dollar for the Americas, and the Euro for everywhere else. And perhaps the Swiss franc will become a collectors' item. The vast change in public understanding of hard money, and the resulting stability and lengthening of horizons, is a great accomplishment at the tail end of a century of monetary turmoil.

The State

In response to both the trauma of the Great Depression and a deep skepticism about free enterprise, the state has become a dominant part of economic life. At the outset of the last century, outside periods of war, the state was minimal and so were levels of taxation, government employment, and public outlays. Whereas before business and finance were substantially unregulated, now the state moved to the center in repressing free enterprise and initiative. Whereas before trade and finance flowed freely across borders, now it became national and regulated. Even in the area of production, state enterprise emerged as a response to bankruptcy or private economic power judged excessive. For some, the rise of the state was an ideological response to a loss of confidence in capitalism; for others, it was a pragmatic answer to a collapse of the world economy and of economic activity.

Whatever justification there may have been for big government in the Depression years and wartime, it was clearly gone by the late 1940s. And yet, big government became the accepted paradigm and growing government the rule. But for whatever reason, the state

103

Figure 5.5
SHARE OF GOVERNMENT IN GERMANY

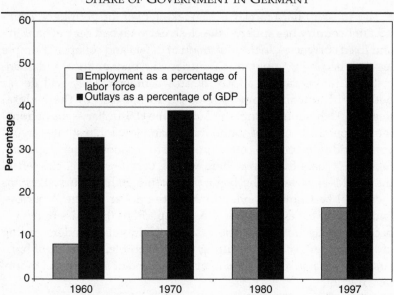

took center place in economic life; in the post–World War II years it has been awfully difficult to roll back the large advance the state made in every dimension. In fact, once the state played a key role in economic life, it was natural to look for ways of expanding its functions and powers to deal with an ever wider range of "problems," substituting government employment, subsidies, or spending for adjustment. The government grew; the private sector shrank in terms of freedom, size, and initiative.

It is interesting to consider just a few numbers marking the case of Germany (see Figure 5.5). By 1960, government employment accounted for 8 percent of the labor force. By 1997 it was 16 percent. And that number does not completely measure the government's largesse since there is in addition the large group of unemployed who are paid not to work and thus keep the status quo and social peace. Government outlays in 1960 amounted to 33 percent of GDP; by 1997 they had reached almost 50 percent. Surely it is not an exaggeration to say that much of the spending is devoted to stopping people from working and that much of the state apparatus does little but slow down private initiative and success. Just what was the problem the government was solving that the private sector could not deal with? The answer is obviously that society rejected adjustment and free market responses as a solution—Why accept hardship if the government commands purse and power to sustain the status quo? People were paid not to work or firms were subsidized to keep producing as if reality had not changed. Regulation completes the picture in the product market by barring initiative and competition.

The fight to restore stable money was much easier to win, particularly in Germany, than the battle for a more productive and financially responsible economy. The reason is obvious: inflation is an immediate threat to the current generation's assets and their sense of stability. They react immediately and give policymakers a mandate to fight for stable prices. But when it comes to government spending and jobs, the choice runs the other way: borrow from the future and support current waste. Never mind that resources are wasted today and create huge tax burdens for future generations; stick with the status quo. It is unlikely that a major boom will resolve these problems and afford an easy adjustment. Communism has fallen, but capitalism is still not accepted in large parts of the world, notably in Europe, where statism continues to be entertained as a "third way." But it is not a third way; it simply amounts to shifting burdens to future generations. The reality is that the bad habit of bloated public sectors and bloated unemployment rolls, and the lack of individual initiative and responsibility, are a dramatic mortgage on future generations and the incoming century.

Inequality

Inequality in the world economy is real. It is there across countries, between the rich center and the poor periphery. And it is there within countries where wages are often highly dispersed. Inequality, of course, must not be confused with poverty even though at the bottom they might feel the same.

The most immediate pass at this issue is to look at the distribution of world income and population (see Figure 5.6). Not surprisingly, high-income countries have the overwhelming share of world income, nearly 60 percent, but have barely 15 percent of world population. By contrast, the poorest countries in the world have 35

Figure 5.6
SHARE OF WORLD INCOME AND POPULATION

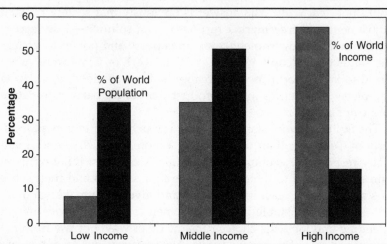

SOURCE: World Bank, *World Development Report, 1998–99* (New York: Oxford University Press, 1999).

percent of world population but less than 10 percent of world income. And these averages disguise the even more striking differences between the upper-income groups in rich countries and the poorest in poor countries, a contrast as sharp as day and night. Clearly, there is nothing remotely resembling equality nor is there a trend in that direction.

Within countries, comparisons of poor and rich tell a more favorable story, at least in the past 30 years (see Figure 5.7). Of course, the poor have a far smaller income share than the rich, but everywhere the discrepancy has declined. In Latin America, where the poor used to have 5 percent of the income of the rich, they are now up to nearly 8 percent. In the far more equal Asian region, the poor have moved from 16 to 22 percent of the incomes accruing to the rich.

And there is a third dimension of inequality. How do the top and bottom deciles of the labor force compare in earnings? Are wages highly compressed by custom or unions or the fact that one worker is just like any other in skills and motivation or anything else that counts? Or are wages dispersed with stars and losers? Across industrial countries we see dramatic differences (see Figure 5.8). As expected, the United States has the largest dispersion, almost twice

Figure 5.7
POOREST-RICHEST INCOME COMPARISON

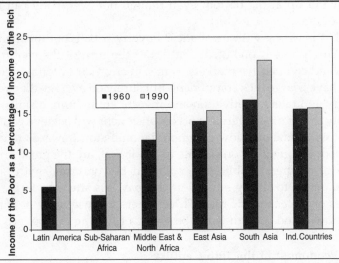

SOURCE: World Bank, *World Development Report, 1998–99* (New York: Oxford University Press, 1999).

Figure 5.8
EARNINGS DISPERSION

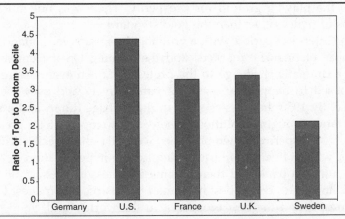

SOURCE: World Bank, *World Development Report, 1998–99* (New York: Oxford University Press, 1999).

that of Germany. Not surprisingly, German workers resist the American model because pessimistically they believe that somehow they will wind up at the bottom even though not everybody can be at the bottom.

What is wrong with inequality? Poverty is bad, but inequality is not. Surely this is one of the battles of the turn of the century. In open and competitive markets, wages in any year or for any person may have a large luck component. But surely on average they reflect energy and talent, motivation and investment in human skills. Any society that limits rewards to accomplishment will achieve equality, but it will come on a low common denominator. Rewards to excellence, or inequality if one wants to call it that, are the great driving force of progress. Public policy should be concerned with giving broad access to strong education and pay less attention to the outcomes of the economic race. Three cheers for inequality; it is good for growth and growth is the best way of rooting out poverty.

The Economist in the 20th Century

A century of dramatic economic events can be viewed in terms of its great economic controversies and the leaders that have emerged in the profession. From that perspective, the century started with Victorian calm—everything was known, Alfred Marshall of Cambridge had codified it and there remained only the details to be filled in. Free enterprise, stable money, and an open world economy were the playing ground for prosperity. There was not much in terms of policy other than the gold standard.

The inter-war period, with a growing depression in England, the collapse of financial markets, and the ensuing Great Depression, was a dramatic challenge to the profession. Such events were not supposed to happen, at least not cumulatively and ever for the worse. By 1930 the classics were in the garbage dump and a new generation brought revolutionary new ideas to cope with the greatest threat to prosperity in memory. They were all rather special. Schumpeter, who as finance minister failed to stop hyperinflation in Austria, ruined a bank and then became a professor. He said he had three hopes—to be the best horseman in Austria, the greatest lover in Europe, and the best economist in the world—and claimed to have succeeded at two of them. John Maynard Keynes was as much an intellectual, brilliant writer, and financial wizard (he lost two fortunes and made three, mostly in the German hyperinflation) as a deep-thinking economist and astute policymaker. And then there was Irving Fisher of Yale, famous inventor of the Rolodeck, who went bankrupt three times (with his own money, Yale's, and that of his wife) in misjudging the stock market, and believed the answer to living a healthy life involved sleeping outside, in particular in the winter.

While Keynes comes away as the winner in the contest for dramatic and practical ideas, Schumpeter and Fisher left important legacies in the way we think today about business cycles, growth processes, and the interaction of deflation and economic activity. Keynes clearly dominated the scene: his focus on inflexibility of wages and prices and the limits to monetary policy in a depression (now rediscovered in Japan) brought fiscal spending to the foreground. Leave gold and start spending. He believed governments should pay people to dig holes (never mind that nobody needs the holes), pay them to fill them in again, and the incomes earned will be spent. If done on an ambitious enough scale, the economy can spend itself out of recession or depression. This was radical thinking, both in fiscal terms and in the role of government. No surprise that governments for decades bought into Keynesian ideas until public debts had become too high and waste too great to give it further credence.

The next generation of formidable economists included Paul Samuelson and Milton Friedman, the heroes of the 1960s and 1970s. Friedman was the free-market and hard money advocate, brilliantly articulate, and the very incarnation of the Chicago School. Samuelson, of the Massachusetts Institute of Technology, by contrast, was the modern Keynesian, a Democrat in politics and a formidable thinker about how to formulate a modern and mathematical rendition of economic theory. Both had their victories: Samuelson won in the 1960s when he (along with many others) urged the Kennedy administration to spend its way to prosperity—and it got there. The only rival to that expansion is what is still under way today. But overexpansion gradually built up wage and price inflation and by the early 1970s, with the dollar collapse and oil price shocks, the experiment became largely discredited. Pump priming with monetary accommodation can go some way, but if overdone, will crash.

No sooner had inflation emerged than Milton Friedman had his time on the stage. Monetarism was the rage; the quantity theory of money was back in full swing. But his contribution, and that of other scholars at the time, went further. Crudely summarized, it said you can fool some people all of the time and some people some of the time but not all people all of the time. More technically, the public catches up with what governments do because it (ultimately) has rational expectations. The practical implication was to minimize the scope for government cyclical policy.

Friedman's contributions became the background for a dramatic period of rethinking economic doctrine: the leadership was provided by Robert Lucas of the University of Chicago. Taking rational expectations to the rigorous extreme, his theories concluded that government should adopt a monetary rule, an unchanging flat tax rate, and be done. In other words, government activism merely confuses, misfires, and distorts: government, get out of the way! Economic agents are rational, they do not leave $100 bills lying on the floor, and the economy does better without activism in policy. Few, at least of my generation, would believe the starkest renditions of this view. But the truth is that our profession by and large views Keynesian economics with deep skepticism, accepts monetarism by and large, and assumes that government has a proclivity to make things worse. The profession has become deeply conservative just as it had been at the beginning of the century. And governments are going that way too, from the care in creating a tamper-proof ECB to the Waigel pact, balanced budget amendments, currency boards, and overarching respect for the bond market.

Angst 2000: Who Is in Control?

People of middle age and above around the world perceive that globalization undermines the stability of their lives and that volatility, falsely perceived to be higher than ever, puts them at grave risk. They feel they have lost control and they perceive the same is true of their governments. They want assurance that security is regained and that someone will do something. Surely these sentiments will get far worse if and when Japan crashes. That is altogether possible since Japan's debt is huge, its budget deficit is mind-boggling, its financial institutions are a bust, its investments have been bad, its policymakers are unconnected to reality, and its loss of confidence is pervasive.

And there is the potential of a U.S. crash, which is less likely because monetary and fiscal policy can respond (but never say never). Even with all the U.S. prosperity, the world today has had an overdose of finance and hence it is far more likely that a serious accident can happen. And if it does, we can be sure the fallout will be worldwide and we must fear that the first instinct will be to play the defensive and destructive strategies of the Great Depression.

Citizens want to know who is in charge. The answer is nobody; the United States cannot lead Japan, and Europe cannot lead the United States. The United States urges Europe to move to prosperity policies but has no resonance; the United States urges Japan to move out of recession but gets no hearing and surely no success. Europe is critical of the huge U.S. trade deficits and lack of saving, not recognizing that if the United States started saving, the dollar would come down and Europe would lose jobs on a large scale. The Japanese dream of not buying U.S. Treasury bills, not realizing that the yen would go through the roof and the Nikkei through the floor.

The world does not need more regulation and agreements to fix this or that; it does need a heavy dose of prosperity policies. Milton Friedman, in commenting on the Great Depression, criticized the Fed for not printing money massively. That is the message to Japan. And to Europe: get deregulation under way so that dynamism in business and employment starts freeing up the fiscal side for emergency use. If Japan and Europe start moving, it will be time for the United States to think of a smaller trade deficit; that will come automatically as the rest of the world recovers. The U.S. role today is to assure that stock market problems at home do not become world problems, to make certain that ideas to peg exchange rates get nowhere, and, along with its partners, to insist that the world economy remain open.

Notes

1. Joseph A. Schumpeter, *The Theory of Economic Development*, translated from the German (Cambridge, Mass.: Harvard University Press, 1955).

2. Angus Maddison, *Monitoring the World Economy: 1820–1992* (Paris: Organization for Economic Cooperation and Development, 1995).

3. Quoted in Karl Hardach, *The Political Economy of Germany in the Twentieth Century* (Berkeley, Calif.: University of California Press, 1963), p. 145.

PART II

CASES

6. Failure and Progress in East Asia

William McGurn

When Lee Kuan Yew addressed the Asian financial crisis at a meeting of the Council on Foreign Relations, the audience was packed. It was one year into the crisis, and Singapore's senior minister minced no words. Singapore's Asian neighbors hit hard by the crisis, he said, needed to find whatever benchmarks the world— primarily the International Monetary Fund (IMF)—was setting for them, embrace these benchmarks, and then move their countries fast and hard in that direction. Whether these standards were fair or not was not the question, he noted. Presuming the goal was to reestablish investor confidence, there was simply no other way.[1]

Lee did add one caveat for his mostly American audience. If the IMF prescriptions failed, he warned, the countersolutions—most notably, the capital controls imposed by, say, Prime Minister Mahathir Mohamad of Malaysia—would gain credibility in Asia. In other words, the crisis was testing the credibility not only of the affected Asian economies but that of Western institutions that presumed to advise them.

During the question-and-answer period, someone put it to Lee that there might be a third way (not *the* third way, but *a* third way) between the IMF and Prime Minister Mahathir, a way Lee had not discussed, a way that recognized that markets were better at sorting out economic problems than politicians and international bureaucracies. That, of course, was just what former Citibank head Walter Wriston, former Secretary of State George Shultz, and former Treasury Secretary William Simon suggested in early 1998 in the *Wall Street Journal*. In one of the earliest commentaries on the Asian financial crisis, the three claimed that it was the "IMF's promise of massive intervention" itself that "spurred a global meltdown of financial markets."[2]

Lee gave the idea short shrift. And before dismissing that answer out of hand, it is worth considering the context. Clearly, Asia's

115

economies have been afflicted to varying degrees with inefficiencies and corruptions that have made recovery difficult. And politically, Lee's response is right on the mark, however dubious may be the Hobson's choice between Mahathir and the IMF. Whatever Milton Friedman and the rest of us might know to the contrary, the IMF is perceived within Asia as an institution of Western capitalism prescribing Western capitalist medicine. Thus, its failures are taken to be failures of capitalism itself.

But it is also worth returning to Lee's framework for another reason. For it points to a subterranean debate about what went wrong in Asia, to wit, the bitter dispute over what went *right* in Asia. Many observers see the crisis as powerful evidence that thou ought not to tamper with markets. But there is another interpretation, regrettably more pronounced. To these people, the crisis vindicates the idea that the "Asian miracle," to use the World Bank term,[3] was a fraud. Scratch below the surface of many of the indictments of Asian-style capitalism and what you will find is an indictment of capitalism itself.

The problem is that there was just enough corruption in the system to lend these wholesale indictments some outward plausibility. Worse still, the ill-advised rhetoric of Asian political and business leaders who predicted Asia's rise atop the ashes of a West brought down by democracy and welfare policies has fueled resentment. For many of those who had to bite their tongues as Asian stock markets skyrocketed in the first part of the 1990s, the crisis became payback time.

The truth is that Asia's sins are now exaggerated as much as its successes, and the word "miracle" only muddies the debate. For years the *Far Eastern Economic Review* and the *Asian Wall Street Journal* consistently criticized the Japanese model and its in-built inefficiencies in allocating capital, though they were lone voices in the wilderness.[4] These inefficiencies continue to plague Asia, exacting a social cost in terms of public resentment perhaps even higher than the economic one. Still, the Asian achievement in lifting its peoples out of desperate poverty, while far from a miracle, was very real.[5] What is needed is not so much wholesale revision of the Asian experiment but the kinds of economic reforms and liberalizations that the pressures from an increasingly globalized market were already beginning to bring about even before the first signs of crisis—let alone before the application of standardized IMF austerity programs that exacerbated existing problems. Had the IMF not intervened as it did, foreign creditors would have had to renegotiate their debts without benefit of the IMF gun to the debtors' heads, and with little of the attendant moral hazard.[6]

The Varied Landscape

Not least of Asia's difficulties today stems from the noxious idea that a globalized market *caused* the Asian financial crisis. To the contrary, the truth is that neither Asia's undoubted corruption nor the equally undeniable fact of rapidly globalizing markets caused the crisis; it is more accurate to say that the crisis brought these phenomena to view. In fact, to define the problem as simply one of crony capitalism leads to disasters such as we saw in Indonesia, where IMF interventions provoked riots overnight, a military-tolerated (if not led) pogrom against the ethnic Chinese minority, and the wholesale collapse of a government which, whatever its other sins, had over the course of its time in power brought poverty down from about 60 percent of the population to less than 15 percent in little more than a generation. Not least of Asia's problems is the loss of such distinctions in the panic of a crisis, not simply by New York fund managers who do not know the difference between a Philippine and Mexican peso but among a public that does not discriminate among the various Asian governments.

Not all East Asian governments are as misguided as they have been made out to be. Some of them, notably Hong Kong and Singapore, boast free and open markets, at least in the area of traded consumer goods. Others, most notably Taiwan, have holdovers from previous interventions but are moving fast toward liberalization; all three countries mentioned, as trading economies, have suffered not so much for their own sins but for the sins of those around them. Japan too must be factored out, for although it had virtually no growth throughout the 1990s it too retains many strengths, not least of which is its approximately $11 trillion in household savings— nearly two and a half times its gross domestic product (GDP)—that if put to productive uses would power not only Japan but all of Asia. At the extremes, Korea and Indonesia, the biggest recipients of IMF largesse, remain among the biggest problems. For most of these countries the central problem was a structure that did not allocate capital efficiently and a monetary policy that covered up the problem. Over time investment mistakes were compounded, so that many inefficient companies got fat while many of those that would have been competitive were squeezed out.

That has certainly been true of Japan, the region's most successful economy, whose example many Asian countries tried to follow. Ever since its bubble burst in 1991, the Japanese economy has stagnated, increasingly exposing the fault lines of a model that helped transform Japan into an economic superpower. In the beginning, the state-directed allotment of capital may have organized the industrial machine, but it did so with tremendous inefficiencies. The *Harvard Business Review* noted that well over a third of Japan's white collar sector would have to be laid off for Japan to be competitive.[7] Essentially, the Japanese have compounded their problem by hiding the bad debts of their banks and industries. Even today no one can agree on the size of Japan's total bad debt exposure: the Financial Services Administration says that the bad loans held by banks amount to about 62 trillion yen,[8] while Standard & Poor's suggests the true figure may be as high as 140 trillion yen.[9] Not a small reason for the lack of confidence in the government's figures is that every time a Japanese company has been permitted to go belly up, the world discovers that its bad debts are several times the reported level.

For a people that have time and again distinguished themselves as incredibly tough business competitors, Japan's political class has proved itself incredibly pigheaded in sticking to a failed revival strategy. What Japan needs, of course, is a more dynamic business sector, one that rewards pluck and initiative on the individual as well as corporate level. Instead, Japanese people are treated as automatons, unresponsive to the same laws of economics that all other peoples obey. Two superb films by Juzo Itami, *A Taxing Woman I* and *A Taxing Woman II*, both romantic comedies about tax inspector Ryoko Ikatura's efforts to nail enterprising tax dodgers, reveal how the Japanese feel about their relationship with the government. "You are so polite but you are really just a bloodsucker," says a small shopkeeper whom Miss Ikatura audits. Even when the government does cut taxes, the avowed aim is never to devolve economic decisionmaking back to the people whose money it is. Instead, tax cuts have always been temporary (and reluctant affairs), designed purely as a government lever to move consumption up and down as it sees fit.

At the moment we are in the midst of the latest multibillion dollar stimulus package, the sixth or seventh in a long line of failures. Dubious on their own merits (it is not clear that Japan needs all the roads, bridges, and public works the spending envisions), the more than 100 trillion yen spent on these pump-priming efforts would have been much more profitably devoted to writing off the bad debts at the outset of the crisis—much as the United States did in the savings and loan scandal. Instead, all this pump-priming government spending has dug Japan deeper and deeper into the hole, with virtually nothing to show for it save a debt that has moved from about 70 percent of GDP in 1992 to 120 percent today to what the IMF says will be 138 percent by 2003.[10] Nothing thus far has induced the Japanese people to spend, because they know two things: that any relief is temporary, and that the government will not have the wherewithal to provide for them in what is a rapidly aging society. So—perversely, but reasonably—they save even more. Japanese behavior may be creating a vicious circle, but it is far more rational than Japanese officials care to admit. Thus, the Japanese are fully preoccupied with their own problems and not much help to the rest of Asia.

Korea and Taiwan

A Japanese recovery would help the region, but there are still plenty of measures East Asian countries should undertake on their own to improve their respective situations. Many Americans, for example, consider Korea and Taiwan as interchangeable economic units. And a glance at the two economies indeed shows the two compete in many of the same markets: chemicals, textiles, electronics, and chips.

But the similarities hide more than they reveal, especially in considering why Taiwan largely escaped the ravages of the Asian crisis while Korea was among the hardest hit. Adapting the Japanese model—indeed, trying to out-Japan the Japanese at their own game—the Korean system has been dominated by the allocation of credit by government authorities and government-controlled banks to favored *chaebols*, or large industrial conglomerates that produce everything, as the saying goes, from ships to chips. Taiwan, by contrast, tends to find niche markets within these industries. Thus, a sudden change in the market, such as the 70 percent drop in DRAM prices in 1996, can devastate Korea.

This difference is exacerbated by another crucial difference in the efficient allocation of capital: bankruptcy. For years we at the *Far Eastern Economic Review*, where I worked, used to write that while Asia certainly knew how to succeed, it had yet to learn how to fail.[11] That is, it had not yet recognized that allowing inefficient businesses to fail was part of a healthy economy, taking the inefficient out of production and feeding the rise of the competitive.[12]

With the exception of Thailand, almost all of the countries hardest hit by the Asian virus have been those with nonexistent bankruptcy laws. The result is that it is almost impossible for creditors in Asia to collect on assets, whatever the laws may be on paper. Even the Bank of Japan has had to ask for help. In this way the main benefit of bankruptcy is thwarted. That benefit, of course, is a market pricing that transfers assets from the hands of those who cannot make a go of things to those who can.

We see this quite clearly in the case of Korea and Taiwan. For example, Hanbo Steel filed for bankruptcy in February 1997 after having built up a debt 22 times its equity (again, due to a government-dominated system of credit allocation) in an effort to create the world's largest steel company. A year after Hanbo filed for bankruptcy, I traveled out to its plant at Asan Bay, where I found it was still producing steel. Bankruptcy, in fact, had proved liberating for the company, by freeing it of debt payments. The upshot was that Hanbo was undercutting many steel companies, which had not been economically irresponsible but could not effectively compete with a plant free of all pricing constraints. Finally U.S. trade negotiators forced the Koreans to shut production down in the summer of 1998, and the assets were finally sold to a U.S. consortium for $480 million—less than a tenth of its debt.

In Taiwan the environment is completely different. In 1996, just before the crisis hit, Taiwan saw some 25,272 companies go out of business, about 4.7 percent of the total. The comparable Korean figure was less than a tenth of that. The churning implicit in such numbers attests to Taiwan's strength and flexibility. A recent productivity survey published by the U.S. National Bureau of Economic Research found that bankruptcy plus ease of market entry allowed new market entrants to compete in and dominate their fields. In

120

1991, for example, 38 percent of textiles and 54.2 percent of fabricated metals in Taiwan were produced by companies that had not even been around a few years before.[13]

Hong Kong and Singapore

Other comparisons highlight similar differences, not always to the advantage of the presumed market leader. Hong Kong, for example, is much more open than Singapore. But in those areas in which Singapore does intervene, it tends to do so in more sophisticated ways. In health care, for example, Hong Kong's response for years was simply to provide double-digit budget increases, a practice that is no longer sustainable.

Indeed, one of the more interesting comparisons has to do with public housing. Hong Kong's free market notwithstanding, some 39 percent of its population lives in public housing, and despite a great deal of dissatisfaction, this percentage does not appear likely to move downward for some time. So cheap are these apartments that they are handed down, and it is not uncommon to go to a parking lot in a Hong Kong public housing estate and find a Mercedes Benz with a Jockey Club membership insignia on the bumper.

Singapore's public housing is far more extensive—some 86 percent of the people live in publicly built and managed flats—and far more integrated into the Singapore model. But this too can hide more than it reveals. Although about twice the percentage of people live in public housing in Singapore as they do in Hong Kong, Singapore's ownership rate is also about twice that of Hong Kong's. In other words, 9 out of 10 people actually own the units in which they live.

Indeed, Singapore's laws encourage people to maintain and purchase the unit in which they live, quite unlike Hong Kong where those interested in buying wait for new stock to go up and, as a result, have less of an interest in maintenance and improvement. True, Singapore's continued management of housing units does give it a lever of control over citizens that a free people would not want. From an economic view, however, the in-built incentive system does seem superior to that of Hong Kong, which, when it does intervene, seems to have no better idea than to throw money at the problem. Unfortunately, at a moment when the Hong Kong model has vindicated itself, Hong Kong appears bent on copying Singapore in other areas; witness the 1998 government decision to allow Richard Li,

121

the son of Hong Kong's leading tycoon, Li Ka-shing, to buy government land for the development of a "cyberport"—without the burden of competitive bidding.

The Structure of Asian Capital

Finally, the role of capital structure is worth mentioning. The most spectacular disaster in Indonesia before Suharto's fall was not the May 1998 riots but the spectacular crash a year earlier of the Hong Kong–based investment bank Peregrine. In scarcely a decade, Peregrine's aggressive pursuit of market share had catapulted it to the top of the heap, and it became Asia's largest independent investment bank. But the company's downfall, virtually overnight, is perhaps even more illustrative of the misallocation of capital at the heart of the Asian crisis, in both its micro and macro dimensions.

When Peregrine started up, it had the right idea: to cultivate (and dominate) a long-term bond market for the region. In pursuit of this vision, alas, Peregrine allowed decisions to be made on the basis of pride rather than profit; the firm was notorious for paying any price to muscle out foreign competition, transforming itself into a huge player but also leaving itself with bond issues that were hard to resell on the secondary market. Peregrine's downfall neatly intertwined the problem of Asia's immature capital markets with Indonesia's crony capitalism: the crunch came when a $270 million issue to an Indonesian taxi company—made on the basis that it had a Suharto family member on its board—went south and Peregrine found itself overexposed and underfunded.

To put this in perspective, it is worth recalling that in Asia bond markets are quite undeveloped. Whereas in the United States they account for about 110 percent of GNP and in Germany about 83 percent of GNP, in East Asia (excluding Japan) bond markets account for only about 20 percent.[14] The consequence in Asia was an overreliance on banks, which by their nature as deposit-taking institutions are geared to the short term. On top of this, in Asia many of these banks were not even banks at all, at least in the sense of mobilizing savings for productive activities. Instead, many were simply funnels for government investment decisions. Still, even where bank credit does function, it can be a crude pricing mechanism. One of the great benefits of an active bond market, by contrast, is that the constant reevaluation and trading of debt leads to more accurate pricing.

When capital was cheap and banks were shoveling the money in, this didn't appear to be a problem; when debt came due companies merely repaid it or rolled it over. But when the Asian economies began to fall and credit dried up, even healthy companies faced liquidity problems. That most of the debt was denominated in U.S. dollars hit Asia with a double whammy, given the collapse of exchange rates. Had Asia had a bond market it might not have avoided the crisis we have seen. But much of the so-called "hot money" that flowed in—and was jerked out in panic—might have found a place in longer-term financial instruments. Bonds alone would not solve Asia's problems but a more developed capital market would at the least contribute to a much more accurate system of pricing.

A Brighter Asian Prospect

Although real problems remain in Asia, the real danger is that of confusing the symptoms for the causes. However flawed and inefficient the various Asian economies were, their problems would not have escalated into a full-fledged contagion had the market been left to operate. Though perhaps more painful in the short term, such a remedy would have come without the moral hazard that has today become a central feature of IMF rescue packages.

Clearly, Asian economies have a long way to go before they have fully developed, something that requires moving away from the foolish belief that the wisest of bureaucrats can bend markets to their will. But it does no one good to deny the achievements that got them as far as they have, or to pretend that a collection of international bureaucrats, however sharp or well intentioned, will be any more efficient than local ones. Its crisis notwithstanding, Asia still retains significant advantages, not least, a broadly shared work ethic and a penchant for savings. Over the past 30 years Asia proved what it could do even in spite of the handicaps mentioned. We can only imagine what it might do with those obstacles removed.

Notes

1. Lee Kuan Yew, "The Asian Financial Crisis" (address to the Council on Foreign Relations, New York City, October 13, 1998).

2. George Shultz, William Simon, and Walter Wriston, "Who Needs the IMF?" *Wall Street Journal*, February 3, 1998.

3. See the World Bank, *The East Asian Miracle: Economic Growth and Public Policy* (New York: Oxford University Press, 1993).

4. See, for example, "Whither Japan? Whatever Happened to Japan, Inc.?" (Editorial), *Asian Wall Street Journal*, December 2, 1993; and "Tokyo's Real Scandal: Japan, Inc. Encourages Business-Government Graft" (Editorial), *Far Eastern Economic Review*, January 21, 1993.

5. "Sayings of Chairman Milton (Friedman): 'Asian Miracle' Was Real" (Editorial), *Far Eastern Economic Review*, March 26, 1998.

6. A similar point was made by former Federal Reserve Governor Lawrence Lindsey. See Lindsey, "The Bad News about Bailouts," *New York Times*, January 6, 1998.

7. Shintaro Hari, "Fixing Japan's White-Collar Economy: A Personal View," *Harvard Business Review*, November–December 1983, p. 162.

8. Toshio Aritake, "Bad Loans at Japan's Banks Shrinking, But Remain High at 11.7 Percent of Loans," *BNA's Banking Report*, February 7, 2000, p. 276.

9. Anthony Rowley, "Banks' Bad Debts Worse Than Admitted: Tokyo," *Business Times* (Singapore), December 28, 1998.

10. Sheryl Wu Dunn and Nicholas Kristoff, "Japan's Private Savings Enormous, But So Is Public Debt," *San Diego Union-Tribune*, October 1, 1999.

11. Consider the following excerpt from "The Will To Fail: South Korea Versus Its Chaebol," in the February 9, 1995, issue of the *Far Eastern Economic Review*:

South Korea's state-directed capitalism has imposed a hefty political cost as well. Whenever businessmen depend on government for credit, political connections become more important than market merit. Graft inevitably follows. The public is well aware of this relationship, which explains why Koreans remain so antagonistic towards the very businesses that built their country. Indeed, economic life remains heavily politicized. Not least of the reasons Hyundai has been so eager to downsize is that it has been out of favour ever since its founder, Chung Ju Yung, ran for president against Mr. Kim.

Overregulation is not a problem that can be solved with regulation. For almost a decade, Korean governments have tried to rein in the chaebol with no success. Tighter regulations on ownership will simply drive the process deeper underground by creating an artificial paper trail. A far better solution would be simply to open up the economy and get the government out of the business of allocating credit. A chaebol competing at home for market share— with no hope of a government bailout—would concentrate on its core strengths quickly enough.

The point is that South Korean Governments have been working from the wrong side of the equation. Without doubt, President Kim is right to point out that Korea today is ill-suited to the challenges it will face in a post-Uruguay world market. In that world, however, failure is as critical to the process as success. By now we have learned that the market makes these decisions with far greater efficiency and far less pain than governments. As Mr. Kim wrestles with preparing his country for the 21st century, our advice would be to leave Korean business alone. It's Korea, Inc. that needs reforming.

12. On the importance of the role of failure in a successful economy, see Dwight R. Lee and Richard B. McKenzie, *Failure and Progress: The Bright Side of the Dismal Science* (Washington: Cato Institute, 1993).

13. Bee Yan Aw, Xiaomin Chen, and Mark J. Roberts, "Firm-level Evidence on Productivity Differentials, Turnover and Exports in Taiwanese Manufacturing," National Bureau of Economic Research Working Paper 6235, October 1997.

14. Ismail Dalla, *Asia's Emerging Bond Markets* (London: FT Financial Publishing, 1997).

7. Asia's Crisis of Corporatism

Tomas Larsson

> There are some things with which governments ought not
> to meddle, and other things with which they ought; but
> whether right or wrong in itself, the interference must work
> for ill, if government, not understanding the subject which
> it meddles with, meddles to bring about a result which would
> be mischievous.
>
> —John Stuart Mill (1848)
>
> In nearly every economic crisis, the cause is political, not
> economic.
>
> —Lee Kuan Yew (1997)

The Asian economic crisis broke out on July 2, 1997. On that day, Thailand's central bank severed the baht's ties to the U.S. dollar and let the currency float. The event was reported—if at all—in minimal paragraphs in most Western newspapers. Few realized the full implication of the event: that the *Titanic* of economic growth, the Asian "miracle," had hit an iceberg and started to sink.

A few years after the crash, only a few of Asia's leading economies—China, Taiwan, and India—still managed to keep their noses above the surface. "Miraculous" Asia had been transformed into an economic disaster area. For those involved, the Asian dream had become a nightmare. The Asian drama was no longer a bright success story, but a bitter tragedy. When, where, how, and why did things go wrong?

Many argue that Asian economies, much like U.S. ships at Pearl Harbor, became subject to unexpected attacks from nefarious individuals. In this case they were not Japanese bomber pilots serving the emperor, but unscrupulous currency speculators led by George Soros. The only way to stop those types of financial terrorists from causing untold damage is to regulate capital markets. Unruly market

125

forces must be reined in by politicians taking decisive action on national and international levels.

On the other hand, some argue that the Asian miracle met a fate similar to that of the royal Swedish warship *Vasa*—the largest, most powerful and heavily armed of its day—which went down in the Stockholm harbor within minutes of the launch of its maiden voyage in 1628. According to this view, Asia, like the *Vasa*, foundered because of errors in design. The marvel had proportions that were inherently destabilizing. In Asia, the state intervened too much in the economy: politicians and bureaucrats did not allow the market to function. The Asian boom was doomed to end in sudden disaster. Like Soviet communism, it was impossible to gradually reform Asian capitalism—it could only collapse. It is only from the ruins of the old system that new and improved political and economic systems can rise. And it is only then that the international community has a role to play as a provider of advice and aid. Since crises are often a condition for the evolution—and progress—of societies, it may not even be desirable for the world community, in the form of the International Monetary Fund, for example, to take action to prevent turmoil.

Yet others suggest that the Asian crash is more akin to the explosion of the space shuttle *Challenger*, which was caused by a faulty O-ring gasket. When something small went wrong, perhaps because of carelessness, the entire system stopped functioning, with fateful consequences. In this case, it is possible that a small, corrupt Thai bank played the role of the malfunctioning gasket. When it collapsed, it affected the psychology of the market: people began to panic and soon everything started to go wrong. Panic spread from one bank to the next, from one stock to the next, from one country to the next—and soon from one part of the world to another, as witnessed when the "Asian flu" hit markets in Eastern Europe, Latin America, the European Union, and the United States. There is not much that can be done about market psychology. But both investors and regulators of financial markets now realize that it is vitally important that even the smallest parts of the financial system be scrutinized thoroughly.

Some say that the Asian miracle, like the *Titanic*, was the victim of too little attention to the surrounding environment. If the people on Asia's "captain's bridge" had been more alert, they would have realized that it was impossible to keep Asian currencies linked to the U.S. dollar after it gained strength against the Japanese yen and the German mark beginning in the mid-1990s. Unable to increase productivity commensurately, Asian currencies became overvalued as the U.S. dollar appreciated. This, it soon became evident, weighed heavily on Asian export industries while stimulating wasteful consumption of imported goods. The crisis could have been avoided if the Asians had just cut the moorings to the U.S. dollar while there was still time, instead of desperately holding on to them—and being dragged down. The lesson here is a simple one: floating currency exchange rates are better than pegged ones. It is only under pegged currency exchange rates that large macroeconomic imbalances can build up; in economies with flexible exchange rates imbalances will be adjusted before they grow to disastrous proportions.

All of those interpretations contain grains of truth. But the overarching lessons of the Asian crisis are the following:

- The Asian "tigers" lacked political and institutional preparedness for a major economic slowdown. Very deep and radical reforms are required if the tigers are to regain their former vigor.
- State intervention and regulation of capital flows created imbalances in the tiger economies. Economic liberalization is the only solution to Asia's structural problems.
- The Asian crisis is not a crisis of the global market economy. It is rather the Asian model of state capitalism that is in crisis. More globalization and more free markets—not less—are the keys to a prosperous Asian future.
- The Asian crisis illustrates the need for fundamental reform of the global financial system. The IMF's role as lender of last resort is highly dubious. Either the IMF should be scrapped, or its functions should be heavily cut back.

The Tigers' Lost Trust

When the Asian miracle economies grew by leaps and bounds during the first half of the 1990s, many observers were deeply intrigued by how wrong Gunnar Myrdal had been. In his mammoth study, *Asian Drama: An Inquiry into the Poverty of Nations*, the Nobel prize–winning Swedish economist explained that the countries of that region had *soft states* and that, as a result, they would be permanently excluded from the exclusive club of economically modern and prosperous societies.[1]

For observers of the Asian scene who were not more intimate with *Asian Drama*, this theory bordered on the ridiculous. A popular—but debatable—explanation of South Korea's, Taiwan's, Singapore's, and Hong Kong's record-shattering economic performances was that the states in these societies were "hard." Politicians and bureaucrats had their way with companies and markets, but they were disciplined enough to ensure that they did not become tools of narrow vested interests. Thus, the intervention of the tiger states did not stand in the way of export success or structural adjustment but rather accelerated it. In other words, Myrdal had been utterly wrong.

But it was not that simple. Developments after 1968 have to a considerable extent confirmed Myrdal's conclusion. The cases of South Korea, Taiwan, Hong Kong, and Singapore do not illustrate how wrong-headed Myrdal was. In fact, Myrdal was not interested in these four original Asian tiger economies. Of the countries that Myrdal did study—India, Pakistan, Ceylon (Sri Lanka), Burma (Myanmar), Indonesia, Malaysia, the Philippines, Thailand, Cambodia, Laos, and South Vietnam—there are few that even prior to the Asian crisis would have been described as economic "miracles." On the contrary, of those 11 countries there were only 3—Indonesia, Malaysia, and Thailand—that had managed to shatter the stereotype of Oriental stagnation. Those three Southeast Asian countries even managed to become emblems of dynamism, rapid modernization, and unbounded faith in the future. They made up the second generation of Asian-tiger economies. Otherwise things remained more or less unchanged since 1968. The Philippines could perhaps be said to almost qualify as a new tiger cub—but it still had some distance to go. And India, Pakistan, Sri Lanka, Myanmar, Cambodia, Laos, and Vietnam were by 1997 just as irrelevant as models of economic development as they had been 30 years earlier.

In 1997 *Asian Drama* made an intellectual comeback. It was a conspicuously soft state—Thailand—that tripped up the Asian tigers in the middle of their explosive dash toward prosperity. Like Thailand, other tigers started to lose their teeth and claws. Indeed, Thailand, Indonesia, and South Korea were admitted to the IMF's financial intensive care unit. And the Philippines, Malaysia, Singapore, Hong Kong, and Brunei were hit hard by the problems in the neighboring countries. The leading Asian economies started to shrink, including Japan's, the world's second largest. Japan had since the early 1990s managed to avoid dealing with the consequences of a punctured speculative bubble—bankrupt property and construction companies and insolvent banks. By the new year of 1997, six months before the onset of the real Asian crisis, the Nikkei index of the Tokyo stock market remained stuck at around 50 percent of the record level it had reached in 1989. The already enfeebled Japanese economy did not possess the strength to withstand the harsh winds blowing across Asia. The largest and fastest growing share of Japan's exports (44 percent) was destined for the rest of Asia. When the economies of Thailand, Indonesia, and South Korea collapsed, Japan was hit by an industrial crisis on top of its unsolved financial crisis.

Until recently, the fast-growing Asian economies were models for the world. It was in Asia that the multinational corporations saw their future. It was there new prosperity and new jobs were being created. It was hardly surprising that Western politicians and opinion makers of both left and right sought to claim ideological paternity of the Asian success story. Indeed, many even argued that their own stagnating countries should become "tigers." Today, many distance themselves from the Asian economies, which are not models but examples of what to avoid.

But exactly what is it that Asian countries are examples of? The crisis-hit countries have little in common—historically, politically, and culturally. As regards levels of economic development and economic structures, there are really more differences than similarities among them. Why were Thailand, Indonesia, and South Korea the first tigers to fall? But after a closer look at the tumultuous chain of events that led to the regional economic collapse, a relatively clear pattern emerges.

A Pattern Emerges

If chaos theorists are correct, the wing of a butterfly in Bangkok could unleash a storm in New York. And the storms on the world's stock markets during 1997 and 1998 gave weight to that argument. The chain of events began on May 8, 1996, when Suthep Thueksuban rose in the Thai parliament and announced that he wanted to say something about one of the country's smaller banks, Bangkok Bank of Commerce (BBC). The Thai parliament member waved a document he said was a copy of a confidential report from Bank of Thailand, the central bank. The report described how BBC over a period of years had been plundered by its owners and managers—with the aid of friends in political circles. And this went on with the full knowledge of the central bank governor. Suthep warned that the BBC could collapse any day.

In international media, this juicy Thai scandal hardly registered. But in hindsight it is clear that the BBC scandal can be compared to the wing stroke of that ill-fated butterfly. News about the criminal mismanagement of the BBC—and about the Thai central bank's involvement—got savers' and investors' attention. During 1996, the year *before* the real crisis hit, the Bangkok stock market's leading index fell by more than 35 percent.

The Bangkok scandal's implications for the rest of Asia were frightening. If a commercial bank could be looted right before the eyes of what was then probably the most respected central bank in Asia, then what was not possible elsewhere in Asia where banking systems were watched over by less revered central bankers? What other financial skeletons had Asia's central banks hidden during the region's long boom?

One answer to that question came in early 1997, when the South Korean steel manufacturer Hanbo went bankrupt. It was then revealed that the company's president had borrowed close to $6 billion for his company—by paying hundreds of millions of dollars in bribes to secure new loans. Was Hanbo an isolated case? Hanbo was probably more of a rule than an exception.

The roots of the South Korean crisis went back at least to 1993, when Kim Young Sam became president. To lift the country from what was then a mild recession, he ordered the country's leading conglomerates to make massive new investments—in car factories, semiconductor plants, steel mills, and so forth. The companies obeyed, assisted by large loans from local and foreign banks. When crunch time arrived in 1997, the largest South Korean companies were saddled with debts that were four times larger than their own capital, an enormous debt burden by international business standards. South Korea's economic advances from 1993 and onward were rightly likened to a "false boom."[2]

The false boom, driven by cheap credit, was not a uniquely South Korean phenomenon. In fact, large parts of Asia during these years experienced something like a "false boom." Foreign banks increased their lending to Thailand, Indonesia, South Korea, and the Philippines by 24 percent during 1996 alone, and during the first half of

1997 lending grew at an annual rate of 10 percent.[3] And where did all this money end up?

The answer is that it ended up in the wrong places. Partly in real estate and stocks, creating a speculative bubble. Partly in "white elephants," industrial projects of doubtful profitability. Among the Asian white elephants were, for example, Indonesia's Chandra Asri, a petrochemical complex on Java; and Malaysia's steel industry Perjawa and the "national car" Proton. These and many other dubious schemes attractive to vain politicians (and businessmen) had been financed by state subsidies, shaky domestic banks, and cheap, short-term foreign loans. Trade protectionism contributed to the channeling of foreign funds into industrial schemes that produced more prestige than profit. Generally, the tigers opened up their capital markets at a quicker pace than they did their trade regimes. One study of Indonesia, Malaysia, the Philippines, and Thailand concluded that those countries thereby put the cart before the horse, with the result that too much capital ended up in heavy, technologically advanced industries like automobiles, steel, and petrochemical products.[4]

The extent of the hubris that beset the tigers in the mid-1990s can hardly be exaggerated. Speculative property "bubbles" have occurred all over the world. But according to a team of researchers who investigated the issue on the behalf of the World Bank, it is unlikely that an oversupply of new buildings as large as the one currently facing Bangkok has ever before been witnessed in history.[5] Other tigers were not far behind, though. In Malaysia, for example, the world's largest building, Petronas Towers, was constructed—an initiative I described elsewhere as "a symbol of a self-righteousness, arrogance, and hubris that has reached dizzying heights."[6] Enormous overcapacity developed also in other sectors. In December 1996 it was reported that prices for petrochemical products during the year had fallen by 35 percent, while prices for DRAM chips had tumbled by 82 percent.[7]

Foreign banks and fund managers started to get cold feet. Slowly, the insight spread that the early 1990s euphoria over tiger prospects had resulted in too many white elephants. That a new, more disciplined age had arrived became evident when Malaysia failed to convince foreign investors to finance the Bakun dam, a giant hydroelectric power project on Borneo.

131

To the Asian public it became increasingly clear that local banks were being crushed by the weight of the industrial white elephants, especially as air started to seep out of the speculative bubbles. People had always known that the extravagant facades of many Asian banking palaces hid shoddy fundamental structures, but now they started to suspect that they were rotten from floor to roof. The reaction came quickly. Savers withdrew their deposits. Foreign creditors recalled their loans. Shareholders sold their positions. The panic spread from bank to bank, from finance company to finance company, from Thailand to Indonesia to South Korea to Malaysia, and so on. Stable and healthy banks, companies, and countries, however, were not hard hit. Taiwan and Singapore (as well as Australia) continued to do quite well in the circumstances. It was not blind panic that swept Asia in the second half of 1997.

Addressing the Banking Crisis

Severe, systemic banking crises can be solved relatively quickly and easily. Once things have gone awry, there is, in fact, little choice but to ensure that the banking system (but not necessarily every bank) keeps operating. However, when banks are "saved" with this objective in mind, it is desirable that the owners first lose their capital, writing down existing shareholder capital to zero before the state injects new capital.

In Asia, the authorities have found it impossible to save the banks in a quick and elegant manner. One obstacle was the fact that governments in all the hardest hit countries have a reputation for corruption. According to Transparency International, Indonesia has the world's fifth most corrupt public administration.[8] Thailand ranked a hardly flattering 14 and South Korea came in as number 42. In Japan (60th position) corruption was found to be as prevalent as in Botswana and Estonia.

Due to the corrupt image, there was much unease over the prospect of sending in politicians and bureaucrats to clean up the banks. That would be like letting the fox into the chicken coop. Asian equivalents to the institutions set up to handle the savings and loan crisis in the United States in the 1980s would easily have fallen prey to suspicions regarding honesty and political neutrality. In order to create trust, it would be necessary to launder the banks' dirty linen in public. But such an accounting was (and is) not something that would interest the political elites that benefited from the mismanagement of the banks. Furthermore, the problems at the banks are to a large extent a result of their close ties to the state.

At the same time it was politically impossible to let the banks crash and burn. The owners of the banks were too politically influential—or useful. Either they were powerful because of their links to industrial and economic interests, or they were useful because they willingly ran errands for the politicians and bureaucrats. More or less instinctively, Asian governments therefore reacted to the banking crises by using carrots and sticks not to save the banking system as such, but rather to save the banks' owners in general and their clients in particular. For this reason, the needed radical surgery on the banking sector has not been performed to this day. Instead, half measures and cosmetic interventions were used to hide the obvious ill health of the banks. Politicians from Tokyo to Bangkok have, for example, tried to force healthy (or at least less ill) banks to take over sick banks. In this manner, government leaders have hoped to contain the situation and perhaps even make the problems go away by themselves. So the banks have remained rotten and the banking systems shaky. And the crisis of trust has become permanent.

Trust and Institutions

This is a rough schematic description. There are of course differences among the countries. Japan has managed to keep its moribund banks alive since the financial and real estate crash of the early 1990s, when they should have been allowed to go bankrupt. After much agonizing and delay, Thailand, Indonesia, and South Korea finally managed to respond to the real issues and acted to shut down some of the worst banks and finance companies. Finance companies have been liquidated and some banks have been nationalized. Others have been forced to raise new capital by selling shares to foreign investors. But much remains to be done. Almost three years since the crisis erupted, some of the banks may appear more stable, solvent, and liquid. Interest rates have come down. But the banks still will not lend to healthy businesses.

In October 1997, when it was evident that the crisis was not an isolated Thai crisis, but rather an Asian crisis, IMF first deputy managing director Stanley Fischer said he expected the crisis to last three or four months.[9] One year later, the *Far Eastern Economic Review* published a special section analyzing Asian banking systems. The magazine's finance editor was highly critical: "Since the crisis began some 15 months ago . . . [t]here has been virtually no progress on the region's problems."[10] The prospect that capital would start to flow into the Asian economies and recapitalize the financial systems anytime soon was "more remote than ever."

Since then, the picture has become less grim. Thanks to lower exchange rates and to interest rate cuts in the United States and Europe, which flooded the world's financial markets with cash, many hold out much hope for Asia. Nevertheless, fundamental structural reforms in Asia have yet to be introduced. Why have the Asians been unable to turn the situation around, despite record-breaking rescue packages from the IMF? One important reason is that Asia is woefully short of certain vital institutions.

In the United States and in western Europe, banks take it for granted that they can check the credit background of any potential customer. It is the easiest thing in the world to find out if an individual or a company has been negligent with payments in the past. In large parts of Asia, it is entirely impossible to find out such information. Credit information bureaus simply do not exist. No one gathers and sells information of this nature. In some countries, such as in Thailand, such activities were even prohibited by law. However, in countries with well-functioning credit information systems, the wealth-creating effects can hardly be overestimated. According to one Taiwanese banker, the existence of a good credit information system is one of the main reasons behind the continuing success of Taiwan's economy.[11]

In crisis-hit Asia, the lack of credit information systems meant that banks and companies had to take extreme measures of caution: they stopped providing new credits. As long as the economies grew and the value of collateral (mainly real estate) was heading for the sky, there was little risk perceived with extending loans or selling on generous credit terms. But as soon as the economies turned south, this blind trust evaporated. Blind trust was replaced by total skepticism, paralyzing the commercial system. The market did not receive the oxygen it desperately needed: information. Even when—or if—the banking systems of Asia are sufficiently recapitalized, Asian banks will be hard-pressed to start lending again because they still will not have access to information on potential clients.

Trust will not return easily, especially if the corporate sector remains insolvent, as is likely to be the case given another Asian institutional weakness. The most affected countries all lack efficient bankruptcy laws and procedures. In theory, there may exist legal avenues for creditors to start bankruptcy proceedings against defaulting debtors. However, as is the case in Thailand, it might take more than five years to get the case through the courts. And by that time most of the assets would probably have been squirreled away or lost value. So bankruptcy is no real alternative. Rather, it is in the interest of the lender to ensure that projects of old clients are kept alive as long as possible, in the desperate hope that they may one day generate sufficient incomes. These perverse incentives have filled Asia with "zombies," companies that belong to the living dead. Since the crisis broke out, we have frequently read news reports of South Korean conglomerates, Japanese banks, and so on, that have gone belly up. And they are indeed bankrupt. But they often continue operating. The factory wheels keep turning. The corporate machinery keeps cranking.

When the first reports of alarming levels of overcapacity in Asia started to arrive in 1997, a reasonable reaction may have been: "So what? May the best man win!" In a functioning market economy, oversupply problems are solved in a natural manner: unprofitable and bankrupt companies are shut down; industries are rationalized and consolidated. In short: the old falls by the wayside and the new rises from the rubble. Unfortunately, in Asia that is a naïve assumption. As columnist James Glassman said, capitalism without bankruptcy is like Christianity without hell—it does not work. The stewards of Asian capitalism over the years have done their utmost to avoid corporate closures and industrial rationalization. Thus, what we have in Asia is not capitalism. The "creative destruction" that economist Joseph Schumpeter described as the essence of capitalism is not permitted.

Societies that do not allow the process of creative destruction to operate face stagnation. They become rigid. They become preserving societies, not creating societies. What the Asian "miracle" hid was that large parts of Asia in this crucial respect are driven by the instinct to preserve the old rather than create the new. It should, however, be noted that not all Asian nations exhibit the same institutionalized aversion to owning up to corporate failures. The Asian economy that has so far managed the crisis best, Taiwan, is also the country in which bankruptcy procedures are the easiest to initiate.[12]

Alan Greenspan, chairman of the Federal Reserve, has noted that the Asian crisis is a striking example of the role trust plays in an economy. When trust disappears, we withdraw from the market. If for some reason you are unable to trust that contracts will be honored, then you will also stop making long-term business agreements. In Asia there were two kinds of trust that disappeared in the course of 1997, prompting people to flee the markets. First, trust in the appreciation of asset values was lost as expectations of future economic growth were revised downward. Second, trust in the *functioning* of the market was lost: the governing authorities and the legal frameworks were found to be inadequate. They could not ensure the continued efficient operation of markets during the bust.

The latter loss of trust had worse consequences than the former. If it had been only the faith in eternal record growth that had been lost, there would have been a short, not very sharp recession. In 20 years' time, the Asian crisis of 1997 would be reflected in a short V formation in the graph illustrating Asian GDP trends. But it is trust in the market as such that has been lost. The depth of the Asian crisis can be explained largely as a total crisis of confidence. This is the fundamental reason why the virtuous cycles of the Asian miracle could so rapidly turn vicious. In the rearview mirror of economic history, the Great Asian Depression will turn up as a U- or maybe an L-shaped graph.

The root of the Asian crisis cannot be found in the market itself, but rather in institutional frameworks that are the products of political processes: central banks, regulations, legislation, and so on. The Asian crisis thus puts a spotlight on the role of the state in a market economy. The question is perhaps not so much one of whether a state is appropriately "soft" or "hard," as Myrdal had it. What is vital is that the state creates an economic environment filled with trust and in which the market is allowed to operate in good times as well as bad.

Financial Chemotherapy Is the Wrong Medicine

In the aftermath of the Asian financial hurricane, many called for international regulations on the movement of capital. The Asian crisis and its globally contagious effects have contributed to a back-lash against globalized financial activities.

On the political front, the first barrage was fired by Malaysia's Prime Minister Mahathir Mohamad. At the 50th annual meeting of the World Bank and the International Monetary Fund in Hong Kong he said that "currency trading is unnecessary, unproductive, and immoral."[13] Mahathir argued for a ban on such activity. Later, Mahathir claimed that speculators, led by George Soros, had attacked the currencies of the ASEAN countries (Association of Southeast Asian Nations) because they had extended membership in the regional cooperation organization to the military dictatorship in Myanmar in the summer of 1997. The philanthropical work of Soros is, among other things, focused on promoting human rights in Myanmar. Mahathir further stated that the raids on the Malaysian currency were part and parcel of Jewish capitalism's conspiracy against Islam. That Soros's and many other hedge funds lost vast amounts of money as Malaysia's ringgit and other tiger currencies tumbled (because they had bet that the currencies would rise, not fall) did not impress Kuala Lumpur's leading conspiracy theorist.

As time passed, Mahathir began to receive surprising intellectual support from well-known economists such as free-trade theoretician Jagdish Bhagwati of Columbia University and Paul Krugman of the Massachusetts Institute of Technology. Bhagwati fired the first shots against free capital mobility. In an article in *Foreign Affairs* he explained that free capital flows were supported only by political ideology, not scientific theory.[14] Krugman's argument against free-dom for capital was based not on theoretical considerations but practical ones. In an article in *Fortune* he argued that the reintroduc-tion of capital controls would give the Asian tigers breathing space, which they could use to undertake needed reforms.[15]

During a visit to a business conference in Singapore, Krugman likened temporary capital controls in the sick tigers to chemotherapy given to cancer patients: "Sometimes, the very bad things are what you need to weather the storm."[16] The proposal won strong backing among the 250 bankers and corporate managers who had gathered at the conference; an instant electronic opinion survey found that 47 percent agreed with Krugman that the control of capital was the right medicine for the sick Asian tigers. But some viewed the pro-posal with skepticism. Krugman was asked why a managed

137

exchange rate system should be reintroduced, given that it was the various "bands" and "pegs" to the U.S. dollar that had masked the region's inefficiencies in the first place. Krugman replied: "If [the current economic climate] is what revealing inefficiencies does, then maybe it's better we didn't know." The problem, of course, is that we know.

On September 1, 1998, Mahathir introduced strict capital controls. Malaysia's prime minister explained that the free market had failed his country:

> Malaysia cannot wait. Malaysia has chosen to become a heretic, a pariah, if you like. Our appeal to the world community to regulate and bring order to the market has gone unheeded. If the international community cannot change, then Malaysia must undertake its own reform.[17]

The winds had changed. Just a year earlier free capital movements had been high orthodoxy. At the meeting in Hong Kong Mahathir's cursing of Soros and hedge funds had made him seem like Asia's neighborhood lunatic. Now he was suddenly in respectable company. Remember that Malaysia is no ordinary banana republic. The Malaysian stock market has been one of the largest and most developed of all the so-called emerging markets. In 1994, Malaysia was the country with the single largest weighting (23 percent) in Morgan Stanley's index of emerging markets.[18] In September 1998, the country was removed from the benchmark index because of the new restrictions. Just as sensational was Hong Kong finance secretary Donald Tsang's taking offence at speculative activities and his demands for stricter international regulations.[19] Hong Kong had previously been perceived as the land of laissez faire. No longer.

Malaysia has long been an example other countries in the developing world have tried to follow. The country represented a modern and pragmatic form of Islam, an alternative to extreme fundamentalist versions. The ethnically complex Malaysian society has in our ethnic cleansing–scarred age acted as an inspiration, showing that ethnic tensions can be controlled using peaceful means. The former British colony has demonstrated for countries in Africa and Latin America that a traditional exporter of agricultural commodities can, given the right policies, be rapidly transformed into an industrial nation of international rank. It is not unfair to label the man who shaped modern Malaysia in these ways—Mahathir—Asia's most interesting politician.[20] With its revolt against the free market, it is fortunate that Malaysia has not become a trendsetter in the Third World.[21] Despite the Japanese government's suggestion that other emerging markets follow Malaysia's lead,[22] doing so would be unnecessary and unfortunate.

Capital Controls and Development

Currency controls are not associated with the promotion of economic development and welfare, though they may provide some protection against sudden market swings. But at what price? Advocates of restrictions have approvingly pointed out that China and India, two countries with strict capital controls, have so far been able to avoid the fate of the tigers. And, indeed, China and India prove that capital controls can protect societies against external economic shocks. But they also illustrate the fact that such societies are hindered from reaping the fruits of prosperity that global markets offer. Capital controls are part and parcel of an inward-looking economic development strategy that is incompatible with strong, sustainable economic growth. Neither in India nor China have capital controls contributed to economic and social progress. What is protected and preserved is not prosperity but poverty and underdevelopment. Even after the tigers crashed and burned, they remained well ahead of India and China in terms of material and social well-being.

Apologists for currency controls have pointed out that both South Korea and Taiwan experienced some of their most economically "miraculous" periods under strict capital controls. That is true. But it is equally true that these developmental phases of the South Korean and Taiwanese economies coincided with harsh military dictatorship and martial law, respectively. Yet who would take this as evidence of the general utility of dictatorship? South Korea and Taiwan only illustrate that both currency controls and authoritarian rule can be compatible with rapid economic growth. They do not prove that these arrangements are preferable to economic and political openness.

India's isolation, China's public enterprises, the martial laws of Taiwan, and the generals' South Korea have drawn the admiration of many.[23] In the case of Malaysia, some admired the prime minister's increasing defiance and uncompromising rhetoric. But other wounded tigers were quick to explicitly declare that they did not intend to follow in Malaysia's footsteps. In the Philippines, for instance, people have vivid memories of the currency controls introduced in the 1950s and abolished only in 1992. Talk of currency controls reminds people of the bad old days, of economic stagnation under Ferdinand Marcos. The restrictions were counterproductive: capital did not remain in the Philippines, it fled. The recent economic boom in the Philippines is partly the result of the fact that fortunes, which under Marcos left the country for safe havens in the United States and Switzerland, started to return once controls were lifted. In other words, open borders discourage capital flight, while closed borders stimulate it.

Capital Controls and Government

The only government that can use regulation to stop capital from fleeing is one that exercises almost totalitarian control over the economy. Indeed, one of the preconditions for capital controls to be successful is the existence of a strongly authoritarian state with an enormous, disciplined bureaucratic apparatus at its service.[24] As Philippine economist Bernardo Villegas observed, "Countries with a strong state may benefit from currency controls. You can only do it if you have a reign of terror. I think Malaysia can do it because there you can be arrested without any warrant."[25]

There was great doubt concerning the Malaysian example also in Indonesia. "The Krugman thesis has some validity for countries with good regulatory procedures, legal infrastructure, enforcement, and good data transparency. . . . In ASEAN it is questionable whether controls can benefit when there are so many factors we have to struggle with," said a director of the Indonesian central bank.[26]

How then, should one evaluate Malaysia's isolationist gambit? If only a reign of terror is required, then its prospects are good. During the years following the imposition of currency controls, Malaysia developed in a less-than-democratic way. Political power has been increasingly concentrated into the hands of one man; for months, Mahathir acted simultaneously as prime minister, interior minister, and finance minister. The Malaysian state—including the police and judiciary—allowed itself to be used like gestapo in a political campaign against the deposed deputy prime minister and finance minister Anwar Ibrahim. Mahathir's political enemies were arrested by the hundreds under the country's draconian security laws, a relic of British colonial rule. In the center of the capital, Kuala Lumpur, water cannons, tear gas, and police batons have been used against peaceful demonstrators demanding an end to corruption and nepotism associated with the Mahathir regime. Malaysian citizens began to fear their government. "Rule of fear" became an apt description of Mahathir's Malaysia within weeks of the introduction of capital controls. In this respect, the country may "succeed" with capital controls. But is this success something others should emulate?

Let us assume that it really is the case, as Bhagwati argues, that free capital movements are motivated only by ideology, not theory, and that the benefit of free flows is not supported by any conclusive scientific evidence.

A strong case can in fact be made for not approaching the issue of capital controls from a strictly scientific and utilitarian standpoint. Just consider that there is no inconclusive evidence that democracy leads to economic growth and welfare. Research has concluded that democracy "is neither negative nor positive for economic growth."[27] But surely this scientific finding should not be taken as evidence that western democracy could be scrapped. People do not become democrats or autocrats because they have been presented with scientific evidence. In the final analysis, ideological and moral considerations are often more important than scientific conclusions when core values are in the balance.

The same considerations apply to capital movements. Great effort has been made to prove that free capital flows lead to prosperity, and there is compelling evidence to support that notion. The rich democracies are also the countries that have allowed capital to freely cross international borders. Without the possibility of borrowing money abroad, Western countries would have been much harder hit, for example, by the oil crises of the 1970s than was the case. Since they started to relax capital controls in the late 1980s, the countries of the developing world have achieved welfare gains that have been unprecedented in history. There are striking pragmatic arguments in support of liberalized foreign exchange markets. But the strongest and most fundamental arguments against capital controls are not of a practical or utilitarian nature. They are ideological. Strict currency controls are incompatible with ideologies that value freedom and internationalism.

As noted above, a nonliberal currency regime is in most countries incompatible with a liberal democratic order. One consequence of capital controls is that the ability of people to travel is restricted. In South Korea, for example, which until recently operated the strictest capital controls in Asia, it was only in 1989 that passports were made available to the general public. And Malaysian travelers are prohibited from spending more than a certain amount when traveling abroad. The good, open society must be open not only for information, ideas, and people but also for capital.

The parallel to democratic processes can be developed further. In a way, free capital movements create an avenue for direct democracy. In most democracies, general elections are held every fourth year or so. But in open societies, citizens can vote in the markets every day with their money. On September 1, 1998, Mahathir decided to take this right to vote away from the citizens of Malaysia. It is easy to understand why authoritarian political leaders should want to deprive their subjects of such a potent democratic instrument. But it is not easy to understand why intellectuals in the democratic West should smile approvingly at the autocrats' autarkic revolt against globalization. Perhaps it is because they, like the editor of *Le Monde Diplomatique*, long for the bygone era when power was "hierarchical, vertical, and authoritarian."[28]

Subsidizing Hot Money

There are different kinds of capital flows. Critics of free global capital flows rarely want to put restrictions on all kinds. In general, they want to put clamps on inflows and outflows of "hot" money, movements of capital across national borders that are not directly associated with "real" economic transactions. Certain movements of capital are exempt from criticism: for example, those that arise when a person in one country buys a product made in another country, or when a company in one country builds a factory in another. Bhagwati and others do not doubt the theoretical soundness of such types of capital flows, but such critics believe that the Asian crisis shows that it is time to make short-term, purely speculative activities on currency and stock markets subject to extensive government regulation and control.

Perhaps there are good reasons for restricting the flows of "bad" or undesirable capital. But the Asian crisis hardly supports that notion. On the contrary, the crisis shows that governments should not subsidize the inflow of hot money as the Asian countries were doing. Market actors simply reacted to the ultimately unhealthy incentives that tiger politicians had created. Among the factors that contributed to the creation of distorted capital flows, two warrant special mention: pegged exchange rates and various kinds of protectionism.

All of the crisis countries engaged in attempts to defend pegged exchange rates. It is in these rigid exchange rate mechanisms that the roots of the Asian crisis are to be found. The pegged exchange rates of the tiger states created an illusion of safety: the illusion that foreign exchange risks had been eliminated. When tiger currencies were as good (or bad) as the U.S. dollar, there was no reason for companies that borrowed U.S. dollars to finance ventures that generated income in local currency to hedge their exposure. Why should they, if government authorities had promised no changes in the currency exchange mechanism?

Of course, currency risk cannot be abolished. But in the tiger countries, politicians and central bank governors were very skillful at creating the illusion that such risks had indeed been eliminated. This stimulated the inflow of foreign capital, spurring economic growth.

By the early 1990s, the fixed exchange rates had already become subject to extensive critique. But tiger politicians were unwilling to change course. One reason was that those countries experienced strong inflows of foreign capital, which raised the specter that they might start suffering from the so-called Dutch disease. If they allowed their currencies to float, the gush of foreign capital would force tiger currencies to appreciate against other currencies. This would in turn have undermined the export-oriented growth strategy pursued by these countries, requiring a radical change in the development paradigm.

It is often said that there are no free lunches in this world. But during the 1990s Southeast Asia has served up lots of free meals. In fast-growing Thailand, this phenomenon occurred as a result of the government's exchange rate policy. It worked quite simply: the central bank intervened to suck up the capital that had flowed into the country from abroad and that threatened to overheat the economy. The resulting rise in interest rates made it even more attractive

143

for foreign investors to change their dollars into baht and park them in bank accounts in order to take advantage of the higher return. In other words, the actions taken by the central banks became counterproductive as they stimulated further inflows of hot money. The policy, followed by all of the region's countries, significantly increased the vulnerability of those countries.

That something had to be done in order to avoid a sad ending was rather evident, particularly so in the case of Thailand. Early on, the IMF issued warnings to the Thais that their currency policies were unsustainable. But it was by no means an isolated Thai phenomenon. Sunanda Sen of the Jawaharlal Nehru University of New Delhi warned, in a 1996 report dealing with Indonesia, Malaysia, and Thailand, that "the current scene requires, rather urgently, strategic measures, so that the growth achieved in these countries over the last 15 years does not disappear as a result of sudden shocks generated in their financial systems."[29] Needless to say, no urgent strategic measures were taken. We know now how fateful the consequences of this Asian mistake were.

Trade Barriers and Hot Money

In addition to the effects of pegged exchange rates, incentives were distorted by protectionist policies affecting the tigers' banking and finance sectors. The desperate attempts by central banks to suck liquidity from the financial markets were not the only factor contributing to high domestic interest rates. Given the scope of protection in Asian banking and finance industries, local companies could either borrow money in local currency at sky-high interest rates or borrow in foreign hard currencies at low interest rates. Because of the illusion that exchange rate risks had been abolished as if by magic, financing operations through direct foreign borrowing appeared as a highly attractive option. It was, however, an option available only to the larger Asian companies. In addition, the big interest rate gap stimulated local banks to borrow capital overseas and relend it to smaller local companies and consumers. The gush of hot money benefited many, which may explain why politicians were so reluctant to change policy direction.

Another just as damaging aspect of protectionism in the banking sector was, paradoxically, linked to the liberalization of the banking and finance sectors. In Thailand, the ministry of finance promised local finance companies and foreign banks with offshore banking licenses that some of them would be given access to the lucrative domestic market. One reason local finance companies and foreign banks poured so much capital into Thailand was that they hoped to become market leaders and, thus, leading candidates to receive the profitable new banking licenses. Since finance companies were not allowed to take deposits from ordinary savers (a privilege reserved for banks) and since the offshore banks were not allowed to raise funds locally by any means, liberalization (and the promise thereof) created perverse incentives for market players to bring ever more foreign hot money into the country.

Strangely, these unhealthy incentives in the finance and banking sectors were created at the very same time analysts and observers began to feel uncomfortable with the setup. In other words, the measures were introduced against better knowledge.

Thus, the tigers with the severest wounds were the ones with weak and protected banking sectors. The tigers have gone all out for industrialization, but they have neglected modernizing the service sector. Indeed, common prejudice in the region is that the financial sector is "unproductive." A telling example is offered by Mahathir's response when asked why foreign bankers were not offered easier access to the Malaysian market:

> Why do you want to go into banking? We would like people to come here and invest in productive activities. Just imagine, we have tiny little banks. Some huge banks come in. Our banks cannot fight against them. They will lose out. Our banks will collapse, probably be absorbed. Then we will have very big, efficient, powerful banks, but they won't belong to us. And banks are very important instruments in the development of a country like Malaysia. It is the banking system that helps to finance certain priority areas which we determine.[30]

But the truth is that it has been the banks that have paved the way for the crisis not only in Malaysia but also in South Korea, Thailand, and other Asian countries. Indeed, it was impossible for the tigers to become world-leading industrial nations while retaining their primitive banking systems. Besides the effects of governments channeling bank financing to pet projects, protectionism itself created huge inefficiencies in the economies. The scope for rationalization can be illustrated by South Korea: When the crisis hit, the country had 25 major domestic banks, 3,000 smaller banks, and 20 large stock brokers.[31] This means that there was one financial institution for every 6,000 South Koreans—5 times the average for all the OECD countries.

Economic theorists agree that the inflow of capital invested for the long term is beneficial. Unfortunately, Asian politicians did not take notice. Laws and regulations have, to an astonishing degree, hindered foreign companies and investors willing to risk their money in Asia. Some sectors have been entirely closed off to foreign players. And in those that have been open, other restrictions have applied, such as bans on foreign majority share holding. In ventures geared toward the local market, foreign ownership was often restricted to less than 50 percent—in order to give local *compradors* the chance to put their fingers in all the pies. Those companies that were willing to make long-term direct investments were not allowed to do so to the extent that they would have liked. This led to a situation where factories and construction projects were financed through foreign loans to a greater extent than necessary or desirable.

New regulations are not needed to control the hot money problem. But, at the very least, those regulations that turn hot money into a highly attractive alternative to colder dollars should be removed.

The Death Throes of State Capitalism

Many voices have hastened to echo Mahathir's lamentations and argued that the crash of the Asian "miracles" signifies a failure of global capitalism. In the *International Herald Tribune*, Marshall Auerback, a consultant, and Patrick Smith, a journalist, wrote that Asians had realized "that globalization caused the Asian crisis and cannot logically be its cure."[32] Auerback pointed to Japanese finance minister Kiichi Miyazawa's statement that "I'm an outdated Keynesian" who favors "economic recovery, not reform," meaning that Asia will not swallow the medicine called "globalization"— especially not if in reality it is equivalent with "Americanization."

But the Asian crisis is not the last gasp of economic liberalism. In fact, it represents the death throes of the Asian model of state capitalism. Put bluntly, the American model has won, and the Japanese model has lost. Americans may perhaps feel some schadenfreude because of this victory, but mostly they seem surprised. As Bill Clinton noted when contrasting Asian fragility and the economic strength of the United States, "It is a great irony that we are at a moment of unsurpassed economic strength at a time of such turmoil in the world economy."[33] The surprise is caused by the same phenomenon that caused surprise following the collapse of communism. Many westerners had imagined that their competitors had an advantage. When the collapse came and the truth was revealed, people did not know what to believe anymore.

Asia has for a long time been regarded as a challenger—not a representative—of orthodox "Anglo-American" economics. Led by Japan, Asia followed economic principles derived not from Adam Smith but from the German economist Friedrich List. This German-Asian model was characterized by the following commandments: economic development must be guided; producer interests are more important than the interests of consumers; do not trust individuals to know what is good for them, put your faith in state paternalism; put the nation ahead of the individual citizen; business is war; morality is less important than power and concrete results.[34] According to journalist James Fallows, East Asian capitalism was headed for collision with the Anglo-American model, which is why the West, led by the United States, needed to abandon its ideals about free trade and free competition, or it would go down with its ideological flag held high.

Those contentions were appealing on the surface. It is beyond doubt that many successful Asian economies during their heydays were subject to heavy state intervention and guidance. Robert Wade described this situation in East Asia in general and in Taiwan in particular in his controversial book *Governing the Market*.[35] However, the presence of state interventionism does not by itself provide a causal link with economic success. Wade admits as much and thereby devalues his own theory:

> I should stress that the organization of firms—their size, the way they grow, their methods of doing business, and the relationship between them—is a major gap in the argument of this book. Any discussion of an economy's development should give a central place to the organization of firms and industries. But since little evidence is available on this subject for Taiwan, and since my primary interest is the uses of public power, I say little more about it.[36]

147

The Growth of White Elephants

Many like Wade have closed their eyes to economic reality and focused their attention on political illusions. This has been common not only among economists and social scientists but also among politicians and journalists.

The fact that some of the tigers followed Japan's lead to varying degrees does not mean that this is what caused their erstwhile success. More likely, they reaped their successes despite, not because of, political and bureaucratic attempts at "guidance." It was not the Thai auto industry that created that country's economic "miracle." It was not the Indonesian aerospace industry that underlay Indonesia's success. It was not the Proton car or the Petronas Towers that made Malaysia a winner in global export markets. And it definitely was not the region's antiquated and corrupt banks that were the source of regional dynamism . . . , and neither were the property bubbles that they produced. On the contrary, these and other white elephants—touted as shining examples of Asian success—were allowed to grow so big that they crushed the sound and substantial parts of the region's economies.

The Asian crisis proves that a certain set of legal and institutional structures is required before a country can participate in the global economy. Note that no one ever forced Asian countries to open up their economies. They were not clients of the IMF, subject to outside pressure for change. They opened their capital markets of their own free will. And, as in Europe, they did it for competitive reasons. Thais, Malays, and others saw the prosperity that openness to capital flows had created in neighbors like Hong Kong and Singapore. They wanted their countries to be similarly successful.

To open capital markets to foreign money was and remains a sign of the maturity and sophistication in a country's economic policies. And initially, in Asia the effects of opening up were positive; capital arrived in unprecedented volumes. Only after Asia had suffered the most painful market bust in half a century did the tigers come to realize what it takes to play in the higher divisions of global finance. As Jeffrey Garten of the Yale School of Management observed in the early days of the Asian crisis:

> The global markets . . . are saying something that is totally
> unambiguous: If the emerging markets want to play in the

global financial marketplace, they are going to have to emerge. And they are going to have to do it overnight.[37]

The Tigers' Choice

Now the tigers (and Japan) have a choice to make: they can either proceed with the greatest possible speed to adjust their institutions or withdraw, as Malaysia did, from global markets.

South Korea's president Kim Dae Jung is probably Asia's strongest advocate of openness and change. In 1998 he remarked, "We must practice democracy and the free-market system in unison. Even though it is a bit late, we have no choice."[38]

Kim did not blame the crisis on immoral foreign speculators but rather on deep structural problems in the South Korean economy. The crisis was created by South Korean hands—many blackened by corruption—not by invisible hands in New York or London. The problems faced by South Korea will not be solved by turning inward. On the contrary, Kim argued, his country must proceed with building the nation.

> We can no longer survive international competition with today's economic system characterized by high cost and low efficiency. If we are to raise national productivity and strengthen our competitive edge, structural reform is indispensable. Through our second nation-building efforts, we must establish a genuine market economy whose development was suppressed by the previous governments.[39]

Kim has not promised any quick fixes. There are none. Kim therefore speaks about fundamental changes to South Korea's political and economic institutions, a reinvention of the entire social system in which government control over the economy is replaced by market mechanisms and market discipline. But, according to Kim, the need for change goes even deeper than that. "We must establish a new value system based on universalism and globalism," Kim says, "shedding self-righteous nationalism and other anachronistic ideas."

This is not the voice of a "neoliberal." Kim Dae Jung's ideology is best described as social democratic. His political base is with the labor union movement. His reform agenda faces the stiffest political opposition from the country's top corporations. It should be mentioned, however, that Kim was a small-business owner before he became a dissident in the generals' South Korea. In other words, he knows how difficult it is to be an entrepreneur in a top-heavy, authoritarian society in which the entire economic-political system has been rigged to cater to the needs of a handful of giant companies.

It is by no means certain that Kim will succeed in overhauling South Korea from the top to the bottom. South Korea is a country that has taken the Japanese model to the extreme—indeed, further than has Japan itself. The structural imbalances are so great and have such deep roots in South Korean society that they will likely prove long-lived, especially in the face of a recovery led by devaluation.

The Western left depicts "globalization" as the biggest threat of the new millennium, yet it is in the forces of globalization that Kim puts his hope for South Korea. In many Western countries it is now fashionable to argue that globalization is incompatible with genuine democracy and humanism. In South Korea, people know from bitter experience that the global market economy offers the best chance to create a just society.

The IMF's Unclear Place in the Global Market

The Asian crisis has led to demands that the world economy be reformed. In September 1998 U.S. President Bill Clinton declared that "this is the biggest financial challenge facing the world in a half century." That assessment differed dramatically from the one he made less than a year earlier, when he argued to the surprise of many Asian leaders that the region's problems were just "a few little glitches in the road."

What, then, is on the reform agenda? According to Clinton, nothing less than to "adapt the international financial architecture to the 21st century."[40] British Prime Minister Tony Blair also believes that "the existing international financial system . . . needs to be modernized to meet the challenges of a new century," and has called for the creation of a "new Bretton Woods."[41] And just one day after the victory of the Social Democratic party in the 1998 German elections, the new chancellor, Gerhard Schröder, argued that he regards the control of financial speculation as one of the most important tasks of his government.

For his part, French President Jacques Chirac wants to transform the IMF's interim committee into a global economic central bureau with vast powers. According to Chirac:

> The International Monetary Fund and the World Bank have served world interests well for the past five decades. . . . Now they need to be adapted to suit a new global climate. The current financial crisis shows that we need a profound dialogue among us all as well as a decisionmaking mechanism that will give the markets strong political signals. The transformation of the interim committee on the IMF into a decision-making body at ministerial level . . . will meet this objective.[42]

In short, in the wake of the Asian crisis, four of the Western world's most influential politicians had begun to appreciate the point made by Mahathir: that the status quo is not an option.

The IMF: Unequal to the Market

It is widely accepted that the IMF has not handled the Asian crisis adequately, in spite of organizing rescue packages to Thailand, Indonesia, and South Korea worth more than $110 billion. The unequal relationship between the markets and the IMF prompted *Financial Times* journalist Edward Luce to champion the idea that the agency should engage in a sort of race with the markets. According to Luce, the IMF should be transformed into something called WOOF (World Organization of Finance), a supercop with the power to intervene in global capital markets when major financial accidents occur. Among other things, WOOF would be empowered to impose currency controls and debt moratoriums on crisis-stricken countries.[43]

Of course, the turmoil in Asia cannot be entirely blamed on the IMF. In Thailand, Indonesia, and South Korea the roots of the crisis lay in mismanaged banking systems. But the IMF had not previously shown a deep interest in Asian banking systems and financial markets. The competence and experience of the IMF were limited to dealing with government finances and the macroeconomic situation.[44] In Asia, government finances were in good shape when the crisis hit. It was only Asian banks and major corporations that were on the edge of a cliff. Instead of addressing the main cause of the Asian disease, the IMF prescribed the same treatment to its tiger patients that it had given to African and Latin American governments in the past.

Clearly, the IMF lacked sensitivity to the Asian political scene. An obvious faux pas was committed by IMF managing director

Michel Camdessus in Jakarta, when he stood with arms crossed and looked down on President Suharto as he, seated, signed the latest IMF agreement. To many observers, and not only in Indonesia, the gesture signified that the IMF was an imperialistic agency. As a consequence, it became virtually impossible for Suharto, a proud nationalist, to follow the IMF regime. The IMF official's imperious gesture undermined the reform agenda of the IMF throughout Asia.

But the problem is more fundamental. Do we really want a world where bureaucrats from the IMF, WOOF, or other multilateral agencies are so powerful that they travel the world appearing to tame leaders of great nations? Would it not, one is prompted to ask, have been easier for Suharto to bite the bullet if a faceless "market" had exerted the pressure, rather than "suits" just off the plane from Washington, D.C.? When the IMF came to Asia, its mission was to restore confidence and calm markets. Instead, the organization behaved like an elephant in a china shop: what confidence had not already been shattered, was shattered; what capital had not already fled, fled.

Many would be loath to sympathize with Suharto had only he been insulted, but the IMF displayed similar arrogance in South Korea. There, the most acute phase of the financial crisis coincided with a presidential election campaign. There Camdessus demanded that all three presidential candidates agree in writing to follow the dictates of the fund. Given its vast financial resources, the power granted to the IMF easily comes into conflict with the principles of democracy and national sovereignty.

The IMF as Global Lender of Last Resort

It seems, however, slightly unfair to criticize the IMF since the fund is neither omniscient nor omnipotent. But these human weaknesses are problematic: being omniscient and omnipotent are almost job requirements if the IMF is to handle its duties.

It is often argued, for example, that the IMF is the world's *lender of last resort*, an entity that we cannot do without. But a lender of last resort must be omnipotent in the sense that it can create the resources it needs. A national central bank, which can print money, has a kind of omnipotence: If it decides to rescue a bank from liquidity problems, it will have sufficient money to do so. And a lender of last resort must be practically omniscient. It must be able to quickly determine whether a bank in trouble is just illiquid or if it is in fact insolvent. Banks that are insolvent should not be given access to liquidity support. To gain such information, any lender of last resort must have in-depth, continuous knowledge of the financial realities of the institution it may rescue.

But the IMF does not act, nor has it the ability to act, as a lender of last resort. The IMF has a finite amount of resources since it cannot print money. And the IMF lacks the ability to regulate the economic policies of independent nations or their financial institutions. Furthermore, IMF funds have bailed out clearly bankrupt institutions.

In Bangkok, Jakarta, and Seoul, drawn-out IMF negotiations hammered out the actions governments would have to take to earn international support. The results were then taken by IMF officers back to the "shareholders" (member governments) of the organization, who had to give their blessing before any funds could be released. Then, schedules covering months and even years were drawn up, in which dollars were apportioned as countries implemented the required reforms. The complexity and slow pace of IMF action created yet greater uncertainty in the region, demonstrating that the IMF was ill-suited to serve as a lender of last resort. Its painful interventions prompted proposals for reforming the fund and strengthening it and other international institutions.

Tempering the Ambitions of the World's Politicians

Jacques Attali, once a top aide to French president François Mitterrand and a founding president of the European Bank for Reconstruction and Development, is one of those who want to go the furthest down this road. He argues that our "global village" now "needs a mayor, a police force, a justice system, a bank, one currency, and taxes."[45] In other words, the Asian crisis convinced him that we need a world president, a world police, a world court, and a world currency minted by a global bank. This, according to Attali, is the only way to prevent economic "disorder."

Yet in the light of the failure of the IMF and of Messrs. Clinton, Blair, Kohl, and Hashimoto to avoid financial turmoil in Asia, Russia, and Brazil, would it not be more reasonable to temper the ambitions of bureaucrats and politicians rather than to boost them?

The illusion that more regulation of the global financial markets— not less—is needed may stem from the fact that the IMF, especially in Europe, is regularly touted as a "neoliberal" organization. For example, Swedish National Radio's Asia correspondent, Staffan Sonning, called IMF chief Camdessus "the high priest of market liberalism."[46] In fact, few market liberals would regard Camdessus as a guiding light. By all means, IMF officials may sometimes *sound* liberal, but the rhetoric cannot disguise the fact that the IMF lies entirely outside of the market. It is an instrument for government guidance of economies. Thus, to describe the Asian crisis and its effects as a failure of *both* the IMF and the free market is patently absurd.

But is there truly a rationale for the governments of the world to come together to do something about wild swings in currency values? If reasons exist for such a strategy, the Asian crisis does not provide them. In fact, East Asia's crisis can to a considerable extent be blamed on earlier attempts to regulate exchange rates and trade flows through international cooperation. In the mid-1980s, when people in the United States were gravely worried about a bulging trade deficit with Japan, the "problem" was solved with a seemingly elegant political maneuver. In the Plaza Hotel in New York in September 1985, the finance ministers and central bank governors from the world's five leading industrial nations agreed that the U.S. dollar was too strong vis-à-vis the Japanese yen and that the yen should be strengthened.

But as the yen grew stronger, the Bank of Japan lowered interest rates to record lows. The rapid expansion of credit that ensued fueled a Japanese boom and an enormous Japanese industrial expansion throughout Asia (where currencies remained tied to the falling U.S. dollar). Money from Japan swamped South Korea, Taiwan, Malaysia, Singapore, Indonesia, and Thailand. In Thailand the increase was dramatic: in 1989 Japanese companies invested 25 times as much as they had done just four years earlier. Within a few years after the New York meeting, East and Southeast Asia had become cluttered with new Japanese-owned factories. Since then the inflow of Japanese capital has continued, not least because it was arranged so that the Japanese yen would remain strong even after the Tokyo bubble burst in the early 1990s.

In later years, the Japanese central bank continued to contribute to the creation of the Asian bubble economy through the extremely low-interest policy it pursued from 1995 onwards. Wave upon wave of cheap Japanese money continued to wash up on Asian shores. Today's strident calls for global currency regulation, cooperation, and coordination sound peculiar. Government leaders from Germany to Tokyo apparently want to intervene in the markets in order to come to grips with the unintended consequences of earlier government interference.

The way forward does not lead to increased government regulation or direct involvement in capital markets. On the contrary, market actors have to learn to live in the new world which was born out of the Asian crisis: a world without illusions about fixed exchange rates or the IMF as its ultimate savior. Politicians from Bangkok to Moscow must also learn to live in the new world. They must learn how to manage their economies in ways that promote stability and growth by building the political and legal institutions of a market economy. Ultimately, countries must be allowed to make their own mistakes and learn from them. Policy competition among countries, rather than coordination, is as important to the global market economy as is economic competition itself.

Conclusion

Many analysts believe that the fall of the baht in July 1997 was just as key a watershed event in Asia as was the fall of the Berlin wall in Europe.[47] It represented the end of a certain way of organizing society, politically and economically. Since the crisis, Asia's political landscape has undergone tremendous changes. Democracy has been strengthened in Thailand, Indonesia, South Korea, and Taiwan. The levels of economic openness have increased remarkably from Seoul to Singapore as capital markets and industries have been liberalized. However, as was also the case in Eastern Europe, not all the old ways will disappear in one stroke. The forces of conservatism are fighting back, trying to roll back reform. And it must be recognized that policy reform and the creation of new institutions is a slow process.

If Asia can achieve lasting change, then its crisis will have had a bright side: a freer, richer, more democratic Asia. The outlook is generally positive. There is a strong base from which to build, thanks to economic progress made in recent decades. That base now includes better-educated, more well-nourished, and healthier populations than ever before; better road and telecommunication networks than could be imagined just 20 years ago; global business relationships; a solid work ethic; and so on. Even after the economic setback, the welfare levels in the tiger nations are much higher than in typical Third World countries. What the tigers achieved was, and still is, very impressive. Further globalization, requiring fundamental structural reforms and cultural change still lacking in most of the East and Southeast Asian crisis countries, can help the region continue to make remarkable progress in the new century.

Notes

This chapter was originally published in Swedish as *Asiens kris är inte kapitalismens* (Stockholm: Timbro, 1998), and has been revised from the original.

1. Gunnar Myrdal, *Asian Drama: An Inquiry into the Poverty of Nations*, 3 vols. (New York: Pantheon, 1968).
2. Mark Clifford, *Troubled Tiger: The Unauthorised Biography of Korea, Inc.*, rev. ed. (Singapore: Butterworth-Heinemann Asia, 1997), p. 340.
3. Steven Radelet and Jeffrey Sachs, "The Onset of the East Asian Crisis" (paper presented at National Bureau of Economic Research conference, February 6–7, 1998), pp. 5–6.
4. William James, "Trade and Financial Market Reforms in ASEAN: Putting the Cart Before the Horse," *Asian Economic Bulletin* 14, no. 3 (1998).
5. Bertrand Renaud et al., *How the Thai Real Estate Boom Undid Financial Institutions — What Can Be Done Now?* (paper presented at a conference arranged by the World Bank and National Economic and Social Development Board in Bangkok, May 20–21, 1998), p. 2.
6. Tomas Larsson, "Höjden av Hybris?" *Svenska Dagbladet*, April 29, 1996.
7. Pete Engardio, "Time for a Reality Check in Asia," *Business Week*, December 2, 1996.
8. Transparency International, "TI Press Release: 1998 Corruption Perception Index," September 22, 1998, http://www.transparency.de/documents/press-releases/1998/1998.09.22.cpi.html.
9. Quoted in Ricardo Saludo and Assif Shameen, "How Much Longer?" *Asiaweek*, July 17, 1998.
10. Henny Sender, "The Storm Intensifies," *Far Eastern Economic Review*, October 1, 1998.
11. Jirasakunthai Choosak, "Taiwanese Back Plans for Credit Bureau," *The Nation*, September 17, 1998.
12. "The Flexible Tiger," *The Economist*, January 3, 1998.
13. Quoted in Saludo and Shameen, "A Question of Openness," *Asiaweek*, October 3, 1997.
14. Jagdish Bhagwati, "The Capital Myth: The Difference between Trade in Widgets and Dollars," *Foreign Affairs* 77, no. 3 (May/June 1998): 7–8.
15. Paul Krugman, "Saving Asia: It's Time to Get Radical," *Fortune*, September 9, 1998, http://www.pathfinder.com/fortune/investor/1998/980907/sol.html.
16. Quoted in *Nation*, "Economist Calls for Currency Controls," August 27, 1998.
17. Mahathir Mohamad, "Call Me a Heretic," *Time*, September 14, 1998.

18. To be compared, for example, with South Korea, which had a weighting of only 3.1 percent. Greece, Portugal, and Turkey did not add up to more than 5 percent of the index.

19. "HK Finance Chief Urges Global Measures to Fight Speculators," *Bangkok Post*, September 9, 1998.

20. See "Mahathir's High Hopes," *The Economist*, July 8, 1995.

21. Not surprisingly, capital flight accelerated in other Asian nations—Indonesia in particular—following the Malaysian action, out of fear that Malaysia's abandoning the road of globalization would prompt others to follow.

22. Alan Friedman, "G-7 Spars over Reshaping of Financial System," *International Herald Tribune*, September 30, 1998.

23. Chile's tax on capital inflows has also been held out as a potential model for other countries. However, Chile has been reducing its currency controls in the face of the Asian crisis.

24. Capital controls are a relatively new phenomenon. According to Milton Friedman, the nonconvertible currency was invented by the German Nazi regime's finance minister, Hjalmar Schacht. As Friedman noted: "The most effective way to convert a market economy into an authoritarian economic society is to start by imposing direct controls on foreign exchange." See Friedman, *Capitalism and Freedom* (Chicago: Chicago University Press, 1962), p. 57.

25. Quoted in Cesar Bacani, "The Road Less Traveled," *Asiaweek*, September 18, 1998.

26. Quoted in Faith Keenan et al., "Desperate Measures," *Far Eastern Economic Review*, September 10, 1998.

27. Svante Ersson and Jan-Erik Lane, "Democracy and Development: A Statistical Exploration," in *Democracy and Development: Theory and Practice*, ed. Arian Leftwich (Cambridge: Polity Press, 1996), p. 64.

28. Ignacio Ramonet, "A World Transformed," *Le Monde Diplomatique*, October 1997, http://www.monde-diplomatique.fr/en/1997/10/leader.html.

29. Sunanda Sen, *Growth Centers in South East Asia in the Era of Globalization*, UNCTAD Discussion Papers, no. 118 (Geneva: UNCTAD, September 1996), p. 34.

30. "I've Lost My Voice," Interview with Mahathir Mohamad, *Asiaweek*, March 27, 1998.

31. Steven Brull and Keumhyun Lee, "Why Seoul Is Seething," *Business Week*, January 27, 1997.

32. Marshall Auerback and Patrick Smith, "It's One World, Ready or Not But Some Are Not," *International Herald Tribune*, September 9, 1998.

33. Bill Clinton, "Remarks by the President to the Council on Foreign Relations," September 14, 1998, http://www.pub.whitehouse.gov/uri-res/I2R?urn:pdi://oma.eop.gov.us/1998/9/15/2.text.1.

34. James Fallows, *Looking at the Sun: The Rise of the New East Asian Economic and Political System* (New York: Vintage Books, 1995), pp. 182–190.

35. Robert Wade, *Governing the Market: Economic Theory and the Role of Government in East Asian Industrialization* (Princeton: Princeton University Press, 1990).

36. Ibid., p. 70.

37. Alan Murray, "New Economic Models Are Failing While America Inc. Keeps Rolling," *Wall Street Journal*, December 8, 1997.

38. Quoted in Chongkittavorn Kavi, "Kim Advocates Free Market," *Nation*, September 18, 1998.

39. Dae Jung Kim, "The 50th Anniversary of the Founding of the ROK Government," August 15, 1998. http://www.korea.emb.washington.dc.us/speech/speech.wcgi?98v.

40. Clinton, 1998.

41. Tony Blair, "Speech to the New York Stock Exchange," September 21, 1998, http://www.number-10.gov.uk/public/info/releases/speeches/.

42. Jacques Chirac, *Bangkok Post*, September 26, 1998.

43. Edward Luce, "Age of Uncertainty," *Prospect*, July 1998.

44. It should be noted that the IMF's track record was hardly promising even before the organization tackled the tigers. Over the past 30 years, the IMF has only rarely managed to bring its patients back to health. Of the 89 developing nations that received IMF support anytime between 1965 and 1995, 48 countries have yet to register any material improvement since they received IMF "help." Of the 48 countries, 32 are poorer than they were before they received IMF loans. And of the 32 countries, some 14 countries have suffered economic contractions of more than 15 percent. See Bryan Johnson and Brett Shaefer, "The International Monetary Fund: Outdated, Ineffective, and Unnecessary," Heritage Foundation *Backgrounder* no. 1113, May 6, 1997, http://www.heritage.org/library/categories/trade/bg1113.html.

45. Jacques Attali, "When Free Markets Fail: World War or World Govt?" *Bangkok Post*, September 27, 1998.

46. Staffan Sonning (radio report in *Godmorgon, världen!* on Channel 1, Swedish National Radio, September 27, 1998).

47. See José Piñera, "Asia: The Fall of a Second Berlin Wall," *Cato Journal* 18, no. 3 (Winter 1999): 399–403.

8. Korea's Choice: Creative Destruction or Destructive Reform?

Byeong-Ho Gong

The past 10 years have been a "lost decade" for Koreans. During that period, the international economic environment has witnessed some remarkable changes. They include the powerful emergence of the Chinese economy, explosive growth in a number of developing nations, the deployment of innovative communication and information technologies, aggressive rationalization initiatives by enterprises in the advanced nations, and the emergence of the global economy. Koreans have spent that time trying to maintain the government-led model that in the past enabled our nation to achieve high growth.

But the Korean economy has rapidly lost its competitiveness due to the direct and indirect involvement of politicians in allocating funds. Government-controlled finance, heavy involvement of the state in the capital market, artificial exchange rate policies, complex regulations and the resulting corruption, powerful labor unions, and unfair bankruptcy policy are all examples of political influence in the marketplace.

Koreans have known for years about the problems in their economy, as drastic reforms were repeatedly advocated to fix the "Korean sickness," whose symptoms were high costs and low efficiency. However, the initiatives of past governments turned out to be short-term episodes due to the lack of political leadership, opposition from special interest groups, and distorted views of the principles of a market economy. The currency crisis in Southeast Asia, which started in July 1997 and spread to Korea in November of that year, dried up the nation's foreign currency reserves. The immediate result was Korea's request for a bailout from the International Monetary Fund (IMF). More important, the country could no longer afford to ignore the main cause of its crisis: the structural weakness of the economy.[1]

Table 8.1
GROWTH RATE, INTEREST RATE, AND FOREIGN
CURRENCY RESERVES

	1996	1997	1998	1999*
Economic growth rate (%)	6.8	5.0	−5.8	4.4
Current account (bil. U.S. dollars)	−2.3	−8.1	40.0	20.0
Foreign currency reserves	33.0	20.4	52.0	20.0
Stock price index (KOSPI)	844.9	654.5	406.1	721.0
Corporate bond yields	11.9	13.4	15.1	8.3

NOTE: As of December 1996, 1997, and 1998 and as of end of April 1999.
*Korean Development Institute estimate.

The Korean government has closely followed IMF recommenda-tions since the inception of the financial crisis.[2] In particular, it has initiated various measures to restructure the *chaebols*, or large Korean conglomerates, that far exceed IMF conditionality. As a result, the macroeconomic indicators rapidly improved. In 1998, the nation's gross domestic product (GDP) dropped by 5.8 percent, a truly unprecedented decline. In the second half of 1998, however, the rapid deterioration of the economy came to a stop, slowly reversing its course along with a noticeable recovery in the manufacturing sector. In 1998, Korea's current account surplus was $40 billion, resolving its chronic trade deficit problem. It is also quite encourag-ing that the nation posted a current account surplus of $20 billion in 1999.

Meanwhile, Standard & Poor's and Moody's, two premier credit evaluation companies, upgraded their credit ratings for Korea from "inappropriate for investment" to "appropriate for investment" as early as February 1999. As a result of such positive views, foreign direct investment in Korea has been steadily increasing along with active foreign participation in the Korean capital market.

It appears that the Korean economy is in good shape, with stable exchange rates, low interest rates, an appropriate level of foreign currency reserves, and a rapid recovery of the stock market (Table 8.1). However, to conclude that the government's economic reforms have strengthened the fundamentals of the Korean economy would be misleading.

Because of the devaluation of the Korean won, which had been overvalued for a few years, the competitiveness of Korean products sharply improved in the short term, increasing the current account surplus. As a result, liquidity has dramatically improved, and the lack of demand for funds from Korean enterprises that are restructuring has resulted in lower interest rates. The available funds that have entered the securities market due to lower interest rates have created a boom in the stock market. The subsequent bullish Korean stock market may also be attributed to sharply increased investments in Korea by international funds looking for opportunities in emerging markets. Foreign investors seem to believe that Korea may be a relatively safer place for investment compared with other emerging nations.

In evaluating the Korean economy, it is important not to ignore the fundamental causes of the economic crisis. It is also very important not to overemphasize short-term improvements of the macro indicators. Monitoring those indicators may be necessary, but to deal with or prevent future problems, it is still more important to examine the factors that led to the "Korean sickness."

Some industrial experts believe that the Korean economic crisis was caused by excessive capital investments by the Korean *chaebols*. However, behind the *chaebols'* excessive borrowings lies the Korean government's powerful role in disrupting the market order and creating an economy of high costs and low efficiency.

For the Korean economy to become fundamentally sound, a paradigm shift is required. The country must move from a government-led economy to a private-oriented one. Unless market decisions are separated from politics, Korea will not regain its competitiveness in the mid- or long term. Indeed, nations that borrow money from the global capital market must ultimately repay the principal and interest due. The ability to do so depends largely on a sound economic system. Thus, an examination of the Korean economic recovery should take into account the effectiveness of the reforms initiated since the crisis erupted and whether the reforms are going in the right direction.

The Financial Crisis and Government Failure

Many consider Korea an example of the success of a government-led economy. A close look at the history of Korean industry, however, reveals few success stories of specific industries whose development was "helped" by the government. Tremendous social costs were incurred as a result of the government's shift from market-friendly policies in the 1960s to a government-led policy in the 1970s to develop heavy and chemical industries.[3] Economist Young Back Choi refutes the idea that Korea's industrial policy should be viewed in a positive light. "We ought to be very cautious," says Choi, "in suggesting that industrial policy is desirable for economic development. Moreover, as Korea has narrowed the gap between itself and the more developed countries, and the gap between its potential and actual attainment, it has become more and more difficult for discretionary policies of the government to be of much use. If anything, dirigiste governments tend to be hindrances rather than sources of help to entrepreneurs wishing to exploit the opportunities they discover."[4]

Central to the government's industrial policy was its determination of exchange rates and influence over lending decisions. Government policies, for example, forced businesses to depend heavily on funds borrowed in foreign currencies, which could be obtained only through local banks. The heavy involvement of the government in the foreign exchange market and the capital market played a decisive role in causing the currency crisis.

Governmental Interference in the Exchange Rate

Before the crisis, the won maintained an exchange rate of 800 to the dollar. Consumers recognized that the dollar was cheaper than the won, and manufacturers expanded their facilities relying on dollar-based loans. The general public also sharply increased its overseas travel, a phenomenon that soon spread like an epidemic. Although increased demand for the dollar and efforts to defend the won caused a near depletion of foreign reserves in October 1997, President Kim Dae Jung was apparently unaware of the exact amount of foreign currency holdings up to the brink of the currency crisis.

Why did foreign banks increase their loans to Korea? Until the outbreak of the crisis, accurate information about Korea was quite difficult to obtain. Increased foreign lending may have been due to misinformation and a lack of transparency. In addition, the high growth of the Korean economy during the previous 30 years may have instilled overconfidence in the economy. A situation in which not even the president or economic experts were aware of the serious problems in the economy would have been difficult for foreign banks to properly diagnose. Naturally, moral hazard at the national and international level, through the IMF, played a prominent role in encouraging unwise investment.

The situation would not have become as serious as it eventually did, however, had the Korean government left the exchange rate to the market instead of determining it artificially. Only in December 1997, after the beginning of the crisis, did the Korean government adopt a floating exchange rate system. The exchange rate plummeted to 1,530 won per dollar in January 1998, but it has stabilized in the 1,200 range since July 1998, and subsequently leveled in the 1,100 range. The new exchange rate system, determined by supply and demand, has helped the won find the value that correctly reflects the actual condition of the Korean economy. It also helped Korean products rapidly regain their competitiveness and led to a surplus in the nation's current account.

Foreign Loan Restrictions

Foreign banks did not need to meticulously inquire about the state of Korean businesses. Their main clients were Korean banks that received direct and indirect support from the government. Two problems thus arose. First, foreign banks issued excessive loans regardless of the local banks' financial standings since the government stood as the ultimate payment guarantor. Second, Korean banks were influenced by political power, causing a tremendous distortion in the allocation of funds. The bad loans and bribery scandals of Hanbo Steel and Kia Motors revealed the extent to which both poor lending decisions and corruption resulted from official government policy.[5]

Following the foreign currency "liberalization" agenda announced in June 1998, the Kim Dae Jung government allowed businesses to obtain foreign loans directly from foreign banks (with less than one-year maturity and based on their credit). That measure invalidated the law that entirely prohibited Korean companies from direct foreign borrowing except for facilities investments. Had the Korean government acted earlier in granting permission for direct

163

borrowings from overseas, private enterprises without governmental guarantees would have had their credit thoroughly investigated by foreign banks. Investment risk appraisals and accounting especially would have improved.

Economic Reform in Korea

Since November 1998, the government has implemented the conditions agreed to with the IMF, while initiating reform measures in four critical sectors: finance, the *chaebols*, labor, and government.

Financial Market Reform

Removing government controls and political involvement in the financial sector is urgent for the recovery of the Korean economy. In April 1998 the Korean government established the Financial Supervisory Commission (FSC) to restructure the financial industry. The commission has closed 5 commercial banks, 16 merchant banks, 5 securities firms, 2 investment trust companies, and 4 life insurance companies that were experiencing serious financial problems. So far, it has raised 64 trillion won in public funds, distributing 32.5 trillion won for restructuring bad loans, 22.5 trillion won for capital increases, and 9 trillion won for deposit security.[6] In addition, the commission has directed the sale of Korea First Bank to the Newbridge-GE Capital Company of the United States, and Seoul Bank to the Hong Kong Shanghai Bank.

The commission's actions, such as selling commercial banks to foreigners and closing financial institutions, were unprecedented and hardly imaginable in the pre-crisis era. Improvements have been made in disclosure and accounting and in initiating a "prompt corrective action" system. Also, strict regulations were provided to classify unprofitable loans.

Some of the measures will help create a more rational financial system in Korea. Indeed, over the past several decades, the Korean financial industry has witnessed a complete separation from market principles in various areas, such as human resources management and business administration, as a result of excessive government influence.

But major banks would still be hesitant to claim that they are autonomous. In electing executive officers and key employees of banks, there are indications that the government is still deeply involved. There are many complaints that the government is giving instructions to banks in the form of unwritten orders. The government's involvement extends to such details as the organization and authority of the board of directors.

In the process of reorganizing bad loans, of course, many of the banks have been thoroughly nationalized. Yet, as long as the banks remain subject to the government's making decisions on business matters, it is quite probable that the banks will once again face financial jeopardy. Without a fundamental change in the structure of bank ownership and governance, it will be difficult to find a bank that adheres firmly to business principles.[7]

To achieve substantial privatization, the stocks of semi-governmental financial institutions must be sold. In the present half-governmental and half-private form of ownership and governance, state-controlled and politically influenced finance will simply not be able to outgrow tradition.

To get from here to there, then, the most important immediate concern is ensuring the political independence and neutrality of the Financial Supervisory Commission. However, the commission has cast aside its original work in maintaining the health of the financial industry and has instead been unnecessarily meddling in *corporate* restructuring, which reflects a political agenda. Economist Soo-Chan Chae expresses why that is disturbing: "The problem is that the FSC, utilizing the restructuring planning body as a leverage, is excessively involved in corporate restructuring, which is not its own business. Consequently, its ultimate objective of securing soundness of financial institutions has been put on the back burner."[8] Thus, the elimination of politically controlled finance is a long way away.

Chaebol Reform

On January 13, 1998, then president-elect Kim Dae Jung and the heads of the top 5 *chaebols* (Hyundai, Samsung, Daewoo, LG, and SK) reached a five-point accord, and on February 6, 1998, the president-elect and the heads of 30 *chaebols* entered into the same agreement.[9] The agreement included the following *chaebol* reform:

(1) Improve the transparency of corporate management: adopt combined financial statements, enhance transparency and reliability of corporate accounting practices according to international accounting standards, and hold corporate management accountable to shareholders by appointing independent outside directors to corporate boards and by strengthening shareholder rights.

(2) Eliminate cross-debt payment guarantees: rectify the traditional practices of intragroup subsidization among subsidiaries, strengthen the financial independence of individual subsidiaries, and abolish the practice of debt-payment guarantees among subsidiaries.

(3) Improve the financial structure: reduce dependence on debt financing, strengthen the financial condition of corporations by lowering their debt-equity ratios, and promote profit-oriented management by liquidating unprofitable business lines and assets.

(4) Concentrate on core businesses: focus on main business areas, move away from diversified business portfolios, and strengthen cooperative ties with small and medium-sized corporations.

(5) Strengthen the accountability of controlling shareholders and managers: specify the accountability and legal responsibility of de facto controlling shareholders, who in most cases serve as group chairmen, and place personal wealth of controlling shareholders into recapitalization and loan guarantees.

To promote the goals of the five-point accord, the government has changed pertinent laws and regulations. However, regulatory changes begun in 1998 were only part of the effort the Korean government has made to promote corporate restructuring. Other official efforts include announcements by policymakers, agreements with corporate leaders, discretionary law enforcement, and administrative guidance of corporate restructuring through financial institutions that are increasingly under the direct control of the government. Despite a new administration, it is disheartening that discretion, coercion, and compulsion are still extensively relied on in Korea.

The five-point accord is expected to improve the structure of Korean businesses. However, a close look at the accord reveals that it contains several unattainable official demands. For example, the government demanded all businesses to uniformly reduce their debt-equity ratios to 200 percent by the end of 1999. Indeed, the average debt-equity ratio for the Korean *chaebols* was 379.8 percent in mid-1999. That ratio must be quite astonishing to American scholars and others who have been accustomed to lower percentages. The average debt-equity ratio for the manufacturing sector is 160 percent in the United States, 206 percent in Japan, and 86 percent in Taiwan. But we simply cannot conclude that the Korean percentage is too high on the basis of a facile comparison with advanced nations.

First, the high debt ratio is not only characteristic of the *chaebols* but is also a general attribute of Korean businesses quite unrelated to the *chaebols*. The average debt-equity ratio in the Korean manufacturing sector in 1996 stood at 317 percent, which is slightly lower than the rate of the top 30 largest *chaebols*. Such high debt ratios result from an economy that does not have a developed stock market and is in its early stage of industrialization. Uniformly reducing the debt ratios of Korean enterprises to the levels of advanced nations at a time when the stock market is not fully developed would deter business growth and further intensify unemployment.

However, an even more formidable problem of *chaebol* reform concerns the new industrial policy that is emerging from the reform as well as the undaunted promotion of such a policy despite severe resistance from the relevant parties. Since January 1998, the government has repeatedly urged the *chaebols*, especially the largest ones, to concentrate on their so-called core competence or core business. This principle was included in the five-point agreement between the president-elect and the *chaebol* leaders and later extended to the idea of the "Big Deal," meaning the swap of business consolidations among *chaebols*.

Unfortunately, the so-called "Big Deal" is a revised version of the government-led realignment of investment in heavy and chemical industries that we saw in the early 1980s and of the specialization policy of the early 1990s. The underlying rationale of the "Big Deal" is that the excess and duplicative investment made by the *chaebols* can be streamlined through business trades or other types of consolidations and the consequent rationalization of production will lead to significant economies of scale. It is ironic that the "Big Deal" so closely resembles the "Big is Beautiful" industrial policy tradition that regulated market entry and investment and protected monopolies. Although the Korean government emphasized that the "Big Deal" plan announced by the top five *chaebols* is voluntary, it is an open secret in Korea that government coercion is behind the *chaebols'* perceived willingness to go through with it.

The government's handling of *chaebol* reform has aggravated the already entangled government-*chaebol* relationship and led to the *chaebols'* suspicion that the real intention of the "Big Deal" may be their eventual dismantling. Among the top 30 *chaebols*, more than half of them have already gone bankrupt. Many, if not most, *chaebols*

167

will undoubtedly be dismantled as a result of the crisis. But in dealing with the *chaebols,* the Korean government should have a better understanding of the business environment and take measures to promote the development of new markets, including mergers and acquisitions or corporate exit markets, for example. The transformation of the *chaebols* will then come not as a result of government direction of business affairs but through the inevitable decisions that a laissez-faire economy will force on the *chaebols.*

Of course, no one denies the necessity of government involvement during a currency or financial crisis. However, when government involvement goes beyond supporting a legal framework for restructuring and actually begins to set industrial policies, we can expect a new round of ongoing government interventions of the kind that brought about the Korean financial crisis to begin with. That is an even more likely outcome if the government directs corporate restructuring itself and does so in an arbitrary and capricious way.

Labor Market Reform

Korea has long retained a system that strictly prohibits layoffs. In addition, powerful labor unions, to which less than 12 percent of workers belong, have played a considerable role in making the labor market rigid. Thus, many businesses had a pent-up unemployment problem—or a situation in which firms retain employees in positions that are not competitive—even before the outbreak of the economic crisis.[10] The difficulty of dismissing workers has blocked the restructuring of Korean businesses.

In February 1998, the Tripartite Committee of Labor, Management and Government agreed to accept the IMF's proposal that calls for partial layoffs under certain conditions and the rotation of workers to other work sites. Although restructuring is still not widespread, the introduction of partial layoffs and rotation of workers to other work places is dramatically changing worker-employer relationships. For example, the lifetime employment system has collapsed and an annual-wage or employment system has been introduced. Workers' perception of the flexibility of the labor market is also changing as more and more workers consider employment a contract and accept the annual-wage system as a matter of course.

Nevertheless, the government has accommodated the labor unions to an exceptional degree. In March 1997, the National Assembly

168

passed amendments to labor laws, deleting the clauses prohibiting labor unions from engaging in political activities. Subsequent measures in the years following have allowed union funds to be used for political purposes.

Moreover, in May 1999, a new law made the Tripartite Committee of Labor, Management and Government a permanent organization, adding to the intense debate over the worker-employer relationship model that Korea should adopt. Unfortunately, because of its fundamental characteristics, the Tripartite Committee seems to endorse German-type corporatism rather than the more decentralized, market-based U.S. model of labor relations. If Korea adopts the German system, which acknowledges the labor union's involvement in non-labor areas, Korea will experience considerable difficulty in creating new jobs. To permanently reduce Korea's unemployment rate, which is in the double digits especially for those ranging from 15 to 30 years of age, there is no alternative but to make the labor market more flexible—a challenge to the present government that has thus far expressed a greater urgency to please the labor unions.

Government Reform

From the beginning of its term, the Kim Dae Jung administration has focused on reforming the public sector. Its initiatives concern privatizations and changes in government functions, the civil servant personnel system, government regulations, the quasi-governmental sector, and the financial and political systems. To promote these reforms, the government instituted the Committee of Planning and Budget that presented a vision for government known as "4S" (Small, Strong, Smart, and Sensitive).

It remains to be seen how successful the Korean government will be in this area of reform, though it reduced its own workforce by 11,000 people in 1998. In May 1999, new legislation was passed to reduce the number of civil servants at the central offices (excluding education, army, and police personnel) by 11.6 percent, or 14,800 persons, by the year 2001. A more drastic downsizing is essential because the total number of public servants reached 938,000 by 1999, an increase of more than 50 percent compared with the 1980s. Unfortunately, previous regimes have failed in their attempts to slash the public-sector workforce.

169

Reforming the public sector will be a critical factor for rebuilding the country's economy. It is urgent to adjust the functions of central government offices, to introduce strict evaluation systems for major public projects, and to reform the quasi-governmental sector. This will undoubtedly require strong political leadership, which has been missing in the past.

Avoiding the Fatal Conceit

Many experts warned about an economic crisis in Korea before 1997. It was becoming evident that Korea's politicized economy was creating an "illness" of low efficiency and high cost.

After the outbreak of the financial crisis in 1997, however, the Korean government began implementing extensive reform measures affecting the *chaebols* as well as the financial, labor, and governmental sectors. Had the economic crisis not occurred, such drastic reforms in such a short time would have never been introduced.

The economic reforms initiated by the Kim Dae Jung government, under the slogan of "parallel growth of the market economy and democracy," have received positive appraisals from the international community. Indeed, the Korean economy's macro indicators clearly show signs of improvement. Yet many areas of the political-economic system still require complementary measures. Certain reforms—including privatization and the downsizing of government, for example—contribute to "creative destruction"; but there are other changes contributing to what might be called "destructive reform." Among those are reforms that insist on a high level of political involvement in decisions that would be better made by market participants. Some aspects of the newly emerging labor and industrial policies could be categorized as destructive reform. As long as politicians and bureaucrats continue to believe that they can plan economic outcomes better than the market, they will be suffering from what Nobel laureate Friedrich Hayek called the "fatal conceit."

The Korean government has mountains of tasks to do. It should close insolvent enterprises under fair principles, privatize nationalized financial institutions, reform the public sector, increase the flexibility of the labor market, and reform the pension system, among other measures. Above all, however, Korea's recovery depends on the extent of political influence on the economy. If Korea lets the government resume a pattern of heavy-handed interventions rather than rely predominately on market principles, it is certain to face another fiasco down the road.

Notes

1. Paul Krugman is critical of the idea that the Asian economic crisis was due mainly to structural problems. See Krugman, *The Return of Depression Economics* (New York: W.W. Norton, 1999), pp. 159–61.

2. Although great side effects arose because the IMF's macroeconomic policy is focused on high interest rates and a tight monetary policy, most of the IMF conditions were in line with the principles of a market economy.

3. Young Back Choi, "Industrial Policy as the Engine of Economic Growth in South Korea: Myth and Reality," in *The Collapse of Development Planning*, ed. Peter J. Boettke (New York: New York University Press, 1994), pp. 231–55.

4. Ibid., pp. 252–53.

5. See Jung-Ho Kim and Jae-Wook Ahn, *The Financial Crisis in Korea: Cause and Solution*, The Korea Center for Free Enterprise, 1998 (in Korean).

6. For more on the methods used in restructuring the financial institutions, see Baek-In Cha, "Financial Institution Restructuring: One Year of Assessment and Future Tasks," Citizens' Coalition for Economic Justice and Korea Economics Society, 1999, p. 3.

7. The government, fearing the concentration of industrial capital, pegs the ceiling of the individual equity stakes of the top 30 *chaebols* at 4 percent (15 percent at provincial banks).

8. Soo-Chan Chae, "Financial Supervisory Committee Should Back Its Own Job," *Chosun Ilbo*, May 16, 1999.

9. See Seong Min Yoo, "Corporate Restructuring in Korea: Policy Issues Before and during the Crisis," KDI Working Paper No. 9903, February 1999.

10. "By pent-up unemployment we mean jobs that are already uncompetitive compared with those overseas but that are being sustained either through cross-subsidization or because of frictions that slow the entry of foreign competition. We have encountered this situation in several client industries. Based on our client experience, we estimate that the level of pent-up unemployment is over 40 percent in some lower technology businesses and is probably close to 20 percent in some of the medium technology sectors." Booz-Allen & Hamilton, *Vision Korea*, Mail Economic Daily, 1997, p. 152.

9. Latin America's Unfinished Revolution

Martín Krause

Latin America moved dramatically from development planning to the market in the 1990s. Some countries, such as Argentina, Peru, and El Salvador, significantly increased their level of economic freedom, especially through achieving trade liberalization, privatization, monetary stability, and a liberal investment regime.[1]

During the same period, however, the region has witnessed the Mexican peso crisis, the collapse of the Ecuadorian and the Venezuelan economies, the Zapatista guerrilla uprising, and the fall of the Brazilian real. Obviously, reforms have not been completed in many countries and some have not even started down that path. To understand where the region stands today, and to provide an assessment that is neither naively optimistic nor exceedingly pessimistic, then, it is useful first to look at what motivated the changes of the last 10 to 15 years.[2]

The Cycle of Populism and Austerity

For several decades since the late 1930s, Latin Americans were trapped in a cycle of populist policies—based on economic mismanagement and the resulting higher levels of government intervention, debt, inflation and poverty—and International Monetary Fund (IMF)-supported adjustment programs that tried to put countries on the path to self-sustaining growth. Through successive waves of spending, populist regimes increased the size of governments over the region's economies, only to have subsequent adjustment programs sanction the new levels of government spending through currency devaluations, price controls, and tax increases to eliminate fiscal deficits.

As economists Rudiger Dornbusch and Sebastian Edwards note, " 'economic populism' is a view of the *economy* stressing growth and income redistribution disregarding the risks of inflation and deficit financing, external restrictions and the reaction of economic agents to aggressive policies against the market. The goal of the description of this paradigm is not a moralistic stand for a conservative economy, but a warning that populist policies ultimately fail, and this failure brings always a terrible cost for those same groups which were supposed to be favored."[3] Comparatively, IMF adjustment programs looked as though they made some economic sense. In practice, the IMF merely tried to alleviate the chaos that populist policies ultimately brought forward and financed regimes hardly committed to thorough reform.

Consider Brazil, for example. How could any private sector lender continue to channel funds to a country after so many failures (unless, of course, it has the backing of international financial institutions)? From 1958 to 1998 Brazil and the IMF signed 13 agreements, none of which was ever complied with by the Brazilian government:

- In 1958 the Juscelino Kubitscheck government arranged for a $200 million loan, but the economic measures agreed to were never implemented and the funds never arrived. In 1959 Kubitscheck suspended negotiations with the IMF although they were resumed later and Brazil received $37 million.

- In the early 1960s, under the Janio Quadros government, Brazil got $2.1 billion from the IMF, the U.S. Treasury, and private banks using gold production as collateral.

- With the military government in the 1960s, Brazil received $125 million under Castelo Branco, and later in the 1980s the João Figueiredo administration signed an IMF Extended Fund Facilities program worth $5.5 billion. In 18 months the minister of the economy, Delfim Netto, negotiated seven letters of intent.[4] The IMF did not accept the last of those letters and suspended payments in February 1985.

- When Brazil returned to democracy with José Sarney as president, the government requested $1.4 billion and committed itself to achieving a budget deficit of 4 percent of gross domestic product (GDP). The IMF only got to lend $477 million when it was obvious again that the Brazilian government was not complying with the conditions of the loan.

- By December 1992, under President Fernando Collor de Mello, the IMF was back with a $2 billion credit line and a 2 percent monthly inflation rate target. In September of that year, Collor was impeached for corruption and the program was suspended.

- Or consider the IMF-led package of November 13, 1998, worth $41 billion. Exactly two months later, the Brazilian government devalued its currency, which increased the government's debt by an amount equivalent to the entire tax increase pushed through the congress as part of the agreement.

Brazil's experience with the fund was not unique: "In September 1984 Argentina reached a standby agreement with the International Monetary Fund (IMF). It agreed that the central bank would set the nominal rate of interest approximately equal to the rate of inflation and would, at the same time, allow total domestic credit to grow so that the monthly rate of inflation would converge at 8 percent within a year. In addition, the quasi-fiscal expenditures of the central bank, about 2.4 percent of GDP at the time, were to be cut to −0.9 percent of GDP over the next five quarters while the fiscal deficit was to reach 1.9 percent of the GDP over the same period. The IMF board approved this agreement on December 28, 1984—at about the same time the government of Argentina had stopped fulfilling it: the departures in the first quarter of 1985 were remarkable."[5] Argentina fared only a little better than Brazil. Since 1958 it signed 15 agreements though only fulfilled 3 of them.

Or consider Peru, where the fiscal deficit in 1984 was 12.1 percent of GDP. "The life span of the new IMF agreement was even shorter than that of the last," noted Peruvian economist Richard Webb. "But again, a few months of respectability were enough to obtain fresh money from both the IMF and the banks, though the amounts in this case were small."[6]

Oftentimes, the conditions that countries were supposed to comply with were not really appropriate for their economies, as was the case in Mexico in 1983: "As to revenue policy, the new program tried to address the problems created by the pricing policy. The IMF had required as a precondition for the standby agreement an adjustment in the prices of public sector enterprises, including gasoline and electricity. The tax policy remained basically unchanged, however. Income brackets were once more adjusted to correct for the inflationary effect on direct taxation. Several products that had been exempted from the VAT during the latter part of the López Portillo administration were taxed again."[7]

In the meantime Latin Americans were suffering under deteriorating economic conditions. To be sure, the region's citizens were not exempt from guilt. In many cases, excluding countries ruled by military regimes, it was elected leaders who were ruining their economies in the name of nationalism and the interests of workers and the poor. But populist ideas and adjustment programs were taking their toll, which could be measured in terms of low or negative per capita income growth (Table 9.1).

By the end of the 1980s, with countries experiencing hyperinflation, recession, and financial breakdown, this vicious cycle was reaching its final days.

The New Consensus and Its Sources

A widespread interpretation of the policies that Latin America began implementing in the late 1980s and early 1990s—sometimes referred to as the "Washington Consensus"[8]—is summed up by Argentine economist Ramón Frediani. According to him, the consensus "is a synthesis of the proposals on political economy the IMF, the World Bank and the IDB simultaneously suggested (cross conditionality) to Latin American countries since 1983, under the name of 'Structural Adjustment Loans' or 'Extended Facilities Agreements,' as a precondition to assist them financially to restructure their foreign debts, granting standby loans or specific sector loans or simply recommending them favorably with the international financial community in order to improve their qualification as debtor countries."[9] This consensus consists of the following 10 proposals:

1. Fiscal discipline: keep the consolidated government deficit sufficiently small so as to be covered without the inflationary tax, with an operating surplus and a total fiscal deficit (including debt payments) no larger than 2 percent of GDP.
2. Reassignment of public expenditures: reassign from the central administration, defense, and subsidies to the private sector toward health, education, and basic infrastructure.
3. Fiscal reform: enlarge the tax base while reducing marginal rates and keeping the progressive bias.
4. Financial liberalization: let the market set interest rates, and if subsidized rates are set for some debtors they should be positive in real terms.
5. Exchange rate policy: maintain a unified exchange rate set at a level that preserves international competitiveness and the growth of exports.

Table 9.1
GDP PER CAPITA AND GROWTH RATES IN LATIN AMERICAN COUNTRIES
(percentages and 1975 dollars)

Country	Share of Total Latin American Population 1980	GDP per Capita 1950	GDP per Capita 1980	GDP per Capita Growth Rates (annual percentage) 1950–80	1981–89
Brazil	35.6	637	2,152	4.2	0.0
Mexico	20.2	1,055	2,547	3.0	−0.9
Argentina	8.0	1,877	3,209	1.8	−2.4
Colombia	7.5	949	1,882	2.3	1.4
Venezuela	4.3	1,811	3,310	1.5	−2.5
Peru	5.1	953	1,746	2.1	−2.5
Chile	3.2	1,416	2,372	1.8	1.0
Uruguay	2.8	2,184	3,269	1.4	−0.7
Ecuador	2.3	638	1,556	3.1	−0.1
Guatemala	2.0	842	1,422	1.8	−1.8
Dominican Republic	1.7	719	1,564	2.6	0.2
Bolivia	1.6	762	1,114	1.3	−2.7
El Salvador	1.3	612	899	1.3	−1.7
Paraguay	0.9	885	1,753	2.4	0.0
Costa Rica	0.6	819	2,170	3.3	−0.6
Panama	0.5	928	2,157	2.9	−1.7
Nicaragua	0.7	683	1,324	2.3	−3.3
Honduras	1.0	680	1,031	1.4	−1.2
Haiti	1.6	363	439	0.7	−1.9
Latin America				2.7	−0.8

SOURCES: Robert Summers and Alan Heston, "Improved International Comparisons of Real Product and Its Composition: 1950–1980," *Review of Income and Wealth*, June 1984; and CEPAL, *Preliminary Overview of the Latin American Economy*, 1988.

6. Trade liberalization: eliminate quantitative commercial restrictions and set a uniform tariff level between 10 and 20 percent in a gradual move lasting about 5 years.
7. Foreign investment: eliminate barriers to direct foreign investment and have local and foreign companies compete under the same terms.
8. Privatizations: privatize state-owned enterprises.
9. Deregulation: eliminate regulations that restrict access to the market, keeping only those that preserve security, protect the environment, or provide public services.
10. Property rights: protect legally the right to property without excessive transaction costs.

Many of these proposals have been turned into policies in several Latin American countries, which explains their improved ratings in economic freedom reports.[10] Regardless of the desirability or soundness of portions of the above policies, it is misleading to refer to that set of proposals as a "Washington Consensus," or to claim that those reform measures were imposed on the region. In fact, Washington reached such a consensus only after many of the most important reforms were already under way. The international financial institutions were not actually opening the way to change in Latin America; rather, the IMF's support followed moves made by the region's governments in response to what Latin Americans were demanding.

The Chilean Example Leads the Way

Chile was the first country to introduce market reforms in Latin America beginning in 1973, though unfortunately they were implemented by a military regime. It should be remembered that by 1973 government spending as a share of GDP amounted to 63 percent, international trade was completely under government control, and more than 3,000 prices were set by state agencies.

During the period of market reforms, the IMF first came to Chile in 1981, after many of the reforms and privatizations had taken place, including the privatization of the social security system, which has since become a model for subsequent such privatizations in the region and around the world.[11] Even then, IMF recommendations were not necessarily helpful. According to Chilean economist Felipe Larraín, "The first element of the [1984 tax reform] was the result

178

of the administration's ideology: it was an attempt to promote expansion of the private sector, in the expectation that lower taxes would produce a supply-side response. The reduction in the personal tax rates had to be postponed, however, because of the many restrictions the Chilean economy has faced, not the least of which were the agreements signed with the International Monetary Fund limiting the size of the fiscal deficit. Thus the highest marginal tax rate was still 56 percent in 1987, while the rates in all other income brackets besides the exempted level were higher than the target ones."[12]

Because the Chilean reforms were implemented by a military regime, it was argued that the region's nascent democracies could not stand to introduce policy reforms of such a magnitude. Nevertheless, that view was belied by the next reforming country. In 1985, the newly elected government of Bolivia headed by Victor Paz Estenssoro, the same populist leader who had led the country toward a state-dominated economy at the beginning of the 1950s, was facing hyperinflation at an annual rate of 23,000 percent. In August of that year, through a single decree, it reduced the number of taxes to five, liberated all price controls, slashed government expenditures, and stopped hyperinflation overnight. The IMF arrived one year later with a standby agreement signed in June 1986.

In March 1991 Carlos Boloña was appointed as the minister of the economy by president Alberto Fujimori in Peru, beginning a reform process that lowered annual inflation from 7,650 percent to 57 percent in two years, increased foreign reserves from $100 million to $2 billion, and reduced the fiscal deficit from 16 percent to 2.5 percent of GDP.[13] Import duties were reduced, foreign exchange controls lifted, and public monopolies eliminated; the labor market was deregulated and the privatization process begun. The government started to pay back its foreign debt and in September 1991 a support group was created by the IMF, the Paris Club, and the Inter-American Development Bank. At the end of 1992 Peru signed an agreement with the IMF.

Finally, one of the most important reforms in the region was Argentina's introduction, in March 1991, of a currency board–like system, sometimes referred to as convertibility. Again, the international financial institutions did not support this initiative until after its success in stopping inflation was beyond doubt. An IMF standby agreement was signed by Argentina six months after the enactment of the convertibility law.

Civil Disobedience

If the international financial institutions (IFIs) were not responsible for imposing policy changes in Latin America, what then accounts for the region's dramatic reforms? Civil disobedience played an important role. (With its long historical tradition, civil disobedience has been advocated by noted thinkers from ancient Greek and Roman times, through those of 17th-century England, and through more recent periods, including those of Henry David Thoreau and Leo Tolstoi.[14]) According to political scientist Gene Sharp, there are generally three stages in nonviolent movements of resistance to power: protest and persuasion; social, economic, and political noncooperation; and nonviolent intervention.[15]

During the first stage, speeches are made in public spaces, literature is distributed and, in the case of resistance to military action, friendly links are established with soldiers and other government officials. In the second stage sanctions are harder. There are students' strikes, consumer boycotts, general strikes, refusals to pay levies or taxes, refusals to accept the government's currency, boycotts of legislative elections, resistance to the draft, and purposeful bureaucratic inefficiency and mutiny. The last stage includes more radical forms of resistance to authority: hunger strikes, sit-ins in public places, occupation of government buildings, road blockades, setting up informal markets, and even the creation of a parallel government.

That is what happened in many Latin American countries in the 1980s, with the peculiar characteristic that there was no political movement whatsoever nor leader calling for generalized civil disobedience. The process of civil disobedience was a totally spontaneous one that manifested itself against an array of government policies that imposed heavy costs on the population.

The Rejection of National Currencies

One example was the rejection of national currencies, something with a long history in several of the region's countries. Take the case of Argentina. The ratio of currency and demand deposits (M1) to GDP, which was over 30 percent at the beginning of the century, held at around 25 percent until the end of the 1940s. It then started to fall to 15 percent at the end of the 1950s and to less than 3 percent at the end of the 1980s. The ratio of M3—a much broader measure of money—to GDP went from 43 percent in 1900 to a peak of 70 percent in the 1920s, falling to around 40 percent in the 1940s. By the end of the 1980s it plummeted to an amazing 4 percent of GDP.[16] The more the state issued currency, the more prices increased. Argentines would flee from the inflationary tax by getting rid of the national currency, making the increased emission of the country's money result in a dramatic fall in its value. The more currency the government printed, the less "currency" there was in the market.

Argentines fled not only from the national currency, but also from the regulated banking sector, which prohibited accounts in foreign currency. Although no statistics are available about the amount of dollars in the country, a private bank estimated in 1989 that the value of dollar bills in circulation was seven times the value of the local currency. In 1986 it was estimated that there was $3.5 billion in credits extended in the informal market, and that local residents held $20 billion in foreign currency and millions more in property abroad.[17]

Tax Evasion

The ability to govern ultimately depends on the voluntary acceptance by a certain proportion of the population to be governed. The same notion applies to tax collection. (Many strategies could be devised to force people to pay taxes, but a certain degree of voluntary compliance is required for tax collection to be successful.) Tax evasion became widespread in the 1980s and was considered acceptable. Data on this are hard to come by even today, several years after the crisis of the 1980s. Indeed, the Argentine revenue service is finding that social conduct is difficult to change. It estimates that it only collects revenues on 55 percent of taxable sales, 54 percent of taxable income, 50 percent of personal assets, and 57 percent of the contributions that should be made to social security, amounting to some $36.8 billion.[18] In 1990 it was estimated that 1.5 million users of public services, such as electricity, phones, water, and natural gas, were not paying for them.

According to Frediani, "tax evasion is still high throughout Latin America, fluctuating between 70% in Peru and Bolivia, and 35% in Argentina, with the exception being Chile whose evasion levels are no higher than 20%."[19] When Brazil recently introduced a tax on checks, the amount of transactions was discovered to be much larger than what past tax collection showed. According to a report by the Brazilian treasury, the activity not registered amounted to $495 billion or half of the country's total GDP.[20]

Avoiding Regulations

Prohibitively costly regulations led to the rise of the informal sector, a phenomenon well documented in *The Other Path*.[21] As the number of regulations affecting the functioning of legal markets grew, participants found new ways to avoid them, mainly by generating alternative markets away from the interference of the state.

According to Frediani, "Tax evasion is furthered by the existence of a vast informal economy, which in the case of Peru and Bolivia is as large as 70% of the national economy, 40% in Mexico and Brazil, 35% in Venezuela, Uruguay and Argentina, and 20% in Chile; but thanks to it a large number of people find jobs that would not be available in the formal economy."[22]

Smuggling

Although illegal trade practices could also be included as tax evasion or avoidance of regulations, they should be considered separately to highlight the entrepreneurial spirit and imagination of Latin Americans. For several decades Latin American countries followed the "import substitution" model to the extreme through the application of high import duties, quotas, and prohibitions. As a result, many Latin Americans were born and grew up amid obsolete and expensive products. Many foreign visitors could not help but be amused at the fact that cars, which had been discontinued elsewhere several decades ago, were still being produced locally. Participants avoiding trade controls ranged from those in big business to those involved in "ant smuggling," or smuggling on a small scale. Exporters would underinvoice exports with a double purpose: to pay less taxes on exports and to leave abroad part of the foreign currency the exchange control regime forced them to change into local currency. Importers would overinvoice imports, paying a higher duty but obtaining foreign currency and profiting from the black-market exchange rate differential that was higher than the increased duty.

Some figures were absurd. For example, the Argentine ambassador to Paraguay estimated in 1991 that 150,000 head of cattle were leaving his country every year in Paraguay's direction, an operation that was probably difficult to hide.[23] At the borders, particularly between Argentina and Brazil or Paraguay, ant smuggling flourished among those who went shopping on one side of the border or the other, depending on the exchange rates of each country. An extreme example of this phenomenon can be found in Ciudad del Este, a Paraguayan city bordering Brazil and Argentina, where contraband trade is estimated to amount to $16 billion.[24]

The Rejection of Public Debt

In the 1980s some Latin American countries defaulted on the interest portion of their foreign debts, precipitating the Third World debt crisis. In 1990 Argentina led the world in the amount of overdue interest payments totaling $7.29 billion, followed by Brazil with $7.1 billion overdue, Peru with $2.9 billion, and Ecuador with $1.5 billion. Argentina's arrears were more than Brazil's and more than those of all other debtors in arrears together.[25] Foreign credit was necessary since locals were understandably not willing to grant it. Instead, they were placing their savings in safe havens abroad. A recent report by the Argentine ministry of the economy estimates that Argentinians have $90 billion abroad, equal to about 44 months of exports or 85 percent of the foreign debt.[26]

The Unfinished Agenda

This widespread rejection of interventionism explains the move toward reform in Latin America, even by governments of social-democrat (Fernando Henrique Cardoso) or populist persuasions (Carlos Menem, Paz Estenssoro). But are Latin Americans still practicing disobedience today? In many ways they are, and are thus sending messages that are even clearer than the votes they regularly cast. (Incidentally, the upsurge of "independent" candidates and the rejection of traditional political parties as in the case of Fujimori in Peru, Collor in Brazil, and Hugo Chávez in Venezuela are further evidence of Latin Americans' dissatisfaction with prevailing political and economic paradigms.) The remaining reform agenda is substantial and if left unfinished may lead to the eruption of periodic economic and social problems. The collapses of the Brazilian and Mexican currencies are dramatic examples of what may result from leaving inadequate policies in place.

Fiscal Policy

One broad area in need of reform is fiscal policy. With tax evasion so widespread it is obvious that a thorough tax reform is long overdue. Although governments have eliminated many of the taxes that distorted economic activity and have reduced the highest marginal rates, Latin American governments are still struggling to eliminate tax evasion. But the obstinate attempts to reduce evasion at the present high tax rates will continue to fail. At some point a decision will have to be made to cut the rates in order to reduce the premium for tax evasion.

In conjunction with the tax cuts, government services need urgent reform. Latin Americans do not see their governments giving much back to them, particularly in the areas of health, education, and crime fighting. Besides the reform of social security systems that spread from Chile to Peru, Argentina, Colombia, Mexico, Uruguay, Bolivia, and El Salvador, governments have not followed the same reform logic in the field of social services. In fact, a common approach has been to sell state-owned enterprises to devote more taxpayers' funds to social programs. But with no reforms in the old state-managed systems, there is not much improvement in those services.

Consider public security, for example. A regional poll taken in May–June 1997 revealed that the percentage of people who trust the police is very low. The level of trust in Argentina was 17 percent, in Brazil it was 21 percent, Uruguay 27 percent, Colombia 34 percent, Ecuador 24 percent, Bolivia 18 percent, Venezuela 9 percent, Guatemala 9 percent, and Mexico 5 percent. The big exception was Chile with a 55 percent level of trust.[27] Today, social expenditures are equal to the same share of the budget that state-owned enterprises received before being privatized—with negative or negligible results.

In the face of so much fiscal mismanagement, a couple of countries, Argentina and Brazil, are considering bills that would restrict the ability of their governments at different levels to have fiscal deficits. They would even restrict the growth of government expenditures. Unfortunately in this case, congressional bills are easy to amend and such a commitment would not be sufficiently credible. The resistance to tax compliance has been more effective in controlling spending. Although it would not be a bad idea to impose balanced budget laws, that should be done in conjunction with other institutional reforms.

Foreign debt also continues to complicate fiscal management. The region's governments have made up for the lack of local financing with foreign debt, which attracted eager investors willing to obtain higher rates for their savings than they otherwise could. Latin America's current foreign debt has reached about $650 billion,[28] and servicing it is taking an increasingly large portion of the budget, particularly in Argentina and Brazil. Although local sources of finance have largely dried up, the same did not happen with foreign savings, something that has opened the door to continued deficit financing.

Monetary Policy, Institutional Reform, and Deregulation

Many Latin American countries have experienced dismal monetary policies, sending some countries into hyperinflation. Do the region's nations actually need their own currencies, with the corresponding central banks and set of banking and currency crises that have cost several percentage points of GDP in countries like Argentina, Chile, and Bolivia? The present currency board of Argentina is attracting the interest of an increasing number of countries; even more so are recent proposals to adopt the dollar as a regional currency. Nevertheless, it should be noted that one of the main benefits of the "convertibility" system in Argentina is not the peg with the dollar but rather the freedom it granted to Argentinians to use any currency they wish. In Argentina, the U.S. dollar is the currency mostly widely used; the U.S. Federal Reserve, moreover, is isolated from local pressures and from Latin American lobbies. But since there is no monopoly on the wisest course for monetary policy, a move toward allowing free use of and contracting in the hard currencies of the world would eliminate a major source of instability in the region's economies and any potential danger of pegging Latin America's monetary future to any single currency.[29]

Despite free-market reforms, the institutional framework in a number of countries has deteriorated substantially. In many cases the division of power or the independence of the judiciary is nonexistent and corruption has tainted many reform initiatives. Indeed, several leaders have ended up in jail or in exile on corruption charges (Brazil's Collor de Mello, Venezuela's Carlos Andrés Pérez, Peru's Alan García, Mexico's Carlos Salinas de Gortari, Ecuador's Alberto Dahik). Until governmental institutions are reformed, corruption will not be reduced.

Deregulation must also be more widespread. Many of the most absurd and distorting regulations, like price and foreign exchange

185

controls, have been eliminated. But a heavy regulatory burden still hampers entrepreneurial activity, particularly in the small and medium-sized business sectors that face Kafkaesque bureaucratic procedures in order to obtain legal status to conduct standard business operations.[30] Although many entrepreneurs may end up in the informal sector, they are then prevented access to banking credit or legal dispute settlement mechanisms.

Another area in need of reform affecting the vast majority of workers is the labor market. Regulatory constraints still impede the creation of jobs through the smooth functioning of the market and force many people into unemployment or into the informal sector. High payroll taxes increase labor costs by as much as 100 percent, and many small companies cannot afford the array of mandated benefits that have ended up benefiting that minority of workers fortunate enough to have jobs in large companies or to be members of politically powerful unions. Argentina's chronically high unemployment rate of 14 percent and above, for example, is due precisely to the fact that the labor market is one of the main areas that has not been reformed since Juan Perón was in power.[31]

Finally, although the "import substitution" model has been widely discredited, nontariff barriers to trade reduced, and import duties lowered, many "specific industries" are still protected either directly or under the umbrella of "regional integration." The various regional trade agreements, such as Mercosur, have opened trade among Latin American countries, but they have also raised some regional barriers that will be even harder to remove. The experience of Chile shows, however, that there is no need for bilateral and multilateral negotiations whose conditions on reciprocity are, at bottom, mercantilist. Indeed, one of the great lessons of the Chilean experience is that countries can integrate into the world economy by unilaterally reducing their trade barriers. The region should thus avoid the danger of a hemispheric trade agreement that creates new layers of bureaucracy charged with negotiating and supervising trade arrangements.

Conclusion

It may not be an exaggeration to say that Latin Americans, either by tradition or culture or both, are inclined to look for a leader, a *caudillo*, who will solve their problems from above. But that may overlook deeper undercurrents in Latin American politics and economics. And one of those has been widespread disobedience as a strategy to reject the burden of a growing Leviathan. No wonder that the same kinds of *"caudillos"* who led populist policies in the past have now heard the message from below and are moving in the opposite direction.

But although popular disobedience and dissent have been the driving forces behind the changes we now see in Latin America, they are grounded on weak foundations. Latin Americans have rejected government because of the harsh economic consequences of its unbounded growth, not out of an ideological conviction about the need to respect individual rights, the rule of law, private property, and market economics. The region's citizens still believe governments should provide them entitlements, although they are not much willing to pay for them. These tensions are putting politicians in a bind; something will have to give—either more entitlements or less taxes. That issue is increasingly at the center of the debate in Latin America.

Notes

1. James Gwartney and Robert Lawson, *Economic Freedom of the World: 2000 Annual Report* (Vancouver: Fraser Institute, 2000), p. 3.

2. For an optimistic account of Latin America's turn to the market, see Paul Craig Roberts and Karen Lafollette Araujo, *The Capitalist Revolution in Latin America* (New York: Oxford University Press, 1997); for a more pessimistic assessment, see Plinio Apuleyo Mendoza, Carlos Alberto Montaner, and Alvaro Vargas Llosa, *Fabricantes de Miseria* (Madrid: Plaza Janés, 1998).

3. Rudiger Dornbusch and Sebastian Edwards, eds., *The Macroeconomics of Populism in Latin America*, National Bureau of Economic Research (Chicago: The University of Chicago Press, 1991). Spanish edition (México, D.F.: Fondo de Cultura Económica, 1992), p. 17.

4. Werner Baer, *The Brazilian Economy: Growth and Development* (Westport, Conn.: Praeger, 1995), p. 103.

5. Osvaldo H. Schenone, "Public Sector Behavior in Argentina," in *The Public Sector and the Latin American Crisis*, ed. Felipe Larraín and Marcelo Selowsky (San Francisco: ICS Press, 1991), p. 31.

6. Richard Webb, "The Good News: Peru—the Government, Anyway—Is Going to Have to Do without Bank Money for a Long Time," *Andean Report* (Lima, 1986), quoted in Carlos Eduardo Paredes and Alberto Pasco-Font, "The Behavior of the Public Sector in Peru: A Macroeconomic Approach," in Larraín and Selowsky, p. 220.

7. Jorge Hierro and Allen Sanginés, "Public Sector Behavior in Mexico," in Larraín and Selowsky, p. 174.

8. John Williamson, "What Washington Means by Policy Reform," in *Latin American Adjustment: How Much Has Happened?* ed. John Williamson (Washington: Institute for International Economics, 1990).

9. Ramón O. Frediani, "Planes de Estabilización y Reforma Estructural en América Latina: Una Síntesis" (Buenos Aires: Konrad Adenauer Stiftung A.C. CIEDLA, 1996), p. 104.

10. See Gwartney and Lawson; and Gerald P. O'Driscoll Jr., Kim R. Holmes, and Melanie Kirkpatrick, 2000 Index of Economic Freedom (Washington: Wall Street Journal and Heritage Foundation, 2000).

11. For an account of the privatization of Chile's public pension system, see José Piñera, El Cascabel al Gato: La Batalla por la Reforma previsional (Santiago: Editorial Zig-Zag, 1991). For an assessment of the system's performance, see L. Jacobo Rodríguez, "Chile's Private Pension System at 18: Its Current State and Future Challenges," Cato Institute Social Security Paper no. 17, July 30, 1999.

12. Felipe Larraín, "Public Sector Behaviour in a Highly Indebted Country: The Contrasting Chilean Experience," in Larraín and Selowsky, p. 128.

13. Carlos Boloña Behr, Cambio de Rumbo (Lima: ILEM-SIL, 1993) p. 54.

14. Bryan Caplan, "The Literature of Nonviolent Resistance and Civilian-Based Defense," Humane Studies Review, vol. 9, no. 1, The Institute for Humane Studies, Summer 1994. Greeks like Xenophonte and Herodotus would not hide their sympathy for civil disobedience, and the Romans Cicero, Plutarch, Seneca, and Polybius would support it openly. Thomas of Aquinas and William of Ockham supported a limited right to resistance and, more emphatically, so did the members of the School of Salamanca, Juan de Mariana and Francisco Suárez, the Huguenot Philippe du Plesis Mornay and the Scot living in France, George Buchanan. This tradition of thought continued in 17th-century England through John Locke, Algernon Sidney, and John Milton, and in the following century with more emphasis on pacific resistance by Henry David Thoreau and Leo Tolstoi. In his work "Civil Disobedience," Thoreau argued that if the subject refused to obey, and officials were forced to resign, the revolution would be consummated.

15. Gene Sharp, The Politics of Nonviolent Action (Boston: Porter Sargent Publisher, 1973).

16. Marie-Ange Véganzonès, Argentina en el Siglo XX: Crónica de un Crecimiento anunciado (Paris: OECD, 1997).

17. "Mercado informal de Crédito en Argentina," Reporte No. 18, Instituto de Estudios Contemporáneos, Buenos Aires, August 1988.

18. Secretaría de Seguridad Social e Instituto de Estudios Fiscales y Económicos, cited in El Clarín, August 8, 1996.

19. Frediani, p. 47.

20. Epoca, "O Brasil que o Leao Não Ve," April 22, 1999.

21. Hernando de Soto, The Other Path: The Invisible Revolution in the Thirld World (New York: Harper, 1989).

22. Frediani, p. 47.

23. "Bovinos Argentinos Serían Contrabandeados al Paraguay," La Nación (Buenos Aires), January 15, 1991.

24. Ambito Financiero (Buenos Aires), April 30, 1999.

25. "Argentina a la Cabeza del Ránking de Atrasos," El Cronista (Buenos Aires), September 20, 1990.

26. An estimate from the Ministry of the Economy to the IMF, as cited in Ismael Bermúdez, "Los Argentinos Tienen 90 mil millones Afuera," El Clarín, April 25, 1999.

27. Consorcio Iberoamericano de Empresas de Investigación de Mercados y Asesoramiento, "Informe Anual de Opinión Iberoamericana," 1997–98.

28. Joint BIS–IMF–OECD–World Bank statistics on external debt. Last update: March 15, 1999. http://www.oecd.org/dac/debt/index.htm.

29. For a discussion of this issue, see Steve Hanke and Kurt Schuler, "A Dollarization Blueprint for Argentina," Cato Institute Foreign Policy Briefing no. 52, March 11, 1999.

30. See, for example, Paul Holden, "Argentina's Market Reforms Overlooked Small Business," *Wall Street Journal*, March 15, 1998; and Paul Holden and Sarath Rajapatirana, *Unshackling the Private Sector: A Latin American Story* (Washington: World Bank, 1995).

31. See Fundación de Investigaciones Económicas Latinoamericanas, *El Empleo en la Argentina* (Buenos Aires: FIEL, 1997).

10. Russia's Potemkin Capitalism

Andrei Illarionov

More than nine years ago the Russian people replaced the 70-year-old communist regime with democratic institutions and elected leaders. Tired of the socialist system's economic marasmus, the Russian population embarked with rare enthusiasm on a path toward the creation of a market economy and the restoration of economic growth. Peoples of the former Soviet republics began building national states, in some cases for the first time in their history. After decades of cold war and isolation behind an impenetrable "iron curtain," Russians emerged from their besieged fortress to find that former enemies could become friends (and vice versa).

By late 1991 Russia had experienced almost all possible economic maladies: an inefficient economy, low living standards, a two-year decline in real output, a budget deficit of about 15 percent of GDP, rampant inflation approaching 100 percent per year, a depreciating national currency, rising unemployment, and the government's inability to service its huge foreign debt (which led to a default on the Soviet debt in December 1991). Thus the goals of economic reform in Russia in late 1991 were clear: to improve living standards, increase economic efficiency through privatization of state assets, restore economic growth, reduce inflation, stabilize the exchange rate, reduce or eliminate the budget deficit, provide opportunities for employment, solve or at least soften the problem of foreign debt, restore confidence in Russia among members of the international community, and reintegrate the country into the world economy as an equal and trusted member.

Nearly all the elements required to meet such ambitious goals were available. The country had a well-educated population, a relatively industrialized economy, enormous natural resources, democratically elected authorities, and a rich culture. The euphoria of the outside world and the readiness of the international community to provide substantial assistance were seen as further points in Russia's favor.[1]

The dream of transforming the West's longtime bitter adversary into its reliable and trustworthy ally was enormously challenging, but seemed quite realistic.

It appeared that Russia lacked only a professional government team to implement the needed reforms. Fortunately for the country, it seemed that even this problem had been solved. Of the five groups of economists that surrounded him, President Boris Yeltsin picked the one headed by the young but well-known and respected professor Yegor Gaidar. In September 1991 this team began to prepare an economic program and a corresponding package of legislation. On November 6, 1991, Gaidar was appointed deputy prime minister with overall responsibility for economic policy. In April 1992 he became first deputy prime minister, and in June 1992, acting prime minister. He was replaced in this office by Victor Chernomyrdin in December 1992. Gaidar returned to the government in September 1993 and left again in January 1994.

Gaidar's closest colleague, ally, and personal friend, Anatoly Chubais, worked in the government in various positions (including two sojourns as first deputy prime minister) from November 1991 through March 1998. Chubais became instrumental in implementing the economic policy elaborated by Gaidar and himself. The influence of these two individuals was so strong that even when both of them did not directly participate in the government, as in Sergei Kirienko's government (March–August 1998), they influenced economic policy through adherents in key government posts and behind-the-scenes consultations. Chubais was at the center of economic policymaking in the "hot" summer of 1998 when he was the special presidential liaison for international financial institutions. Gaidar and Chubais played decisive roles in the collapse of the Russian ruble of August 17, 1998.

An Interim Assessment of the Transformation

The results of Russia's much-heralded transformation from the plan to the market are now clear. The economic depression that began in 1990 continued through most of 1999 at a rate roughly equal to that of 1991 (about −5 percent per annum). The ruble has proved unstable, experiencing a devaluation of 75 percent since 1998 alone. In 1999, Russia's inflation rate reached 86 percent.

But there are also other astonishing developments in Russia's economy. Over the course of the post-Soviet years, Russia's GDP has almost halved, breaking the world's record for the longest and deepest economic depression. As a consequence, overall living standards have fallen by at least 15 percent, unemployment has grown tenfold, cumulative inflation has exceeded 10,000 percent, and the Russian population has dropped by 4 million persons. In addition, the national debt has doubled, with the government again unable to service it. The government subsequently defaulted on Russia's domestic debt, restructured leftover Soviet foreign debt, and accumulated fresh Russian foreign debt.

Before the August 1998 financial crisis, Russian reformers could point to a few economic achievements—relatively low inflation, a relatively stable exchange rate, a slight economic recovery of 0.8 percent in 1997, and two economic sectors (export and banking) with visible signs of recovery. The 1998 financial crash swept away all of those modest achievements overnight, and revealed the short-term nature of 1997's prosperity. Since the nation's few successes were based on huge foreign loans taken by both the public and private sectors, Russia was saddled with an even greater debt burden. The crisis set off a new "brain drain" and prompted the emigration of many of the most dynamic young entrepreneurs.

One of the most touted "successes" of Russian reform is the supposedly more efficient allocation of resources due to the record-size transfer of property from the government to the private sector. Indeed, the mass privatization campaign increased the proportion of the work force employed in nonstate firms from 17 to over 75 percent. Similarly, the share of GDP produced by the nongovernment sector jumped to 70 percent. But surprisingly, economic production measured by the ratio of output to any indicator of its costs (e.g., energy consumption, electricity consumption, raw materials consumption, volume of transportation) actually deteriorated sharply. Even more striking, all surveys of comparative performance of the state, private, and privatized companies show unequivocally that privatized Russian companies, unlike their genuinely private counterparts, perform worse than unprivatized state firms.

None of the goals set in 1991 have been achieved; rather, eight years of reform have in fact aggravated Russia's economic, financial, and social turmoil. Moreover, the attitude of Russians regarding a market

193

economy, a democratic society, a liberal political regime, and friendly relations with the West has markedly worsened. The very terms "market," "democracy," "liberalism," and "reforms," as well as the concepts associated with them, have been discredited. The Russian population at large has become receptive to vigorous government intervention in economic and social affairs, theories of a Western conspiracy against Russia, and the idea of a unique "Russian way." The experience of the past nine years has reinforced the argument that liberal market reforms brought about Russia's economic collapse.

One cannot avoid the painful conclusion that the attempt to create a stable democratic society with an effective market economy in Russia has failed. Russia again appears to be emerging as an unpredictable power, whose feared strength (or weakness) poses dangers both to the outside world and to its own citizens.

Official Explanations for Russia's Failure

The failure of the "Russian model" of transformation has stimulated an intense search for an explanation. The August 1998 crisis was the culmination of years of misguided policy and arguably the pivotal moment of the Russian transformation. Citing the Russian experience as well as that of other countries in transition, opponents of market reforms have raised doubts about the wisdom of such prescriptions. Opposition has forced those responsible for the reform policy in Russia—both Russian authorities and influential foreign supporters—to address the question "What went wrong?"

The results of this inquiry have been quite disappointing. The culprits of the 1998 crisis are most often identified as the Asian contagion, the fall in oil prices, the refusal of Russia's parliament to support the Sergei Kirienko government's legislative package, a lack of confidence among foreign investors, pervasive corruption, and the fundamental weakness of post-communist institutions, evidenced by the government's inability to collect sufficient tax revenues and its failure to establish a favorable investment climate. Yet, almost all of the numerous explanations for the Russian collapse offered by Russian authorities, international financial institutions, and the U.S. Treasury Department have missed the mark.

The Asian Contagion

"In January–March 1998 $2 billion invested by Southeast Asian businessmen fled from the Russian market. The Russian financial

194

market—weak as it was—could not withstand the blow," declared Chubais.[2]

Contrary to this widespread belief, Asian contagion did not play a critical role in the Russian crisis. During the most acute stage of the Asian crisis, from its unfolding in Thailand in early July 1997 through the last week of October 1997, all indicators for the Russian financial markets were strikingly calm. Yields on government securities and bonds (GKOs and OFZs) reached historically low levels of 18–20 percent in nominal terms, and 7–9 percent in real terms. The situation changed slightly from November 1997 to January 1998, when signs of destabilization began to show. But even then, Russia was able to withstand the pressure without serious negative consequences. Then, in late spring and summer 1998, after most of the East Asian financial markets had demonstrated a sustainable recovery for several months, market sentiment in Russia disintegrated. Only one country, Russia, succumbed to the Asian malady in spring and summer of 1998, which suggests that the true cause of the August crisis lay elsewhere. Moreover, the $2 billion supposedly withdrawn by East Asian investors from Russia in January–March 1998 was offset by funds borrowed by the Russian government on international markets in the same period (and by additional monies borrowed in subsequent months).

The Fall in Oil Prices

"Tumbling oil prices," Chubais argued, "hit the Russian budget, which, as in the Soviet times, relied largely on oil sales for revenues."[3] A fall in oil prices occurred in 1997 and 1998 but did not provoke Russia's fiscal crash.

Russian export oil prices fell by 31 percent from January to July 1998 compared to the corresponding months of 1997, but the volume of exports of Russian oil increased by 8 percent. Total earnings of Russian oil exports fell by 25 percent, from $8.6 billion in January–July 1997 to $6.4 billion in January–July 1998. Even if all export earnings had gone to the Russian federal budget (rather than being shared with the exporters themselves), budget revenue would have fallen by $2.2 billion.

Surprisingly, the fall in oil prices did not cause a decline in overall federal revenues. A number of revenue-raising measures implemented by the government boosted total budget revenues by $3.1

billion from $24.1 billion in the first 7 months of 1997 to $27.2 billion in the first 7 months of 1998. Moreover, from January to July 1998, the Russian government was able to borrow more than $12 billion on international markets. Therefore, financial resources available to the Russian government in 1998 were significantly larger than in 1997.

And the fall in oil prices did not precipitate a comparable financial crisis in any other oil-producing or oil-exporting country. None of them experienced a sharp devaluation of its national currency, or defaulted on its debt, or imposed a moratorium on repayments of foreign debt by private companies. All of that happened only in Russia. In 1998 a decline in GDP was registered in just one-fifth of net oil-exporting countries (in 8 of 42). However, only in two of them (Venezuela and United Arab Emirates) can the economic downturn be attributed to the fall in oil prices. In at least five other oil-exporting countries with negative growth in 1998 (Indonesia, Malaysia, Kazakhstan, New Zealand, and the Democratic Republic of Congo), the economic depression was to a large extent associated with factors other than the fall in oil prices. The remaining 34 oil exporting countries continued to have positive growth rates averaging 6.4 percent. Even more interesting, countries in which oil plays a more important role in the national economy (as measured by the ratio of net oil exports to GDP) than in Russia had higher average GDP growth rates (6.9 percent) in 1998 than those in which net oil exports play a less important role (2.2 percent). From these data one could argue that the oil factor in 1998 should have had positive rather than negative impact on Russian economic performance.

Refusal of the Parliament to Implement the Kirienko Government's Program

Chubais noted that "the State Duma had cut by two-thirds the revenues that could be obtained as a result of the anti-crisis program."[4] The International Monetary Fund (IMF) observed that "confidence was weakened particularly by the lack of support for the program in the Duma, which forced the president to veto several measures approved by the Duma and to implement a number of other measures by decree, and led the IMF to reduce the amount of a disbursement from the $5.6 billion originally planned to $4.8

billion."[5] This is correct. But it is also true that the remaining two-thirds of the package that was not passed by the Duma was immediately signed by the president in a series of presidential decrees. As a result, the total tax package put into effect turned out to be even larger than initially planned. Moreover, unlike the laws submitted to the Duma that would have come into force in January 1999, implementation of the corresponding presidential decrees (an additional 3 percent of import duties and an increase in the tax rate on foreign exchange purchases up to 1 percent of the volume of the transaction) began just a few days after Yeltsin signed them on August 15, 1998.

A Crisis of Confidence among Foreign Investors

According to the IMF, "The immediate cause of the Russian crisis was the growing loss of financial market confidence in the country's fiscal and international payments situation."[6] But data on the developments of the financial markets indicate that from January 1 through August 14, 1998, the volume of funds invested by foreign investors in Russian government debt actually *increased* by slightly more than $1 billion. The volume of funds invested by private Russian investors remained virtually unchanged. The only investors that did substantially reduce the amount of money they invested in Russian government paper were the Russian Central Bank (CBR) and the group of semi-state, semi-private banks owned by the CBR (Sberbank, Vneshtorgbank, and Eurofinance). The data thus do not support the theory of a confidence crisis among foreign investors. As for domestic investors, the most concerned group was that of the Central Bank, and one could argue that the bank did not feel a lack of confidence, but rather felt secure in their chosen policy.

Pervasive Corruption

Then-deputy-secretary of the U.S. Treasury Lawrence Summers stated: "Worst of all, corruption remains pervasive and fundamentally undermines peoples' faith in the legitimacy of the political and economic system."[7] This argument has recently become one of the most fashionable explanations for the Russian economic crisis. Although corruption may be widespread in Russia, there are two problems with using corruption as an explanatory variable for economic performance. First, the data used to measure corruption, generally the results of opinion polls, reflect public perception of corruption rather than an independent measurement of existing phenomena. Second, extensive international comparisons have not produced convincing statistical evidence that corruption inhibits economic development. Countries with scores on the Corruption Perception Index (CPI) similar to Russia's (e.g., Vietnam, Bolivia, Indonesia, Thailand, Pakistan, Egypt, Latvia), between 2.0 and 3.0 on a scale elaborated by the Transparency International, were able to produce impressive annual growth rates of 4 to 6 percent in the 1990s.[8]

The Inability of the Russian Government to Collect Sufficient Tax Revenues

This point has been repeatedly raised by the IMF and U.S. Treasury officials over the past several years. "At 9 percent of GDP," Summers claimed, "the tax revenues the federal government was able to collect last year is at odds with the role the government and its electorate envision for the state, indeed, it cannot credibly sustain the operations of the most minimal state."[9]

This is one of the great myths about modern Russia. From 1994 to 1998, actual tax collection of the budgetary central government in Russia was at the same effective level as that in the United States— 10.9 and 12.0 percent of GDP, respectively (see Table 10.1). This holds true for total revenue and tax collection of the consolidated central government (which includes social security and extrabudgetary accounts). As for the Russian "general" government (government at all levels), its capacity to collect taxes (30.7 percent of GDP) turned out to be greater than that of the U.S. general government (27.4 percent of GDP). Taking into account the 6-fold difference in the two countries' per capita incomes (by purchasing power parities), it becomes clear that the so-called institutional ability of the Russian government to collect revenues in general, and taxes in particular, is stronger than that of the United States. Suggestions that the Russian government represents a "minimal" state are unfounded. The tax burden imposed by the Russian authorities on the national private sector, and the constant attempts of the IMF and the U.S. Treasury to make this burden even greater, are already unjustifiably heavy.

The Failure to Build and Institutionalize a Favorable Investment Climate

"One interesting anomaly in Russia is that private personal consumption has remained quite strong," according to senior World

Table 10.1
TOTAL REVENUE AND TAX REVENUE AS A PERCENTAGE OF GDP
IN RUSSIA AND USA

Indicators	1994	1995	1996	1997	1998	Average 1994–98
Budgetary central government						
Total revenue and grants						
Russia	12.5	14.2	12.8	12.5	11.0	12.6
USA	12.3	13.0	13.2	13.9	NA	13.1
Russia minus USA	0.2	1.2	−0.4	−1.4	NA	−0.5
Tax revenue						
Russia	11.4	11.9	11.9	9.4	10.1	10.9
USA	11.2	11.5	12.0	12.6	12.9	12.0
Russia minus USA	0.3	0.3	−0.1	−3.2	−2.8	−1.1
Consolidated central government						
Total revenue and grants						
Russia	20.9	20.5	19.8	22.0	20.2	20.7
USA	19.2	19.9	20.0	20.7	20.5	20.1
Russia minus USA	1.7	0.7	−0.2	1.2	−0.4	0.6
Tax revenue						
Russia	19.4	17.9	18.5	20.3	17.7	18.8
USA	17.7	18.2	18.6	19.2	19.6	18.7
Russia minus USA	1.7	−0.3	−0.2	1.1	−1.9	0.1
General government						
Total revenue and grants						
Russia	35.6	33.0	33.0	34.7	33.2	33.9
USA	30.6	31.0	31.6	31.9	32.3	31.5
Russia minus USA	5.0	2.0	1.4	2.8	0.9	2.4
Tax revenue						
Russia	32.2	29.8	31.1	31.5	29.1	30.7
USA	26.9	27.4	27.8	NA	NA	27.4
Russia minus USA	5.2	2.4	3.3	NA	NA	3.6

SOURCES: IMF GFS; IMF IFS; OECD Outlook; Russia's Ministry of Finance.

Bank economist Eric Swanson. "What has really disappeared is investment and government consumption."[10]

One of the possible indicators of the relative favorability of an investment climate is the level of total investment in general and

Table 10.2
PRIVATE AND GOVERNMENT CONSUMPTION AS A PERCENTAGE OF
GDP IN RUSSIA AND USA

Indicators	1994	1995	1996	1997	1998	Average 1994–98
Private consumption						
Russia	47.1	52.9	52.3	53.1	57.9	52.7
USA	67.7	68.2	68.1	67.7	68.2	68.0
Russia minus USA	−20.6	−15.3	−15.8	−14.6	−10.3	−15.3
Government consumption						
Russia	22.6	19.9	20.7	21.6	18.0	20.6
USA	16.1	15.8	15.7	15.4	15.0	15.6
Russia minus USA	6.5	4.1	4.9	6.3	3.0	5.0

SOURCES: IMF IFS; Russia's Goskomstat.

foreign investment in particular. In its level of gross capital formation as a share of GDP, Russia exceeds many other countries of the world including the United States. With the exception of 1998, the Russian level since 1994 has been 4.6 to 8.3 percentage points of GDP higher than the American one. The ratio of foreign direct investment to GDP in Russia (with the exception of 1997) was a little less than the ratio in the United States, where an economic boom has increased such investment over the past few years. But the level of foreign investment in Russia is not exceptionally low by international standards. Among 180 countries of the world, Russia occupies 108th place, not too bad considering that foreign direct investment became legally permissible in the country only in 1991. Note also that a number of countries with levels of FDI as a share of GDP lower than Russia's (e.g., Korea, Turkey, Cyprus, Greece) demonstrated fast and stable growth rates from 1995 to 1997. The level of investment in Russia should be thus regarded as neither extremely low nor an insurmountable constraint on economic growth.

On the other hand, private consumption as a proportion of GDP still lags far behind that of the United States, though it has visibly increased in Russia in the last 8 years (see Table 10.2). From 1994 to 1998, private consumption in Russia as a percentage of GDP was nearly one-quarter less than in the United States (52.7 and 68.0 percent of GDP, respectively). Quite the opposite is the case with

Russia's Potemkin Capitalism

government consumption. Contrary to widespread belief, the share of the government consumption in GDP in Russia (20.6 percent) has been inappropriately high given Russia's level of economic development and is much higher than in the United States (15.6 percent). On average, the portion of the economy consumed by the government in Russia has been greater by 5 percentage points of GDP, or one-third higher, than in the United States. In sum, neither investment nor government consumption has disappeared in Russia.

Official statements have not satisfactorily described Russia's economic transformation or explained the causes of the August 1998 crisis. The resulting confusion has weakened support for liberal reform measures and led some to openly challenge the wisdom of rapid and widespread liberalization.[11] So the question remains: What are the roots of the failure of the Russian model of economic transformation?

Liberalization of the Economy or Liberalization of the State?

Two events transformed the Russian economic system from one driven by a plan to one characterized by a market: the liberalization of prices on January 2, 1992, and the unification of the exchange rate on July 1, 1992. The reduction and elimination of state subsidies to various sectors of the economy, undertaken in 1992, 1993, and 1995, was also critical. Since then, however, the Russian authorities have done next to nothing to expand the role of the market or to reduce government regulation, taxation, government distribution, and government confiscation. Moreover, in the last several years, government intervention in a number of areas has significantly increased, becoming more detailed, sophisticated, and institutionalized.

The policies pursued since 1992 by an impressive array of individuals—including 7 prime ministers, 45 deputy prime ministers, 160 ministers, and 4 Central Bank chairmen—by and large were and remain socialist. These post-Soviet policies have not been identical to those imposed during 70 years of communism, but they have preserved their essentially socialist redistributive nature. The so-called "economy of the bureaucratic market"[12] of the late socialist period has been effectively monetized and adapted to a changed political and economic environment. Bureaucratic arrangements that were negotiated and "traded," such as "plans," "limits," and

201

"funds," have been replaced with "new" securities: budget subsidies, budget guarantees, tax and customs exemptions, export permissions, offsets, government programs, quotas, protectionist tariffs, presidential decrees, government instructions, different types of government credits (including "targeted" ones), and so on.

The absence of tight budgetary constraints for the government has kept its explicit expenditures at levels substantially higher than are sustainable for a country at Russia's level of economic development, and even higher than in the United States (see Table 10.3). From 1994 to 1998 the Russian authorities spent 19.1 and 26.4 percent of GDP at budgetary central and consolidated central government levels, respectively. That is, the Russian government spent on average 5 to 6 percentage points of GDP more than the American government (14.3 and 21.3 percent of GDP, respectively). At the level of the general government the difference between the two countries increases to more than 8 percentage points of GDP—the Russian general government spends 40.5 percent of GDP, while the American one spends 32.2 percent of GDP. Data from Tables 10.1 and 10.3 show that the government in Russia not only collects more revenue as a proportion of GDP than its American counterpart, but also has a far greater appetite for expenditures.

One should bear in mind that official calculations overestimate the size of Russia's real GDP. Besides the real legal economy that is registered and pays taxes, the official numbers include estimates of "shadow economic activity" that are equivalent to approximately 25 percent of the official GDP, plus numbers that reflect a "virtual" economy that exists only in account books, but not in reality and that is equal to another 8 to 10 percent of official GDP.[13] Thus the real fiscal burden on the real economy, which also pays taxes, is much heavier than it appears in official statistics. Seen from that perspective, overall taxation rises from 33 to 35 percent of official GDP to 45 to 50 percent of real, legally produced GDP; while overall expenditure rises from 37 to 40 percent of official GDP to 55 to 60 percent of real legal GDP. In 1992, the first year of the so-called "radical economic reforms," overall expenditures of the general government hit a peacetime world record—they exceeded 70 percent of official GDP and 80 percent of real legal GDP. Even "socialist" Sweden lagged behind "liberal" Russia by relative size of government spending.

202

Table 10.3
TOTAL EXPENDITURE AND BUDGET DEFICIT AS A PERCENTAGE OF
GDP IN RUSSIA AND USA

Indicators	1994	1995	1996	1997	1998	Average 1994–98
Budgetary central government						
Total expenditure						
Russia	23.6	18.1	19.5	18.0	16.3	19.1
USA	14.9	14.6	14.1	13.7	NA	14.3
Russia minus USA	8.8	3.6	5.4	4.3	NA	5.5
Overall surplus						
Russia	−11.1	−3.9	−6.7	−5.5	−5.8	−6.6
USA	−2.5	−1.7	−1.0	0.2	NA	−1.2
Russia minus USA	−8.6	−2.2	−5.7	−5.7	NA	−5.6
Consolidated central government						
Total expenditure						
Russia	31.7	25.1	26.5	25.2	23.6	26.4
USA	22.1	22.0	21.5	21.0	19.9	21.3
Russia minus USA	9.6	3.1	5.0	4.2	3.7	5.1
Overall surplus						
Russia	−10.8	−4.5	−6.7	−3.2	−3.4	−5.7
USA	−2.9	−2.1	−1.5	−0.3	0.6	−1.2
Russia minus USA	−7.9	−2.4	−5.2	−2.9	−4.0	−4.5
General government						
Total expenditure						
Russia	46.2	40.2	40.5	38.8	36.9	40.5
USA	32.8	32.9	32.7	31.6	31.1	32.2
Russia minus USA	13.4	7.3	7.8	7.2	5.9	8.3
Overall surplus						
Russia	−10.6	−7.3	−7.5	−4.1	−3.7	−6.6
USA	−2.2	−1.9	−1.1	0.4	1.2	−0.7
Russia minus USA	−8.4	−5.4	−6.4	−4.4	−4.9	−5.9

SOURCES: IMF GFS; IMF IFS; OECD Outlook; Russia's Ministry of Finance.

At the same time, government pressure on the private sector increased through detailed government regulation, greater trade protectionism, and irresponsible monetary and exchange rate policies. Domestic economic liberalization effectively stopped in mid-1992. The ban on the sale of goods at prices below their production costs led to an overvaluation of the general price level and to a multitier price system. Continuing inflation subjected ruble holders to heavy inflationary taxation that created a flourishing multicurrency payment system. State intervention to control so-called "natural monopolies" has limited market competition and has stimulated the growth of prices.

In mid-1992 the government canceled the zero-percent import tariff policy, which had existed for only months. Since then it has regularly revised its tariff rates upward, making them more detailed and introducing more loopholes in the process. Widespread use of a range of regulatory measures suggests that the actual burden of government on the private sector was and is even greater than fiscal indicators would suggest. The huge reserves of entrepreneurial energy freed by price liberalization and exchange rate unification could have braked Russia's economic crisis, but it has instead been smothered by an ever-expanding state. Russia has unfortunately not experienced the much-touted liberalization of its economy. Rather, it has witnessed what might be called the liberalization (and growth) of the state.

Privatization or Distribution?

The privatization of state property in Russia has led to a sharp fall in the efficiency of privatized enterprises, a mass stripping of their assets, and continuing economic depression. Why did Russian voucher privatization fail to produce the desired results and what kinds of lessons should be drawn from this experience?

First, voucher privatization has been implemented almost as a giveaway—companies were not sold at the highest prices they could fetch, but were given to new owners in exchange for relatively cheap vouchers. As is well known, the higher the price of an investment, the better the incentive for maximizing the return on the investment. If the price of an investment is next to zero, the expected return on investment will be low, as will incentives to improve the acquired property.

Second, companies were offered to everybody. Vouchers were claimed by 144 million people (97 percent of those eligible). While most of the Russian population can be characterized as rational consumers, being a rational producer requires particular skills, knowledge, and character. To drive a car one must pass an exam;

not everyone who wants to drive is capable of doing so. To "drive" a company, and to be a rational investor, is no easier, especially in a country where the market for productive assets disappeared for 70 years.

Third, compounding the problem was the fact that, in most cases, companies were handed over to their managers and workers. Practically all companies needed to adopt extremely painful decisions to restructure, trim staff, and sell off unproductive assets. Yet the voucher privatization program encouraged managers and workers to form a powerful lobby interested in blocking attempts to improve the efficiency of companies. Moreover, one of the most important goals of privatization was the decentralization of economic and political power. However, since most companies were now owned by workers and managers, the Russian privatization process inevitably led to the recentralization of power around the old management elite.

Fourth, the quick speed of Russia's mass privatization program played against long-term economic efficiency. Case-by-case privatization would have meant that state companies accustomed to soft budget constraints would be gradually forced to accept the new market rules of the game. Under mass privatization, by contrast, competition, hard budget constraints, contract execution, and other market rules were never seriously enforced. The mass inflow of state companies accustomed to the old rules into the new market allowed them to use their numerical superiority to avoid playing by new rules. In extreme cases, other market participants were forced to adapt to the rules of game set by the privatized enterprises.

Fifth, mass privatization was performed in a highly inflationary environment, when financial stabilization was far from complete. The situation granted great comparative advantage for entities that had access to the Central Bank and government credit resources— typically enterprises that displayed the old economic mentality and nonmarket behavior.

The later stages of Russian privatization were characterized by the "loans-for-shares" auctions and the "Sviazinvest" auction— scandals marked by inside dealing and lack of transparency. In short, privatization in Russia has been implemented in a generally socialist manner. Assets were transferred improperly, not purchased, and were distributed virtually for free. Property was distributed not to those who would use it most effectively, but to those who were closest to it and best placed to grab it quickly when the opportunity appeared. Those with the best political connections then received protection from the state.

Privatization of the State

Perhaps the most significant peculiarity of Russia's troubled transition has been the privatization of the state itself. By this I mean not privatization of state property and state assets, or privatization of state liabilities, or even the growing disparity between the speedy privatization of state assets and the slow privatization of state liabilities. By privatization of the state per se I mean privatization of the state's core functions: personal security, property protection, law and order, foreign policy, national defense, revenue collection, as well as setting the basic rules governing relations among the state, economic agents, and citizens. The selling of basic state services is not unprecedented in world history; Russia's innovation is the scale and speed of state privatization.

Government decisions, official policy positions, and state institutions have become subject to the supply and demand fluctuations present in any market. Prices have been assigned to practically all actions involving the actual or potential use of state power—from the setting of individual customs exemptions to raids by special forces against offices of competing companies. If there has been any successful privatization in Russia, it is the notable success in the privatization of the state itself. Privatization of the core functions of the state began in the Soviet era, but has become institutionalized in the last few years. The preservation of the state's pervasive role in the economy, along with the privatization of the state per se, has created a new monster that is the most salient feature of Russia's transformation. That monster, politicized economy, set the stage for the spectacular failure of the Russian "reforms."

The actual policies implemented by the Russian authorities have been largely overlooked as public attention has focused on the endless and tiresome melodrama of struggles among so-called "liberal reformers," and "conservative hard-liners," "corrupted officials," and "financial oligarchs." Russia still has people and groups who can be described in such terms. But since the summer of 1992, with few exceptions, the political struggle has not been over whether the government should implement more liberal or more interventionist economic policies. The real struggle has been over a different issue: who or whose team (group, gang, family) would control the state institutions and instruments that control the distribution and redistribution of economic resources. The volume of resources available for distribution not only determines the administrative status of the responsible appointee and his team, but also sets the limits on the exaction of administrative rents. State assets, including appointments, have been used not only for personal gain but also for maintaining and strengthening the social and financial positions of relevant political and economic groups. The only distinction among the groups participating in the Russian transformation was their ability to camouflage their deeds to make them suitable for public consumption in Russia and abroad.

The Mightiest Financial Oligarch

One of the most striking examples of the privatization of state institutions is the effective privatization of Russia's Central Bank (CBR). Privatization of the state monopoly that creates and controls legal tender and manages foreign exchange reserves gave the CBR's administration financial resources that dwarf those available to all the other Russian oligarchs put together. The independent legal status of the Central Bank allows for very little accountability. The process of money creation and its subsequent distribution is subject only to rules set by the CBR itself. Revenues from the bank's operations are not subject to taxation. And while half of the CBR's official profit is transferred to the federal budget, the CBR itself determines the amount of its own operating costs.

The CBR has thus managed to consume huge amounts of financial resources.[14] Its current expenditures (e.g., wages and stationery) alone are 50 percent higher than the total federal expenditure on the nation's administration, and equivalent to approximately one-fifth of the country's defense expenditures. While the average wage in Russia before the August 1998 crisis was roughly 20 times lower than that in the United States, just the cash portion of the official salary of the CBR chairman was almost twice as high as the salary of the chairman of the U.S. Federal Reserve, and higher than the salary of the U.S. president, as well as that of the presidents and prime ministers of most countries in the world.[15]

Its independent status has also allowed the CBR to combine the functions of the executive branch, a supervisory institution, a commercial organization, and a political party. The CBR spends billions of dollars on commercial and investment projects, the construction and purchase of offices and property, the launching of satellites, the acquisition and financing of the media, and political lobbying. In the spring and summer of 1998, for example, the CBR's top officials began open financial warfare against the federal government. They used a variety of weapons including selling off a large package of treasury bills on the market in May, writing off federal government revenues from its accounts in July, and dumping state securities by CBR-owned commercial banks (i.e., Sberbank, Vneshtorgbank, Eurofinance) and then transferring to them $3.5 billion—the lion's share of the first portion of the IMF loan—in the first two weeks of August.[16] The Central Bank's actions culminated in the August 1998 financial crisis and the dismissal of the Kirienko government.

Imported Goods: Interventionism and Populism

The survival of interventionist economic policies in Russia cannot be attributed wholly to corruption, domestic political resistance, and the legacy of communism. Credit also belongs to international financial institutions (IFI). The core policy recommendations of the IMF and the World Bank include economic liberalization, financial stabilization, and the privatization of state assets. But while other IFI client countries were expected to pursue those measures, Russia was largely exempted from doing so. In fact, the IFIs often pressured the Russian authorities to adopt policies that openly contradict the central tenets of the "Washington Consensus" on market liberalization.

For example, financial stabilization requires balancing government revenues and expenditures at the lowest possible level, eliminating budget deficits, achieving low interest rates, and reducing government debt. But by regularly supplying Russia with new credits, the IFIs encouraged policies that preserved the budget deficit, kept interest rates high, and resulted in the accumulation of more government debt. For years, the IFIs have advocated increasing taxation in Russia—already at intolerable levels—thereby aggravating the country's prolonged depression.

In Russia the IFIs opposed domestic economic liberalization when they suggested the acceptance and regulation of so-called "natural monopolies" and opposed external liberalization when they called for increases in customs duties and heavier taxation of foreign exchange operations. The IFIs silently backed the introduction of two foreign exchange trading sessions in August 1998 and Russia's subsequent departure from a unified exchange rate regime. Moreover, while the Washington Consensus stipulates that privatization of state property is necessary to improve economic efficiency, the IFIs subsidize and protect unprofitable coal mines and discourage attempts to privatize them.

The most important policy recommendations of the July 1998 IMF program were to increase taxation and to maintain an overvalued exchange rate.[17] The $4.8 billion tranche of the IMF loan transferred to the Russian Central Bank on July 20, 1998, directly subsidized the ailing Russian banking sector, which had been teetering on the brink of total collapse. The bulk of that money, $3.5 billion, dropped into the pockets of the daughters of the mightiest financial oligarch (Sberbank, Vneshtorgbank, Eurofinance). That IMF program proved valuable mainly in helping to bail out Russia's financial oligarchs. It is not surprising that that IMF package worsened Russia's economic environment, exacerbating the financial crisis and making its resolution much more complicated.

In the last nine years, the lending agencies have credited Russia with more than $25 billion ($19 billion from the IMF and $6 billion from the World Bank). Those credits substantially helped to postpone the implementation of a coherent economic strategy and reduced the willingness of national authorities to make painful but necessary changes in economic policies. Moreover, they have encouraged irresponsible behavior in both the public and private sectors. The Russian political elite is now firmly convinced that Russia will regularly receive international financing regardless of its economic policies. Having effectively spoiled Russian society with practically unlimited financial support, the IFIs have made the transformation of the Russian economy significantly more difficult.

Conclusion

The failure of Russia's transformation does not lie with liberal economic policies allegedly applied in Russia. In fact, such programs have never been tried.

Contrary to widely held views, the economic policies actually implemented represent a distasteful mixture of interventionism and populism aggravated by the privatization of the core functions of the state. Those developments have been generously supported by international financial institutions. Ending such misguided largesse is a necessary step in encouraging Moscow to begin to deal seriously with its ongoing economic problems.

Notes

1. Some observers were skeptical early on of the international community's ability to promote market reforms in Russia, especially through massive foreign assistance programs. See, for example, Nicholas Eberstadt, "Western Aid and Russian Transition," in *Perpetuating Poverty: The World Bank, the IMF, and the Developing World*, ed. Doug Bandow and Ian Vásquez (Washington: Cato Institute, 1994), pp. 89–99.

2. Anatoly Chubais, "Democracy Is Never for Free," Statement submitted to the U.S. House Committee on Banking and Financial Services, *Hearing on International Economic Turmoil*, 105th Cong., 2d sess., September 15, 1998, p. 5.

3. Ibid., p. 5.

4. Ibid., p. 6.

5. International Monetary Fund, *World Economic Outlook*, October 1998 (Washington: International Monetary Fund, 1998), p. 53.

6. Ibid., p. 7.

7. Lawrence H. Summers, "Russia in Crisis," Statement submitted to the U.S. House Committee on International Relations, 105th Cong., 2d sess., September 17, 1998, pp. 2–3.

8. Also, in 1998 Russia's rating in the CPI rose to 2.4 from 2.27 in 1997.

9. Summers, p. 2.

10. Eric Swanson, World Bank senior economist, cited in Robert Lyle, "Has Transition Failed in Former USSR?" *RFE/RL Newsline End Note*, vol. 3, no. 83, April 29, 1999. See also Summers, p. 2.

11. See, for example, Joseph E. Stiglitz, "Whither Reform? Ten Years of the Transition," *World Bank Annual Conference on Development Economics*, April 28–30, 1999.

12. This term was introduced by Vitaly A. Naishul.

13. For a discussion on this matter, see Andrei Illarionov, "How the Russian Financial Crisis Was Organized," Part I, *Voprosy Ekonomiki*, no. 11, 1998.

14. Steve Hanke ranks Russia's Central Bank as one of the most inefficient of the world's largest 50 economies. See Hanke, "Banks That Rob You," *Forbes*, November 1, 1999, p. 188.

15. Yurij Schekochikhin, "VIP-Life," *New Daily (Novaya Ezhednevnaya Gazeta)*, October 1998.

16. RF Federation Council, Conclusion of the Temporary Commission of the Federation Council on Investigation of Reasons, Circumstances and Consequences of Decisions of the Government of the Russian Federation and the Central Bank of the Russian Federation of August 17, 1998, Moscow, February 15, 1999, p. 27.

17. International Monetary Fund, "IMF Approves Financing for Russia," *IMF Survey*, vol. 27, no. 15, August 3, 1998, p. 3. For a discussion of the implications of the July 1998 IMF program see Andrei Illarionov, "Russia and the IMF," Statement prepared for the General Oversight and Investigations Subcommittee of the U.S. House Committee on Banking and Financial Services, *Hearing to Examine the Russian Economic Crisis and the International Monetary Fund (IMF) Aid Package*, 105th Cong., 2d sess., September 10, 1998.

PART III

THE GLOBAL FINANCIAL ARCHITECTURE
AND ITS FUTURE

11. Bretton Woods: A Golden Era?

Francis J. Gavin

What can the past tell us about monetary relations today? On August 16, 1962, the two most powerful economic policymakers in the world—President John F. Kennedy and Federal Reserve Chairman William McChesney Martin—met privately in the White House. The purpose of the meeting was to find a policy to end the dollar and gold outflow that had plagued American foreign economic policy since late 1958. Kennedy and Martin discussed a plan put forward by George Ball, the Undersecretary of State, and supported by the Council of Economic Advisers, to dramatically recast the global payments system. Among other things, Ball's plan envisioned a politically negotiated standstill on conversion of foreign-held dollars into America gold. As dramatic as such a move would have been, to Kennedy's mind, altering the rules of the international monetary system was far preferable to the other policy options he was given: restrictions on trade and capital movements, domestic deflation, or a massive retrenchment of America's cold war security commitments abroad. But Martin warned Kennedy that Ball's plan was dangerous. The position of the dollar and the world's financial architecture was so weak that the Federal Reserve chairman believed that the mere discussion of a gold standstill could send the dollar and the international monetary system into a downward spiral.[1]

The meeting was remarkable in several ways. Imagine how international capital markets would react today if President Bill Clinton and Federal Reserve Chairman Alan Greenspan met privately in the White House. But perhaps more amazing was the subject and purpose of Kennedy's talk with Martin. The president was deeply dissatisfied with the rules of the international monetary system. The year is 1962, the height of America's economic dominance—years before the Vietnam War and the Great Society-inspired inflation that supposedly forced America to suspend dollar-gold convertibility—and

213

the president wanted to drastically alter the world's monetary system.

What was going on here? This meeting and many others that took place among top officials in the U.S. government in the late 1950s and throughout the 1960s reveal a far different picture of America's international monetary policy than we are accustomed to hearing. Economics and history textbooks make no mention of this high-level discussion. Instead, descriptions abound of something called the Bretton Woods order.[2] These textbooks tell about the system that emerged from an Anglo-American conference in 1944, and that it functioned smoothly and effectively until the Nixon administration rudely destroyed it in 1971. In most cases, such texts will also explain that this Bretton Woods system increased trade mobility while maintaining exchange stability, thereby sustaining growth and promoting peace. In short, they describe something much different than the monetary system that so frustrated and worried Kennedy.

A historical examination of the period reveals a much different story. Contrary to the standard view, international monetary relations were not smooth. Top American policymakers did not think the system bestowed great economic advantages on the U.S. economy. Rather, they felt constrained and burdened. Western leaders fretted throughout the period as the system lurched from crisis to crisis (the dollar was threatened in 1960, 1962, and 1968; the sterling was under siege in 1961, 1964, and 1967; and even the French franc was attacked in 1968 and 1969). Each crisis brought with it increasingly complicated and restrictive rules, including controls and limits on capital, trade, and even tourism. Perhaps most disturbing was how this monetary turbulence spilled over into political tension. These monetary problems—which were in large measure caused by a poorly functioning system—acted like an acid on the Western alliance. To give just the most extreme example, monetary conflicts between the United States and Western Europe forced four successive presidents (Dwight Eisenhower, John Kennedy, Lyndon Johnson, and Richard Nixon) to threaten massive troop withdrawals from NATO for balance-of-payments reasons.[3]

Clearly, the conventional wisdom about post–World War II monetary relations is wrong. This distortion is more than a historical curiosity. It has potentially enormous policy implications. That is because the monetary problems of recent years—particularly the turmoil in East Asia and Russia—have inspired calls for a new monetary conference to reform and rebuild our global financial architecture. And more often than not, the Bretton Woods conference and the system the conference supposedly created are held up as the models for how a 21st-century monetary system should be constructed.

This chapter will make four points. First, I analyze how the so-called Bretton Woods system was so poorly designed that it was doomed to failure. Second, I lay out how monetary relations *actually* worked during the post–World War II period. (In fact, a strong case could be made that there really was no such thing as the Bretton Woods system.) Third, I explain why economists, historians, and policymakers have consistently gotten the story of postwar monetary relations wrong. Finally, I connect these lessons of history to current policy debates on international monetary relations.

How Bretton Woods Was Supposed to Work—And Why It Did Not

The Bretton Woods Agreement of 1944 was the most ambitious and far-reaching monetary arrangement between sovereign states in history. American and British financial officials, led by John Maynard Keynes and Harry Dexter White, hoped to set up a system with several goals: stable exchange rates, free trade, and an adjustment mechanism that avoided domestic deflation. But as laudable as these goals may have been, they ultimately contradicted each other.

In the absence of trade restrictions and capital controls, it is impossible to maintain fixed exchange rates and shield national economies from demand shifts produced by gold flows. The Bretton Woods agreement did not provide a way to guarantee price stability across borders (necessary to maintain fixed exchange rates), nor did it offer a mechanism to automatically adjust payments imbalances. Since different countries pursued different national monetary policies (as well as having different national savings rates), some method was needed to adjust for the changes in the relative value of currencies produced by differential rates of inflation. The agreement did allow for International Monetary Fund (IMF)–approved changes in par value. But exchange rate variations were difficult, because they unsettled foreign exchange markets, and it was hard to get countries to agree to shifts because they feared the adverse effects on their terms of trade. Speculators always knew the direction of any revaluation in advance, guaranteeing windfall profits whenever exchange rates were changed. Countries were equally reluctant to sacrifice full employment and social policy goals for balance-of-payments purposes. In the end, this meant that there was no effective means to automatically close balance-of-payments gaps other than trade and capital controls. As the economist Robert Stern has stated, "Since the functioning of the pegged-rate system may appear to avoid rather than expedite adjustment, it might be more fitting to characterize this system . . . as the 'international disequilibrium system.'"[4]

The Bretton Woods arrangement was further complicated by the unusual role of the dollar as an international reserve currency and universally accepted balancing item. During the war, there was a general sense that the world's supply of gold was too small to provide the liquidity needed to finance payments imbalances in a fixed exchange rate system. Therefore the dollar, which was convertible into gold on demand, would supplement gold as a reserve and balancing item. In other words, a nation could finance its deficit with either gold or dollars, and since dollars earned interest and had lower transaction costs, dollars were often preferred in the immediate post–World War II period. This meant that the foreign demand for dollars went beyond what was needed to purchase American goods and services, and that the equilibrium point for the U.S. balance of payments was not zero.[5] Much of the American balance-of-payments "deficit" was not a deficit at all, as excess dollars were desired, at least for a time, by central banks for reserves.

But when did the American deficit exceed international liquidity requirements? The exact figure was almost impossible to calculate. This added a great deal of confusion to the system. At a certain point, foreign central banks would tire of accumulating an unlimited supply of dollars and demand gold instead. The worth of the dollar—its gold guarantee—might be questioned as the U.S. gold supply was run down. A form of Gresham's law could undermine the dollar's reserve status, and the resulting loss of liquidity could set off a mad scramble by central banks eager to acquire scarce gold.[6] "Beggar-thy-neighbor" policies, such as import restrictions, export subsidies, exchange controls, and competitive devaluations, might ensue. Or at least that was the scenario that so scared Western policymakers throughout the 1960s.

Thus, the monetary system designed by White and Keynes had two fatal flaws. It lacked a reliable, automatic mechanism to adjust payments imbalances between countries, and the liquidity needed to maintain fixed exchange rates was provided in an inconsistent and ineffective way. The result was that the Bretton Woods arrangements would work if only two, but not all three, of the following policies were followed: fixed exchange rates, domestic autonomy, and free trade and capital flows. This meant that the Bretton Woods model described in the history and economics textbooks never really existed. So what took its place? And was Bretton Woods a monetary order worth replicating today?

The Real History of Post–World War II Monetary Relations

Clearly, the monetary system that Keynes and White designed at Bretton Woods was unworkable. Two events in the late 1940s made this painful fact obvious. The first was the attempt, in 1946–47, to make sterling convertible on current account. The United States had provided a large, low-interest loan to help the British strengthen sterling during this transition. But the proceeds of this loan, which were supposed to back sterling for years to come, were run down in six weeks. The British abandoned their effort to make sterling convertible for more than a decade. What was worse, Great Britain maintained, and in some cases strengthened, capital controls and imperial trade preferences. This set an unsettling precedent. The free movement of capital and trade remained elusive throughout the so-called Bretton Woods period.

The second event was the massive devaluation of sterling in 1949. The Bretton Woods agreement had allowed devaluations if there was a fundamental disequilibrium in a nation's balance of payments. But "fundamental disequilibrium" was never defined. It was hoped, however, that devaluations would be small and orderly and take place only after consultation and analysis from the International Monetary Fund. The British devaluation flouted both the letter and the spirit of these rules. The change in parity was roughly 30 percent; the IMF was told, not consulted, only 24 hours before the event; and the move deeply unsettled the nascent European economic recovery. But the lesson of this incident was that the cherished Bretton Woods goal of international cooperation and coordination was a mirage. If a nation felt it had to change its parity, it could do so suddenly, massively, and without the approval of the IMF. The pattern was set for the 1950s. To maintain exchange rates, nations maintained trade and capital controls. Ironically, most of these were supported by the United States. The United States encouraged European discrimination against dollar goods in order to encourage European economic and political integration. Japan's trade practices were overlooked so as to compensate for losing its traditional markets in China. Judging by the statistics, it is amazing how little international capital mobility there was. Foreign private capital—the fuel behind the amazing growth of the United States during the 19th century, and one of the engines of East Asia's remarkable growth in the last 25 years—was quite small during the 1950s in relative historical terms. This was due in large measure to the lack of trust in inconvertible currencies and the array of capital controls installed to maintain fixed exchange rates.

At the end of 1958, the larger West European economies finally moved to make their currencies convertible on current account. Not coincidentally, this also marked the beginning of real concern and even panic within the U.S. government over the U.S. payments deficit. This highlights a puzzling situation that is rarely appreciated. The United States maintained a large current account surplus throughout the so-called Bretton Woods period, but every year (except 1957, because of the Suez crisis) had large balance-of-payments deficits. That was the case not just in the late 1960s but in the late 1940s and 1950s as well. So the problem was never trade. But it was only in the late 1950s and early 1960s that a real fear of monetary chaos developed. That fear—first displayed by Eisenhower but continuing through the Nixon administration—was the most important feature of U.S. foreign economic policy from 1958 through 1971.

The dread of what would happen if the U.S. gold supply were run down inspired a whole series of policy distortions in the United States. Capital controls, at first voluntary and then mandatory, were instituted. Foreign aid was tied. Tourists were told what they could spend. West Germany and Japan were strong-armed into holding only dollars in their reserves and not buying gold.[7] Perhaps the most amazing monetary distortions took place in the Department of Defense. Troop withdrawals were always high on the agenda.

But other measures were taken as well. To save foreign exchange, Defense Secretary Robert McNamara, the supposed accounting whiz, ordered the military to "buy American" regardless of budgetary cost.[8] This meant that when a jeep broke down in Japan, it would not be fixed there but sent to Hawaii for repairs and then shipped back, costing two or three times as much. This amounted to a de facto devaluation of the dollar, at least in terms of defense expenditures overseas. Such crazy policy distortions were necessitated by a poorly constructed monetary system. In a system of market-determined exchange rates, none of these measures would have been necessary.

This irrational arrangement could not persist forever and, despite enormous efforts, the system began to break down in the early 1960s. New evidence has emerged that by 1963 President Kennedy was so worried about international monetary relations that he considered letting the dollar float.[9] But U.S. policymakers instead pursued a policy of temporary expedients throughout the 1960s, culminating in the March 1968 decision to have two prices for gold—one determined by the market, the other determined by central banks to remain at $35 per ounce. This decision—taken more than three years before Nixon closed the gold window—marked the real shift in post–World War II monetary relations. The intergovernmental gold price was a fiction maintained between central banks, and in the world of money, fictions do not last long. As the market price for gold increased to $40 an ounce and higher, it would only be a matter of time before a central bank broke away from the two-tier price regime.

Nixon's decision to close the gold window should have surprised no one, and in fact had been considered as early as the late 1950s. The world (and the United States in particular) would have been far better off if the dollar had been set free much earlier. Coinciding with an increase in world inflation and a steep rise in commodity prices, there is no doubt that the post–August 15, 1971, international monetary system took some time to find its bearings. But it is only since exchange rates have been more or less set free that ever-expanding trade accompanied by international investment throughout the world has come to pass. Private international capital flows have increased by orders of magnitude since 1971 despite occasional exchange rate instability.

Why Does the Myth of Bretton Woods Persist?

The Bretton Woods plan was unworkable from the start. The system that did develop was chaotic, unstable, and inefficient. Yet policymakers and even economists still yearn for a return to something they call the Bretton Woods system.[10] Why, despite the rather obvious and overwhelming evidence of the flaws in post–World War II monetary relations, do these myths about Bretton Woods persist?

This phenomenon is puzzling. When the Bretton Woods agreements were considered by Congress, many experts pointed out their evident shortcomings.[11] But after the agreements were passed, the critics seemed to disappear into the wilderness. Throughout the 1950s and most of the 1960s, several economists, most notably Milton Friedman, pointed out the flaws of fixed exchange rates and the virtues of floating exchange rates. But their views were not in the mainstream. Even stranger is the low level of support that the current system of flexible exchange rates received through much of the 1990s, despite its relatively smooth functioning. It should be pointed out, of course, that the monetary crises that have emerged in the past two decades have usually surrounded attempts by states to maintain a fixed exchange rate that the market does not believe is supportable. The United States has faced no such crises since allowing the dollar to float.

Why then is there this nostalgia for Bretton Woods? The overarching reason is the failure to bring historical analysis to bear on the question of international monetary relations. This is a polite way of saying that people just do not understand what happened in the past.

The lack of knowledge and understanding about the past allows certain myths to grow, which become established as conventional wisdom and become almost impossible to dislodge. Of course, this happens in other fields as well. Consider the Munich analogy in international politics, for example. U.S. policymakers and analysts, trying to understand the origins of World War II, found cause in British Prime Minister Neville Chamberlain's attempts to appease Adolf Hitler. When British foreign policy failed, the lesson that was taken from the experience is never to negotiate with dictators. Tyrants must expand to survive, and must be stopped early in the game because their territorial demands are unquenchable. Putting aside the question of how accurately this describes what was going on at Munich, there is little doubt that this analogy—this model for explaining causality in international affairs—has had a profound and, more often than not, misleading effect on American foreign policy in the post–World War II years. U.S. policymakers look at Ho Chi Minh, Saddam Hussein, and Slobodan Milosevic, and they see Hitler. Right or wrong, these historical analogies often cloud the real context and causality behind complicated international relations phenomena. A deep historical examination would reveal that the motivations and circumstances behind all of those cases were vastly different, and that the analogy was more misleading than helpful.

In the same way that a simplified model of the Munich conference was used to explain international affairs, a simplified model of the Great Depression has been used to explain international monetary relations. The problem, of course, is that the wrong lessons were taken from the Great Depression. Post–World War II policymakers believed that the source of interwar monetary chaos had been exchange instability, competitive devaluations, and a free market out of control. But this was not the case at all. Rigid adherence to fixed exchange rates and the gold standard exacerbated deflationary pressures. Central bank cooperation to maintain these fixed exchange rates actually worsened the international financial situation.[12] The Great Depression had many causes, not all of which are fully understood, but it is clear that the attempt to reign in and curtail the market—in this case the foreign exchange markets—made the Depression worse than it would have been. The countries that devalued and went off gold fared much better, and came out of the Depression much sooner, than those that maintained fixed rates. The correct lesson should have been to prevent central bank cooperation and to allow the markets to do their work.

The lack of historical analysis manifests itself in other ways as well, particularly when defining terms and weighing their importance. This is especially true of the terms "conference" and "system." People look at the Bretton Woods conference of 1944 and just assume that the decisions made there were simply implemented. But international monetary relations are far more complicated than that, and no conference can simply change the way international finance works. A good historian of international politics during the interwar period will see parallels to the Versailles conference. Versailles produced the League of Nations, and Bretton Woods created the International Monetary Fund. Versailles set limits on armaments, and Bretton

221

Woods set rules for managing currencies. But simply studying Versailles will tell you little about international politics during this period. The League of Nations was weak and ineffectual and the armaments and reparations clauses were ignored. Factors far more powerful than a simple treaty came into play. The same is true of Bretton Woods. The IMF was weak and ineffectual during its first two decades. In fact, the United States expressly forbade Marshall Aid recipients to use the fund. And, as already mentioned, both the spirit and the letter of the Bretton Woods agreements were largely ignored. A major difference between the two conferences, it seems, is that most people correctly view Versailles as a tragic failure and mistakenly believe the Bretton Woods conference was a success.

The word "system" is likewise misleading. I have already argued that there really was not a Bretton Woods system. To convey a sense of how the conference did not produce a "system," compare monetary relations in 1956 with 1936. The main feature of both periods was that the dollar was convertible on demand into gold at $35 an ounce. Most major countries sterilized their reserve flows. The differences? There were far more capital controls in 1956 than in 1936. But is this difference enough to define a "system"? When de Gaulle gave his famous 1965 speech attacking the role of the dollar in the gold exchange system, the conference he attacked was not the 1944 Bretton Woods conference, but the 1922 Genoa conference. A serious historical analysis reveals all sorts of problems with even defining what the Bretton Woods system was. When did it begin? 1944? 1958? Never? When did it really end?

When all the high-sounding rhetoric surrounding modern international monetary relations is removed, there are lots of details but there is really only one great debate—whether you will have a system based on government-determined fixed exchange rates or flexible exchange rates. The experience of this century should make clear which is better.

Leaving Well Enough Alone

Advocates of a new Bretton Woods conference and a reformed international monetary system should take into account several points. First, the system that White and Keynes designed was flawed from the beginning and never came into operation. Second, the system that did come into being, which was partially based on the

Bretton Woods agreements and partially based on ad hoc expedients, was troubled from the start. The twin goals of domestic autonomy and fixed exchange rates are only possible if the free movement of trade and capital is sacrificed. Many analysts lament the loss of stable exchange rates, but are they willing to pay the price of onerous trade restrictions and capital controls to achieve this stability? If so, then they must also be willing to return to a period when exchange stability required painful domestic policies and troubling foreign policy choices.

In fact, the system of floating exchange rates that exists today is superior to any that came before it. Market-determined exchange rates eliminate the two fatal flaws of post–World War II monetary relations. Payments imbalances are automatically and in most cases painlessly adjusted by the market. And allowing the market to determine exchange rates eliminates the whole issue of liquidity and reserves. Perhaps most important, the whole process has been depoliticized. It is inconceivable to most people living in developed countries that our government could ask us to restrict our investments or travel abroad, and it would seem absurd for our nation's leaders to make foreign policy based solely on balance-of-payments reasons. But that would be commonplace were we to return to anything like the so-called golden era of Bretton Woods.

Notes

1. Discussion between John F. Kennedy and William McChesney Martin, August 16, 1962, 5:50–6:32 p.m., J.F.K. Recordings, Tape 13.

2. See, for example, Alfred E. Eckes, *A Search for Solvency: Bretton Woods and the International Monetary System, 1941–1971* (Austin: University of Texas Press, 1975); Richard N. Gardner, *Sterling-Dollar Diplomacy: The Origins and the Prospects of Our International Economic Order* (New York: McGraw-Hill Book Company, 1969); Margaret Garritsen de Vries, "Bretton Woods Fifty Years Later: A View from the International Monetary Fund," in *The Bretton Woods–GATT System: Retrospect and Prospect after Fifty Years*, ed. Orin Kirshner (Armonk, N.Y.: M. E. Sharp, 1996); Joanne Gowa, *Closing the Gold Window: Domestic Politics and the End of Bretton Woods* (Ithaca, N.Y.: Cornell University Press, 1983); Diane Kunz, *Butter and Guns: America's Cold War Economic Diplomacy* (New York: The Free Press, 1997); John Odell, *U.S. International Monetary Policy: Markets, Power, and Ideas as Sources of Change* (Princeton, N.J.: Princeton University Press, 1982); Judy Shelton, *Money Meltdown: Restoring Order to the Global Currency System* (New York: The Free Press, 1994); Susan Strange, *International Economic Relations of the Western World: 1959–1971*, vol. 2. (London: Oxford University Press, 1976); and Paul Volcker and Toyoo Gyohten, *Changing Fortunes: The World's Money and the Threat to American Leadership* (New York: Times Books, 1992).

3. See Francis J. Gavin, "The Gold Battles with the Cold War: American Monetary Policy and the Defense of Europe, 1960–1963," *Diplomatic History*, forthcoming; and Marc Trachtenberg, *A Constructed Peace: The Making of the European Settlement, 1945–1963* (Princeton, N.J.: Princeton University Press, 1999).

4. Robert M. Stern, *The Balance of Payments: Theory and Economic Policy* (Chicago: Aldine, 1973), p. 152.

5. In other words, if the deficit had been zero, there would not have been enough dollars in the system for reserve and liquidity purposes. Dollars were willingly held, instead of used to purchase American goods and services, by both central banks and private concerns. These dollars counted as a "deficit" but were not a deficit in the sense that they were willingly held.

6. For the contemporary description of this scenario, see Robert Triffin, *Gold and the Dollar Crisis* (New Haven, Conn.: Yale University Press, 1960).

7. See Francis J. Gavin, *Gold, Dollars and Power: The Politics of the American Balance of Payments Deficit, 1958–1971* (Chapel Hill: University of North Carolina Press, New Cold War History Series, scheduled for 2001).

8. Deborah Shapley, *Promise and Power: The Life and Times of Robert McNamara* (Boston: Little, Brown and Company, 1993).

9. Walt Rostow, "Kennedy's View of Monnet and Vice-Versa," in *John F. Kennedy and Europe*, ed. Douglas Brinkley and Richard T. Griffiths (Baton Rouge: Louisiana State University Press, 1999), p. 281; Oral History Interview with Carl Kaysen by Joseph O'Connor, July 11, 1966, John F. Kennedy Presidential Library, Oral History Collection, pp. 87–88.

10. For several examples, see Diane B. Kunz, "The Fall of the Dollar Order: The World the United States Is Losing," *Foreign Affairs* (July/Aug.): 1995; Peter Passell, "Bretton Woods: A Policy Revisited," *New York Times*, July 21, 1994; Judy Shelton, "How to Save the Dollar," *Wall Street Journal*, July 15, 1994; and Volcker and Gyohten.

11. The *Wall Street Journal, New York Times*, and *Chicago Tribune* all ran editorials against the conference and the Bretton Woods agreements. Jacob Viner, perhaps America's most distinguished international economist at the time, expressed serious reservations about the International Monetary Fund. Several of his University of Chicago colleagues, especially the economist Henry Simons, came out against Bretton Woods. Winthrop Aldrich, the chairman of Chase National Bank, delivered a devastating indictment of Bretton Woods in a speech delivered on September 15, 1944. Aldrich supported the key currency approach advocated by Allan Sproul and John H. Williams of the Federal Reserve Bank of New York. For these and other examples, see Eckes, pp. 165–209.

12. This comes through clearly in Barry Eichengreen's excellent account of interwar international monetary diplomacy, *Gold Fetters: The Gold Standard and the Great Depression, 1919–1939* (New York: Oxford University Press, 1995).

12. The International Monetary Fund: Lender of Last Resort or Indispensable Lender?

Onno de Beaufort Wijnholds and Arend Kapteyn

The financial crisis that began in mid-1997 has forcefully demonstrated that in a world of increasing capital mobility there is a premium on sound macroeconomic and financial policies. The crisis has also served as a painful reminder of the futility of defending overvalued exchange rates, although this lesson had to be learned the hard way. The strength and speed with which capital flows and risk premia have reacted to newly detected economic weaknesses have inflicted a combination of surprise, awe, and fear into the minds of policymakers. Given the depth and duration of the crisis, and the number of countries affected, many now believe that surely there must be something wrong with the international "architecture," or, in laymen's terms—"the world as we know it."

The knee-jerk reaction has been to fix whatever is presumed to be broken. While attention has naturally focused on where the fire is—that is, the weaknesses in emerging markets—many have also turned their eyes toward the fire department, the International Monetary Fund (IMF). In this regard, the criticism has ranged from the firefighter not having enough water (money) to extinguish the fires, to blaming him for making things worse. Depending on how one allocates the blame for the crisis, reform proposals range from, at one extreme, abolishing the IMF to, at the other extreme, endowing the IMF with full lender-of-last-resort capabilities. These proposals can also be seen as proxies for the degree of official intervention that could take place in future crises. Should we, for instance, attempt to control capital movements during future crises? Should we limit the effect of financial turmoil by providing liquidity or should we do nothing and let market forces play out?

The crisis of the last few years is not a crisis of capitalism, nor is it a breakdown of the market-based international monetary system. Rather, the lesson of the crisis should be to improve the way in which markets work, to accept that the degrees of freedom in national policymaking are curtailed in a globalized world, and to find a way to make both debtors and creditors more responsible for flawed borrowing and lending decisions. Proposals to turn the IMF into a full-fledged international lender of last resort are misguided. Efforts should focus instead on improving the institutional framework in which markets function.

The Rationale for Official Involvement

The general rationale for any IMF involvement, let alone a lender-of-last-resort role, needs to be grounded in the existence of market imperfections or the inadequate provision of public goods, both of which IMF lending can help to remedy.[1] In the most recent crisis, there were probably three different types of market failure.

The first and most prevalent market failure is imperfect information. For too long markets lent money to emerging markets at spreads that were too low in the mistaken belief that the proceeds were being productively invested and would be repaid in full. When the realization hit that this was not the case, excessive outflow quickly followed the earlier excessive inflow. Lack of transparency was commonplace in emerging economies, not least at the government level. Governments attempted to hide their true reserve holdings, while neither governments nor creditors had a clear sense of the size of the often implicit guarantees or the debt payments falling due. This lack of information is, of course, not so much a "market" failure as a failure by governments to provide sufficient information to the markets. The IMF is now attempting to address this lack of transparency in various ways. First, it has included a special category for "net" international reserves in its special data dissemination standard, to take account of the tendency of countries to hide their exchange rate intervention by keeping it off balance. In addition, countries are being asked to report on their external debt position. Second, the fund is developing standards and good practices for transparency in fiscal policy and monetary and financial policy. This will serve not just as a benchmark for countries to improve their own policies but also, ultimately, as a benchmark against which private markets can assess a country's performance.

The second market failure that the IMF could attempt to address is that of a coordination problem among creditors. Herd behavior, free-rider behavior, and bandwagon effects are the terms that come to mind. If investors believe that other investors will attempt to pull out their money so as to obtain some of the limited resources left at the central bank, or, alternatively, before the exchange rate falls further, then there could be a role for some official coordination. In Korea, Indonesia, and Brazil, for instance, the IMF set up a monitoring system for foreign commercial bank exposure to those countries. Information about rollover behavior of bank claims was then communicated back to the central banks in the countries of the main creditor banks. The central banks, in turn, kept commercial banks informed about aggregate rollover performance of commercial banks in other countries and exerted some moral suasion on their own banks to maintain their claims. The concerted involvement of the monetary authorities of creditor countries and the IMF served to provide some confidence to creditor banks that they would not be the victim of free-riding.

The third market failure could be the existence of multiple equilibria. There may be one equilibrium in which creditors believe in a country's economic prospects and in the policymakers' intentions, and in which money is available on reasonable terms. This "good" equilibrium would apply to Asia pre-1997. There could also be a bad equilibrium, however, in which creditors lose their faith in both economic fundamentals and the authorities' policy commitments. Market access could be cut off and credit withdrawn. There is, in some cases, a priori no reason to believe that the markets will choose the better of the two equilibria. IMF programs, by providing assurances about the course of economic policy, can tilt the balance toward the good equilibrium.

There could also be a role for the IMF in providing public goods. The main public goods that the IMF attempts to achieve are free trade and payments, transparency, and exchange rate stability. By providing some form of insurance against adverse shocks, the IMF can encourage the provision of these public goods. This insurance involves having access to IMF balance-of-payments financing when access to private markets is cut off. Of course, in principle, markets

GLOBAL FORTUNE

should also be able to provide such "catastrophe insurance"[2] but—
with some notable exceptions of private contingent credit lines in
Argentina, Canada, Indonesia, and Mexico—a market for this type
of insurance had not yet developed (which could be as much due
to the inability of banks to provide such financing, locking themselves into a crisis, as it could be to countries' unwillingness to pay
the required premium).[3] The access to additional financing in crises
is welfare enhancing. By allowing countries to smooth out their
adjustment process over time, economic disruption is minimized and
the country is enabled to stay current in its international obligations
without resorting to (capital) restrictions.[4] Indeed, one of the considerations underlying the IMF programs to Asia, Russia, and Brazil
was to mitigate the overshooting of exchange rates and, as such, to
dampen the effects on other countries and contain the crisis.

**Why the IMF Should Not Be an International Lender of Last
Resort**

Although market failure and public good arguments provide a
rationale for an international monetary fund in the global financial
system, it would require somewhat of a leap of faith to argue that
the IMF should have comprehensive lender-of-last-resort responsibilities. Such a role would be neither feasible nor desirable.

Lack of Feasibility

The notion of lender of last resort is best known in a domestic
context, in which central banks stand ready to provide liquidity to
illiquid but solvent banks, usually against collateral and at a penalty
rate. Applying this concept to the IMF is inaccurate on at least
two counts.

First, the IMF, in contrast to a domestic central bank, cannot create
liquidity at will. The IMF's capital consists of member states' contributions, or so-called quotas, which usually require a government
appropriation and sometimes parliamentary approval. Given that
quota increases of the IMF require the approval of 85 percent of the
fund's membership, there is a high threshold for increases in the
IMF's capital. It should be added that increases in the IMF's capital
involve changes in the voting structure of the fund as well as a
country's access to IMF resources because the quotas themselves are
based on a member's economic size, which of course changes over
time. This only adds to the difficulty of getting quota increases

approved. Given the past difficulty in getting even the periodic five-year quota increases ratified by parliaments, it is highly unlikely that a lender-of-last-resort capability to create money at will would be any more acceptable to the governments of the 182 member states that make up the IMF.

There is one other way in which the IMF can contribute to financing deficits or strengthening reserves, apart from increases in its quota base. Since 1968 the IMF has been authorized to create Special Drawing Rights (SDRs). This authority was conferred in response to what was at the time perceived as a global liquidity problem (the Triffin dilemma), but that problem basically disappeared with the breakdown of the Bretton Woods system of fixed exchange rates. Consequently, the SDR never became the "primary reserve asset" it was once envisioned to be. At present, SDRs account for less than 1.5 percent of global foreign exchange reserves. Creating SDRs has proven to be even more difficult than increasing IMF quotas. Not only does it require a finding that there is a *global* liquidity need—which given the abundance of capital slushing around the world is hard to argue—but, as in the case of quota increases, it also requires approval of 85 percent of the voting power. Given that allocations of SDRs, in contrast to quota-lending, constitute a creation of unconditional liquidity, industrial member states have been understandably reluctant to agree to proposals for increasing international reserves in this manner. In the end, SDR creation runs into the same constraint as quota increases, namely that the governments of important shareholders do not favor endowing an international institution with an uncontrolled ability to create liquidity.[5]

Thus, it seems highly unlikely that the IMF's ability to create official financing will ever be able to keep up with the growth of international transactions. To illustrate this point, consider that in April 1999 the IMF's combined quota, or its capital base, amounted to roughly $300 billion. The actual availability of funds for lending is roughly half of that amount, though—a logical reflection of the fact that against countries with balance-of-payments deficits there are countries with balance-of-payments surpluses whose reserves are available for lending to deficit countries via the IMF. This compares, for instance, to an outstanding stock of debt of developing and transition countries of roughly $2.3 trillion and annual debt service costs of roughly $340 billion.[6] Moreover, the share of private sector debt in these totals is growing. Annual emerging market-bond issues, equity issues, and loan commitments already amount to roughly $300 billion, and this figure is growing rapidly. Not only are IMF resources dwarfed by private money, but the gap is also growing. As IMF deputy managing director Stanley Fischer has noted, if the IMF today were the same size relative to the output of its member states in 1945, it would be more than three times larger, and if the size of the fund had been maintained relative to the volume of world trade, it would be more than nine times larger—that is, the size of the fund would be more than $2.5 trillion.[7] Hence, it is clear that attempts by the IMF to provide financing apace with the growth in international transactions are unrealistic.[8]

The second reason that the lender-of-last-resort analogy does not hold up in an international context is that the IMF cannot make a distinction between solvent and insolvent countries. Indeed, the very concept of insolvency is not well suited to sovereign nations. It would not be possible, for example, to remove the government of a country in the same way one could remove the management of a bank. It would also be very difficult, if not impossible, for the IMF to find appropriate collateral against which to lend. Most countries do not have collateral, such as oil or gold, that could be transferred to the IMF when things go sour. Requiring collateral could therefore conflict with the principle of uniformity of treatment among IMF member states. In addition, given that most assets of a country are located within its borders, it would be difficult to actually attach assets when a loan is not repaid, absent the existence of an international bankruptcy court and any means to enforce its decisions.

Lack of Desirability

The foregoing arguments address only the feasibility, or lack thereof, of creating a global lender of last resort. An equally important question is whether it would even be desirable. The short answer, primarily from a moral hazard standpoint, is no.

A world in which the IMF was a full-fledged lender of last resort would presumably be a world in which the financial packages would have been of at least the same magnitude as those disbursed during the Asian, Russian, and Brazilian crises. But they would probably be larger. It is thus useful to start by analyzing whether the fund's existing lending creates an acceptable degree of moral hazard. Inevitably this amounts to a judgment call as moral hazard arises in any situation in which insurance is offered. An acceptable degree of moral hazard amounts to finding the right balance between financing and adjustment. More specifically it is a balance between (a) providing some degree of assurances to borrowing countries to help them gain time to adjust their economic policies in a way that avoids welfare-destroying measures such as trade and payments restrictions, an excessively abrupt reduction of domestic demand, and overshooting exchange rates, and (b) the degree to which such financing shields the private sector from losses, thereby affecting their future investment behavior.

The vast majority of creditors in Asia, Russia, and Brazil, particularly those investing in stocks, time deposits, or local currency bonds, and those with claims on corporations, have experienced a significant loss on their investments. The Institute of International Finance, for instance, has estimated that losses, in mid-1998, since the start of the crisis, could have amounted to about $350 billion, $240 billion of which consisted of equity losses, $60 billion of commercial bank losses, while $50 billion pertained to other foreign investors.[9] That these estimates are vulnerable to the date of measurement, given the prevailing exchange rate and stock market prices (both of which have recovered significantly since mid-1998), is shown by another estimate provided by Federal Reserve chairman Alan Greenspan in February 1998. He estimated that Asian equity losses alone, excluding Japanese companies, amounted to $700 billion between June 1997 and January 1998.[10]

Whether or not moral hazard has occurred is not dependent on the mere existence of losses, however. What matters is whether the degree to which an investor perceives to have taken losses is such that future behavior will be affected. Put differently, an investor who is scrambling to invest in Russian GKOs (ruble-denominated government bonds) at 130 percent interest rates or in Russian Eurobonds with a spread of 2,000 basis points is fully aware of the possibility of a ruble devaluation. Future investment behavior in short-term GKOs could well be unaffected. Similarly, it is entirely plausible that an investor who had been investing since the late 1980s in Thailand, which was growing at almost double-digit growth rates for over a decade, would not hesitate for a second to make that same investment again even though he or she may have taken a loss in 1997. Whether moral hazard arises depends on an individual's risk-return analysis and the extent to which that assessment materializes. Clearly, this is almost impossible to assess, which is perhaps why the IMF has refrained from conducting any serious empirical analysis of the degree of moral hazard arising from its aid packages.

But even if we accept that sometimes significant losses were incurred by certain groups of creditors, it is still possible to identify two groups for whom this was not the case and for whom official financing was likely to have helped shield them from losses: holders of short-term foreign currency denominated debt and domestic residents transferring funds abroad. In all crisis countries official financing facilitated the outflow of capital. Even in Brazil, which still had significant reserves of its own, official money can be said to have financed the capital outflow (as money is, of course, fungible). Brazil in 1998, for instance, was estimated to run a $13.2 billion balance-of-payments deficit that would have entailed an equivalent loss in reserves. Due to some $10.2 billion in IMF and bilateral financing, the reserve loss was limited to $3 billion. Although it is impossible to track down whose dollar paid which creditor, the bottom line is that IMF financing, all else equal, loosens a country's budget constraint.[11]

The only way for the IMF to reduce moral hazard drastically is to cut down on the amount of financing it provides in times of crises. No secret has been made of the fact that not everyone on the IMF's board is equally enthusiastic about the IMF's newly created contingent credit line (CCL).[12] In its most pure form, this credit line is an up-front guarantee that the IMF will bail out a country that has in the past implemented adequate policies. Under such a system it would be difficult to maintain the conditionality associated with normal IMF lending. Stated differently, the CCL is a backward-looking reward program while a crisis is likely to require forward-looking policy adjustments. As such, and in contrast with traditional IMF facilities, the CCL seems to have shifted the emphasis from adjustment toward financing.

Fortunately, compared with the original prototype that was presented to the executive board, the final form of this facility at least constitutes a significant improvement. The eligibility criteria have been significantly strengthened so as to ensure that the fund will use this facility sparingly and, it is hoped, just for the strongest economies. In this regard, there are some requirements for ex ante private sector involvement (sound relations with creditors, limited short-term debt, no arrears, etc.) as well as certain stipulations on transparency and sound economic policy. In addition, it has been decided that if things were to go seriously wrong in a country after the IMF credit line has been committed, there would still be a board review prior to activation in which adjustment measures could be formulated.

The IMF as Indispensable Lender

The focus on large-scale financing by the IMF, particularly in a contingent capacity, does not mesh well with its traditional role as the "indispensable lender."[13] On average, the fund provides no more than 10 percent of the financing requirements of the countries that turn to it for support. The added value of the IMF lies not so much in its temporary liquidity support—although at the margin such financing can be important— but more in the economic dialogue it maintains with its member states and the conditionality it includes under its adjustment programs. This conditionality provides the international community with some leverage over a country's economic policies. As such, it can accelerate economic stabilization and mitigate potentially harmful externalities on third countries. Concerns about depreciating currencies were, for instance, very much at the center of the tight monetary policies prescribed by the IMF in both Asia and Brazil.

Because the IMF's involvement is seen by many as a safeguard against beggar-thy-neighbor policies, and as the best bet toward economic stabilization policies, many official lenders have made their own financing conditional on the existence of an IMF program. The Paris Club of official lenders, for instance, requires an IMF program to be in place before it can approve debt restructuring. The World Bank, similarly, uses IMF programs as a proxy for "a satisfactory macroeconomic situation" that is needed to be able to grant its own adjustment loans. The European Union, for its part, also tends to tie its financing to IMF programs. The private sector has, empirically at least, also tended to tie its financing to IMF programs, although this is, of course, not a formal link.

Thus, the IMF has a catalytic role in generating financing for its member states. But the fund's role as an indispensable lender goes beyond that. The IMF provides the markets with data on its member states and has for the first time recently published its assessment of a member state's economy. This will add to the amount of information available to markets and enable them to make better informed decisions. The fund has also developed the data dissemination standard, mentioned earlier, that serves as a benchmark for industrial countries and emerging markets to improve their frequency, timeliness, and coverage of reporting. Again, this should add to, and improve on, the pool of information available to the private sector. In addition, the fund is developing other standards that serve as reference points for its member states and which could help improve economic policies. In 1998 it already developed the Code of Good Practices on Fiscal Transparency. In 1999 it added a Code of Good Practices on Transparency in Monetary and Financial Policies. The IMF also continues to pressure member states in its regular surveillance activities to remove barriers to trade and capital account liberalization. All in all, the IMF, being a universal institution with 182 member states, is a vehicle for bringing about change in the way countries think about economic policies and the way in which they approach financial markets. As such, the IMF is an indispensable lender.

Private Sector Involvement

To argue that the IMF, that is, the official sector, should finance less is the reverse of saying that the private sector should do more. Not surprisingly, those countries on the IMF's Executive Board that are opposed to the IMF's lender-of-last-resort role are the same countries that have forcefully argued for greater private sector involvement in case of a crisis. But what does that mean? Essentially, it means leaving the markets alone to a greater extent than is currently the case and providing them with the tools to maximize recovery of loans in case a debtor runs into payment difficulties. As the term "private sector" is often misunderstood, however, and as it is critical to the fund's role as an indispensable lender rather than lender of last resort, it is useful to elaborate.

The private sector is, of course, already involved. Net private capital flows to emerging markets in 1996, the year before the crisis in Asia broke, amounted to $327 billion, compared with net official flows of $7 billion.[14] In flow terms, therefore, almost 99 percent of the new contracts with emerging markets belong to private creditors (admittedly this number is estimated to have fallen to 74 percent in

1998 due to a sharp fall in net private flows and a rise in net official flows). The fundamental premise on which the entire debate about "private sector involvement" is based is that these private contracts, or any contract for that matter, should be honored. What we at the IMF have been worried about is what to do when countries, or large groups of debtors backed up by government guarantees, do not honor contracts. How messy should that be? In a domestic context, there is bankruptcy legislation that provides such rules of the game as a standstill to prevent a "grab race" or fire sale of assets, protection of the seniority of creditor claims, equal treatment of foreign and domestic creditors, and so on. In an international context such rules are often absent.

There are two possibilities if a debtor cannot meet its obligations: The first is for the official community to provide temporary liquidity. This essentially prevents the private sector from taking a loss. Perhaps the clearest example is Mexico in 1994–95 when all bondholders were fully repaid according to their original maturity and interest rate coupons. The second possibility is to not put up the bailout money but to "push" the markets to either take a loss or postpone repayment. They are "pushed" in the sense that there is not enough money to go around, and not agreeing to some restructuring of the loans or bonds basically means taking a loss. This is what happened in Korea in December 1997 after a Mexico-type solution had failed first and both reserves and the official financing package from the IMF were exhausted. Those in the *private sector* who oppose private sector involvement—which admittedly is a confusing term—are essentially arguing for a government bailout and unwilling to let investors bear the full responsibility of their investment decisions. Those in the *official sector* who oppose private sector involvement tend to do so out of concern over an extreme economic downturn or loss of market access that can occur after a default and the negative externalities this can generate. This latter point, once again, shows that providing official financing is not a zero-sum game (a dollar less for the private sector does not mean a dollar more for the official sector). The negative effects on moral hazard could well be offset by the social gains from minimizing the crisis.

The debate about private sector involvement is more about the official sector doing less than the private sector doing more. Stated another way, the question is not whether the private sector should put up new money, although maintenance of exposure through a refinancing of existing lines amounts to the same thing, but rather how much money the official sector should put up. Although this is a judgment call, there is a widespread feeling of discomfort about how much money has been put up so far.

The debate about private sector involvement goes beyond the question of how large financial packages should be. Attention has focused, for instance, on preventing crises from happening in the first place and minimizing the group of short-term debt holders that tend to be primarily responsible (together with domestic residents) for triggering a crisis and putting the initial pressure on reserves and exchange rates. Thus, the IMF is now encouraging countries to think twice about what constitutes a healthy debt structure. This does not mean making it illegal for countries to accept short-term loans, but it does mean encouraging them to pay the higher premium associated with longer-term loans. The reasoning is that this higher premium in the short run could be offset by the long-run benefit of their being less prone to crisis and thus minimizing the need for official bailouts.

A variant of this encouragement of a healthy debt structure is the possible adoption of Chilean-type capital controls. Contrary to what seems to have become conventional wisdom in the press, however, there is still no consensus on the benefit of such capital controls because they are costly and over time can be easily circumvented. A more market-friendly approach would be to encourage countries to set up commercial contingent credit lines, such as those in place in Argentina, Canada, Indonesia, and Mexico. A country could buy this type of insurance to obtain access to liquidity if the market environment deteriorates. It is still somewhat unclear, however, if such lines really provide additional liquidity in times of crisis and are not offset by withdrawals from other sectors of the economy. In any case, even if the effect were to be zero, there would still be no harm in encouraging what are essentially private insurance contracts between debtors and creditors. All else being equal, such commercial credit lines, set up ex ante but activated ex post, should serve to make a country's debt structure healthier.

Another form of ex ante private sector involvement on which debate within the IMF has focused is strengthening bankruptcy legislation. By ensuring properly functioning bankruptcy regimes in times of economic calm, mass insolvencies as in the case of Indonesia could possibly be prevented.

An ex post form of private sector involvement includes certain kinds of majority voting clauses, sharing clauses, and collective action clauses in bond contracts that may make debt restructuring less messy, and therefore benefit both debtors and creditors.

Finally, the IMF could play a role as a coordinator in debt restructuring arrangements, as it has in Korea and Indonesia. The IMF helped these countries make presentations about the state of their economies during their "road shows" to investors. In addition, the fund set up a monitoring mechanism of creditor banks' rollover behavior in the run-up to the formal debt restructuring of bank claims and exchanged this information with the monetary authorities in creditor countries. This mechanism provided the various creditors some assurance that free-rider behavior would be limited, and it overcame the coordination problem of banks that would otherwise be tempted to run for the exit before other banks did.

These are all examples of a more modest role for the fund in acting as a "facilitator" and an "encourager," which contrasts with the more ambitious tendencies of lender-of-last-resort advocates.

Conclusion

The real debate about the current international financial architecture is not about whether or not a global lender of last resort should be created, nor is it about whether the IMF should be abolished. Indeed, not one of the governments among the IMF's membership has argued seriously for either of these two extremes. Instead, discussion has centered on the appropriate degree of market intervention, the size of financial packages, and the extent to which the cost of a crisis should be shouldered by the international community or by the private sector. Although this is a judgment call, there is a danger that the IMF could be shifting in the wrong direction. This is highlighted not only by the increasingly large financial packages provided to emerging markets, but also by the recent creation of the CCL, which seems to indicate an inclination on the part of its proponents to play a risky game of bluff-poker with financial markets.

Instead of attempting to assume a role it was not set up to do, and which is neither feasible nor desirable, the fund should return to its core business of being an indispensable lender. By linking its credits to sound economic programs, acting as a conduit for information to financial markets, and performing a catalytic role in involving other parties, the IMF can continue to play a pivotal role in financial crisis management, albeit without providing the bulk of the financing needs.

Notes

The views expressed in this chapter are those of the authors and not necessarily those of the International Monetary Fund.

1. Paul Masson and Michael Mussa, *The Role of the IMF: Financing and Its Interactions with Adjustment and Surveillance,* IMF Pamphlet Series no. 50, International Monetary Fund (Washington, 1995).

2. Catherine L. Mann argues that private sector credit insurance could significantly influence herd mentality. See Mann, "Market Mechanisms to Reduce the Need for IMF Bailouts," *International Economic Policy Briefs* no. 99-4 (Washington: Institute for International Economics, February 1999). Barry Eichengreen, however, points out that there has been little interest from the private sector to provide such insurance. See Eichengreen, *Toward a New International Financial Architecture: A Practical Post-Asia Agenda* (Washington: Institute for International Economics, February 1999). George Soros's proposal for an international credit insurance agency may be seen in this light. Soros's proposal is fatally flawed, however, as it would inter alia further increase moral hazard. See Soros, *The Crisis of Global Capitalism* (New York: Public Affairs Press, 1998).

3. South Africa has in the past also had such contingent lines.

4. Age Bakker and Arend Kapteyn, "Financial Crisis Management and the Role of the IMF 1970–1995," in *Financial Crises Management in Regional Blocs,* ed. Scheherazade S. Rehman (Boston: Kluwer Academic Publishers, 1998).

5. The decision taken in 1997 to allocate SDR 21.4 billion (roughly $30 billion) is an exception in that it constitutes a special one-time allocation primarily aimed at providing SDRs to countries that were not members at the time of earlier allocations (mainly former communist countries). Actual allocation is, however, still awaiting ratification by a sufficient number of member states.

6. IMF, *World Economic Outlook and International Capital Markets; Interim Assessment* (Washington: International Monetary Fund, December 1998).

7. Stanley Fischer, *On the Need for an International Lender of Last Resort,* revised version of a paper for a meeting of the American Economic Association and the American Finance Association (New York, January 3, 1999).

8. The IMF does not finance international trade and capital transactions directly, but only the imbalances that occur in them. Under noncrisis conditions such imbalances might well grow less than proportionally with the volume of trade and payments. Nonetheless, it is hard to see how the IMF could keep up with the (presumably) less hectic growth of imbalances. Moreover, in crisis situations imbalances on account of reversal of capital flows tend to balloon.

9. Institute of International Finance, *Report of the Working Group on Financial Crises in Emerging Markets* (Washington: Institute of International Finance, January 1999).

10. Alan Greenspan, *Testimony before the Committee on Foreign Relations,* U.S. Senate, Washington, February 12, 1998.

11. This leaves aside the case in which the IMF program parameters would be so tight that a country's ability to use the money would be curtailed. This could be done by setting a high net-international-reserves target, pursuing a tight monetary and fiscal policy, and limiting the room under the monetary targets to provide liquidity support to banks or corporations.

12. Onno de Beaufort Wijnholds, "Maintaining an Indispensable Role," *Financial Times*, March 1, 1999, p. 16.

13. We clearly do not share Ariel Buira's analysis of an alternative approach to financial crises consisting of a lender-of-last-resort function to scare off "speculators." See Buira, *An Alternative Approach to Financial Crises*, Essays in International Finance no. 212 (Princeton, N.J.: Princeton University Press, February 1999).

14. Institute of International Finance.

13. Global Financial Markets and the International Monetary Fund

Lawrence H. White

> The right question is how well the financial system and the economy operate in such a regime compared with a relevant alternative, for instance one in which there is neither a lender of last resort nor deposit insurance.
>
> —Stanley Fischer (1999)

Stanley Fischer, deputy managing director of the International Monetary Fund (IMF), poses a pertinent question for the global financial system. How well would *laissez faire* work by contrast with the current regime, and by contrast with a regime in which the IMF takes on the additional role of an international lender of last resort? Specifically, how well do developing economies avoid exchange rate crises and banking system failures in a world without an official international lender of last resort (which, as I will emphasize, is not the same as being without *any* lender of last resort), and without the IMF? Not perfectly, so long as information is scarce. But better, I will argue, than they do in the presence of such institutions. Considering such fundamental policy questions will contribute something, I hope, to the voluminous literature on the instability of the current regime in which the focus is more often on incremental improvements.[1]

Exchange Rates and the Global Monetary System

Let us think seriously about the institutional character of a free-market global monetary system. We can then ask whether such a system would exhibit market failures—whether it would fail to provide public goods in the technical sense—and whether the IMF (once we seriously consider *its* institutional character) is likely to improve long-run economic performance by intervening.

241

A century ago, it would have been natural to assume an international silver or gold standard as the laissez-faire benchmark monetary system. Under a metallic standard, market forces in the mining industry, not government policies, determined the global quantity and purchasing power of metallic money. The forces of arbitrage, known to economists as the "price-specie-flow mechanism," equalized the purchasing power of gold in every country and distributed metallic monetary stocks across countries to match the distribution of the demand to hold them. The exchange rate between any two gold-standard countries was practically fixed by definition, variation being bounded narrowly within the "gold points" determined by shipping costs. The central exchange rate between the dollar and the pound, for example, was fixed by the ratio of the defined gold content of the dollar to the defined gold content of the pound. This, at least, was how the gold standard operated insofar as it was not impeded by central banks.

Today silver and gold have been demonetized. The final act in the drama that demonetized gold began with the Bretton Woods treaty that also created the International Monetary Fund. (How ironic, then, that the IMF's managing director, Michel Camdessus, proclaimed that it would be desirable for the leading central banks of the world to pursue policies providing "greater exchange rate stability."[2])

In a world of national fiat currencies, which exchange rate regime is most consistent with free financial markets? Certainly *not* the sort of regime that has been crumbling throughout the less developed world in recent years, in which the central bank temporarily pegs domestic currency at an artificial price in terms of some foreign currency, but retains discretion to devalue. Not only is this a price-fixing scheme, but even the advocates of that system now appear to recognize that it cannot be sustained without quantitative controls on financial flows.[3]

A country has two noninterventionist alternatives: (1) maintain a distinct national currency and let the foreign exchange market freely determine the appropriate exchange rate against other national currencies, as most developed countries (outside the Euro zone) do today, or (2) adopt an external currency as the definitive money, that is, officially "dollarize" or "euroize." Panama is the most discussed example of a dollarized economy today, and Argentina has been much discussed as a candidate for official dollarization.[4] Like Panama, any member of the Euro zone relies on interregional flows of high-powered money—the fiat-money equivalent of the price-specie-flow mechanism—to maintain external balance.

Because no exchange-rate fixing is practiced under either of these two alternatives, there is no danger of exchange rate crisis (inability to sustain a fixed rate), and accordingly no rationale for imposing exchange controls. Neither system requires any external help in defending the exchange rate. In a world in which all countries practice free floating or dollarization, the IMF's core reason for existing vanishes.

Which of these two alternatives, a free float or dollarization, is better for the public in a developing country? In any concrete case it depends on a number of factors, primarily transactional network economies and the relative trustworthiness of the domestic versus the foreign currency. Members of the public can weigh these factors for themselves. (The traditional analysis of "optimal currency areas," by contrast, focuses on macroeconomic criteria from the viewpoint of a central planner, and dubiously assumes that the discretion to devalue helps dampen business cycles.) In a free economy the national government respects the public's preferences, and does not restrict "choice in currency."[5]

Those who observe that Federal Reserve notes now circulate in Panama often assume that dollarization implies the circulation of foreign currency notes, and that it correspondingly implies the loss of seigniorage to the central bank that issues the definitive money (absent a rebate treaty). They consider the loss of seigniorage a price that must be paid for dollarization. In fact the circulation of foreign notes is entirely the result of avoidable legal restrictions that prevent domestic banks from issuing notes. As they do today in Scotland and Northern Ireland (two "sterlingized" economies), domestic banks can issue currency notes denominated in and redeemable for the definitive foreign money (there, Bank of England notes).[6] In the absence of reserve requirements, competition among the domestic banks will distribute the potential seigniorage on currency to the banks' customers, typically in the form of unpriced services. In Northern Ireland, where four issuing banks are competing for clientele, there are no fees for withdrawing notes from the banks' automatic teller machines, and the machines are easy to find.[7]

Where we observe unofficial dollarization of transactions in financial markets (savings and debts) and commodity markets (cash for goods), and especially where it has taken place despite legal obstacles, we can infer that the public clearly prefers the money produced by a foreign central bank over the money produced domestically. We can infer a clear preference rather than possible near-indifference because people typically incur a non-negligible cost of switching over to a second currency. Where the domestic central bank fails to win a majority market share *voluntarily*, that is, without support from legal restrictions that compel people to accept and use its currency, it has failed the market test. The national government would conform to the market verdict if it were to make the de facto standard the official standard.

There is of course an option short of dollarization that has been viewed as providing immunity from an exchange-rate crisis, namely the "currency board" type of arrangement, most famously practiced today (with varying degrees of orthodoxy) by Hong Kong and Argentina. Because an orthodox currency board backs the domestic monetary base 100 percent with foreign currency assets, it will never run out of reserves even under the most severe speculative attack. Devaluation risk would therefore seem to be zero. And yet in recent years the Hong Kong dollar and the Argentine peso *have* come under attack by speculators fearing devaluation. (At the respective times of attack, Argentina had less than 100 percent reserves, whereas Hong Kong had several times more than 100 percent reserves. Devaluation did not in fact occur in either case.) Nominal interest rates on Argentine peso accounts continue to be distinctly higher than rates on dollar accounts of the same maturity in the same banks, the difference representing perceived devaluation risk. Although a currency board always has the *ability* to buy back the entire monetary base at the fixed exchange rate, and thus is less prone to attack than a central bank that pegs with smaller reserves, speculators may worry about the government's *willingness* to let monetary contraction go very far before choosing instead to devalue.

Dollarization with competitive note issue leaves entirely to commercial banks the eminently commercial business of issuing media of exchange that are claims to dollars. It correspondingly imposes on them the responsibility for holding adequate dollar reserves. There are good reasons to believe that claims on private institutions are generally more enforceable and hence more trustworthy than claims on sovereign institutions.[8] Starting from such a free-market regime, the establishment of a currency board is an interventionist measure in which the issue of currency claims, and the holding of dollar reserves, is inexplicably monopolized and nationalized. (Starting from a central bank, converting it to a currency board is a step toward dollarization.)

The Banking System

Much as speculators may choose to test the commitment of a central bank or currency board to par redemption, holders of the notes and demand deposits of a commercial bank may choose to test *its* commitment. Under dollarization (or a currency board) there is no domestic central bank to act as lender of last resort or to back up any deposit guarantee system through an ability to print cash ad lib. The domestic banks are seemingly on their own. Critics have accordingly suggested that a currency board or dollarization eliminates exchange rate crises only at the cost of more frequent banking crises.

The Argentine banking crisis of 1995, which occurred under a (less than fully orthodox) currency board regime without explicit deposit guarantees, is sometimes cited as evidence of such a trade-off. That crisis, however, was an attack on the peso, not a run on the banks per se. The banks predominantly lost peso-denominated deposits, not dollar-denominated deposits. The attackers doubted the currency board's commitment, not the banks' solvency. Under complete dollarization such an attack would not have occurred.

In my view it is neither necessary (for achieving financial stability) nor desirable for a government to immunize bank creditors from losses, whether through implicit guarantees or through an explicit system of deposit insurance. History shows us many competitive and stable banking systems without deposit guarantees, including the offshore banking ("Eurodollar") market of the last forty years.[9] In the absence of deposit guarantees, banks maintain higher capital ratios and hold safer asset portfolios. A bank's assets are better diversified, more liquid, and lower on default risk, exchange-rate risk, and interest-rate risk (duration mismatch), all of which assures the public of the bank's solvency. If necessary, clearinghouse associations can provide credible third-party certification of solvency and

245

liquidity. Banks that do become insolvent are immediately closed. Shareholders and unsecured creditors take losses, and accordingly depositors and other potential bank creditors learn to be cautious.[10]

In the historical banking systems closest to laissez faire, contagion effects have been closest to absent. As economist Charles Calomiris correctly summarizes the general record, "Random, irrational attacks on financial systems are not evident in financial history. Thus concerns of 'irrational contagion' spreading from one country to another without any fundamental explanatory link connecting the countries are unwarranted."[11] The banking systems that historically have displayed chronic weakness and contagion effects have typically been those subjected to legal restrictions that have prevented banks from diversifying or otherwise from offering adequate solvency assurances.[12] To avoid weakness, a government should not hamstring banks' efforts to behave soundly, or block market mechanisms that punish unsound banks.

Many economists disagree, believing that banks and banking systems *are* inherently fragile, because we do observe historical instances of instability (which they erroneously attribute to laissez faire). Treasury Secretary Lawrence H. Summers, for example, states that "the experience of the 1930s is hardly encouraging regarding the stability of laissez-faire financial systems." It is unclear just where Summers imagines that laissez-faire financial systems existed in the 1930s. If he refers to the waves of banking failures in the United States, it should be noted that those involved small-unit banks whose weakness was the product of geographic (branching) restrictions, not of laissez faire. The freely branched Canadian system had no bank failures in the 1930s.[13]

We do have *theoretical models* of purely self-justifying runs, in which it is arbitrary whether the public runs upon a bank (and so a bad equilibrium occurs) or does not. In the canonical bank-run model of economists Douglas Diamond and Philip Dybvig, rational depositors may run the bank purely out of concern that a run by other depositors will cause the bank to fail.[14] The rationale for deposit insurance is to preserve a good equilibrium by removing the incentive to run. In a world where self-justifying fears are the *only* reason for runs, and runs are the *only* reason for bank failures, deposit insurance does its job without ever actually being called upon to make a payout. Clearly, this is not the world in which we actually live.[15]

In the real world, bank runs have typically been triggered not by purely self-justifying fears but by bad news casting reasonable doubt on the bank's pre-run solvency. Bank insolvency has typically been due not to runs but to bad loans. Deposit insurance is consequently not costless, as U. S. taxpayers learned all too well when the exhaustion of the thrift industry deposit insurance fund in the 1980s left them with a tab of more than $150 billion. Deposit insurance exposes taxpayers to losses and encourages morally hazardous banking by reducing depositor vigilance.

Some economists have likened the 1997 Thai exchange rate crisis to a self-justifying bank run. This is at best an explanation of last resort. The more plausible alternative to the "self-feeding investor panic" account is a "bad news" account: investors and bank depositors received news (for example, news raising the probability that the central bank would pursue easy money to keep the banking system afloat) that cast reasonable doubt on the sustainability of the exchange rate. The "stampede to the exits" was not the realization of a bad equilibrium when a good equilibrium remained equally sustainable, but an information cascade revealing that the fundamentals had shifted far enough to render unsustainable the previous constellation of investor expectations and positions. The flight of capital was a vote of no confidence in anticipated Thai government policies.

Deposit Guarantees

Suppose that a government chooses to adopt a deposit-guarantee system. Does that choice in turn favor a floating exchange rate regime over dollarization because the central bank's ability to print cash ad lib (absent under dollarization) ultimately backs the deposit guarantee? Not necessarily. The ability to run the printing presses does not guarantee that the *real* value of all bank liabilities can be repaid, only that the *nominal* value can be repaid, so it does not completely immunize depositors from potential loss. A government unwilling to monetize the debts of its deposit guarantee fund ultimately backs the fund with its readiness and ability to borrow and to impose future taxes. (For example, the U.S. government was unwilling simply to print the $150 billion required to cover the debts of its savings and loan guarantee fund, because doing so would have meant increasing the monetary base, and ultimately the price level, by about 50 percent. Many developing country bank insolvency losses in recent years have been larger than the U.S. losses as a share of gross domestic product (GDP). The credibility of a deposit-guarantee system is thus largely independent of the government's ability to print cash.

Most important, the discretion to print cash to (nominally) bail out depositors, or more generally to pursue easy money to keep domestic banks afloat, is not a costless option. The option would be costly even if its actual use could be strictly limited. But as is well known, when the central bank seemingly has the option to inflate away real economic problems, solemn promises to strictly limit its use are likely to prove time-inconsistent.[16] In the context of a pegged exchange rate, the option to bail out domestic banks increases the danger of speculative attack on the exchange rate because the discretion to use monetary policy for that (or any other) purpose is the discretion to pursue a policy inconsistent with maintaining the peg. In the context of a floating rate, it increases the perceived risk of exchange rate swings. In both cases it will discourage long-term cross-currency investments. As economist Rudiger Dornbusch puts it, a government "can choose to visit exchange rate surprises on investors but it will be charged for that option with a currency risk premium and a shortening of economic horizons," and consequently a higher cost of capital to its economy.[17] Dollarization provides the most credible precommitment available not to inflate.[18]

The Lender-of-Last-Resort Role

Stanley Fischer raises the question of the need for an international lender of last resort to suggest that the IMF's mission and its resources should be expanded (yet again) to equip it more fully for that role.[19] Somewhat surprisingly, two of the strongest critics of the IMF's current modus operandi have recently suggested that the IMF would change from bane to blessing *if* it became a genuine lender of last resort and nothing else.[20]

The function of a "lender of last resort," in the standard sense of the term, is to address a systemwide liquidity problem.[21] The classic problem is an "internal drain"—most dramatically a banking panic—in which an apprehensive public withdraws funds from banks on a scale that threatens to deplete the (fractional-reserve) banking system of reserves. Unabated, a panic forces a sharp contraction in the quantity of bank liabilities and correspondingly in bank lending. More generally, an illiquidity problem occurs when many holders of short-term financial liabilities suddenly decline to roll them over. The classic solution is an injection of "high-powered money" (the type of money that serves as bank reserves). The injection can be made by lending it to illiquid banks, as the term "lender of last resort" suggests. But if the lender of last resort is a central bank in a modern financial system, it can instead make the injection—and there are strong moral hazard arguments for preferring that it do so—through open-market purchases of securities.[22] In such cases the "lender of last resort" does no actual lending.

What creates the need for a lender of last resort? Fischer and others suggest that a lender of last resort addresses a financial system weakness that stems from some sort of market failure under laissez faire (perhaps a coordination failure or a contagion externality). They cite Walter Bagehot's classic (and still relevant) brief urging the Bank of England to take on the role.[23] But this is *not* the argument Bagehot made. He argued that the bank's acting as a lender of last resort would offset weakness in the system *created by legal restrictions*, namely, the very restrictions that had given the Bank of England its artificially predominant position.

Bagehot argued that "whatever bank or banks keep the ultimate banking reserve of the country must lend that reserve most freely in time of apprehension." The Bank of England through "privileges and monopolies" had acquired the "very anomalous" and "very dangerous" position of being the sole holder of ultimate (at that time, gold) reserves: "Whether rightly or wrongly, at present and in fact the Bank of England keeps our ultimate bank reserve, and therefore it must use it in this manner." A bank in that position is "the only place where at such a moment new [high-powered] money is to be had." It should provide new high-powered money to the market when an internal drain threatens to contract the banking system and commercial credit. Further, it should assure the market in advance that it will pursue such a policy, to allay depositors' apprehensions that if they do not withdraw now their banks will be out of reserves and unable to pay when they do need to withdraw. Such actions would not be a sacrifice but would be in the bank's own interest because they would help to protect *its* reserves.[24]

By contrast to England's anomalous "one-reserve system," Bagehot understood that "the natural system—that which would have sprung up if Government had let banking alone" is a "many-reserve system" in which "no single bank . . . gets so much before the others that the others voluntarily place their reserves in its keeping."[25] As in Scotland, each bank instead keeps its own reserves. Liquidity needs can then be met by an interbank market containing many potential lenders. Thus, contrary to economist Allan Meltzer's restatement, Bagehot did not believe in general that "a financial system requires a lender of last resort to assist financial institutions in a liquidity crisis."[26] In Bagehot's view only an artificial "one-reserve system" requires it.

In cases in which the IMF lent before 1990 to enable a central bank to maintain an exchange rate peg in the face of balance-of-payments problems (an *external* drain), it clearly did *not* act as a Bagehotian lender of last resort. As many have noted, when the IMF lent to Mexico in 1995 and the troubled Asian countries in 1997–98, *after* exchange-rate collapse and capital flight had already occurred, it again did *not* act as a lender of last resort.[27] It rather aimed to recapitalize insolvent banks and to insulate investors and lenders (particularly large U.S. banks) from losses. Again, a lender of last resort addresses an immediate *illiquidity* problem due to an incipient *internal* drain. It does not attempt to finance an *external* drain and does not attempt to fix an *insolvency* problem due to poor lending decisions. It certainly does not seek to insulate international lenders from losses as the IMF has done.

An institution can play the lender-of-last-resort role if and only if it can increase the financial system's stock of high-powered money at the appropriate time. Fischer is correct when he states that this does not strictly require the power to create new high-powered money ad lib, the way a discretionary central bank on a fiat standard can.[28] But the ability of any other institution to provide liquidity will be limited to the amount of stockpiled high-powered money it can disburse. An orthodox currency board, because it is not allowed to go below 100 percent reserves, can act as a lender of last resort only if it stockpiles reserves in excess of 100 percent. The IMF could act as a lender of last resort to a dollar-based financial system only to the extent of its own stockpile of dollars.

The lender of last resort need not be a public agency. It can readily be a private bankers' bank, an institution whose liabilities other banks hold as reserves, as the Bank of England was when Bagehot addressed it, and as private clearinghouse association (CHA) banks were in the late 19th-century United States. A bankers' bank (provided that its members authorize it to do so, as they did in the case of CHA banks) can expand total bank reserves by expanding its own liabilities. As noted, Bagehot urged the Bank of England that last-resort lending was in the bank's own interest. The CHAs in various U.S. cities came to recognize and use to their own advantage their potential to expand the stock of their members' reserves during the banking panics of the pre-Fed era.[29] In ordinary periods, an illiquid bank was expected to borrow from, or sell assets to, holders of existing high-powered money. But in a panic such loans and asset sales were extraordinarily costly because interest rates were high and because potential lenders (other than the CHA, which audited its members regularly) lacked timely credible assurance of the borrowing bank's solvency. Illiquid banks needed last-resort loans to avoid "fire sale" losses from hastily liquidating assets in an extreme buyer's market. Ex ante agreement to a CHA policy of extending loans in panics served as coinsurance against an individual member bank's risk of finding itself in such a bind.[30]

To control moral hazard, Bagehot prescribed that the lender of last resort should lend at a "penalty" rate (higher than the nonpanic interbank rate, and high enough to make the borrower regret having gotten into the position of needing the loan), and should lend only to solvent (but illiquid) intermediaries that would repay. The Bank of England at that time lacked audited financial information on other commercial banks or bill brokers, so Bagehot proposed as an assurance of repayment that the borrower must offer high-quality and sufficient collateral. CHA practice in the United States was consistent with Bagehot's prescription, and the default rate on CHA loans was negligible.

Meltzer proposes an international lender of last resort to address liquidity problems for banks and nonbank institutions with foreign-currency liabilities, but rightly emphasizes the penalty rate and collateral requirements:

> If loans denominated in foreign currencies are withdrawn suddenly, solvent borrowers with excellent long-term prospects are unable to repay their short-term loans on demand. Neither they nor their local banks may be able to obtain sufficient foreign exchange to prevent default.

One solution is to have a true lender of last resort. Unlike the IMF, a true lender of last resort does not subsidize borrowers. It charges a penalty rate—a rate above the market rate—and requires good collateral. It offers to lend at a penalty rate to anyone offering proper collateral.[31]

Together, Bagehot's (or Meltzer's) prescription and CHA practice suggest a simple test for a successful lender of last resort. Because it lends at a penalty rate, and because its clients are solvent and rarely default on their loans, a successful lender of last resort *earns at the least the normal rate of return* on its lending.

But if a lender of last resort can earn a normal rate of return, then there is a private incentive to undertake the role where needed. What rationale remains for assigning the role to a government institution like a central bank or the IMF? There is none.[32] Provided that it can demonstrate its willingness and ability to repay, an illiquid bank in a dollarized economy can borrow from other commercial banks with dollar reserves or (if it is a member of one) from a private clearinghouse association. If timely solvency assurances are difficult to provide on the spot, a prudent bank will arrange standby lines of credit from a correspondent bank or consortium of banks domiciled in the country in which the reserve currency is issued, to which it provides whatever financial information is required. Local branches or subsidiaries of dollar-center banks—that today provide more than half of Argentine bank deposits—will be able to draw reserves on a moment's notice from their parent institutions.

The Moral Hazard of Actual IMF Lending

The moral hazard problem with IMF lending, as it has actually been practiced, is now well understood.[33] A market without deposit guarantees or IMF bailouts would not subsidize risk-bearing and would reward prudence. IMF lending programs, no doubt unintentionally, have by contrast encouraged at least two sorts of morally hazardous behavior: excessively risky (mostly short-term) lending by private creditors (including U.S. banks) who are encouraged to show too little regard for credit and devaluation risks, and gambling by the finance ministers who are encouraged to neglect the risk of the exchange-rate crisis when pursuing monetary policies in conflict with maintaining a fixed peg to the dollar.

Some defenders of the IMF believe that concern with moral hazard is overblown. In the Asian crises, they note, equity investors have suffered large losses, while banks and other creditors have also taken some losses. Regarding government behavior, they argue that governments have also suffered and thus would not have deliberately provoked a crisis. They are missing the point: moral hazard is not all-or-nothing, but operates at the margin. Any IMF policy that promises to reduce the losses of banks and bondholders reduces their prudence in like measure. Any policy that allows finance ministers to delay the day of reckoning reduces their caution, especially so where political instability makes their planning horizons short. It is no coincidence that since 1982, as the IMF has shifted toward a policy of intervening more actively in exchange rate and banking crises as they arise, insulating lenders from losses in the hope that this will stem short-run "contagion" effects, the frequency and size of crises have increased.

Is it likely that the IMF could switch from the imprudent lending it has practiced to prudent last-resort lending? To succeed, a lender of last resort must accurately identify viable borrowers from among institutions viewed as nonviable or doubtful (hence denied funds) by ordinary creditors. As Federal Reserve economists Stephen Smith and Larry Wall put it, a successful lender of last resort must "know, at least temporarily, more than the market."[34] Otherwise its lending will prolong the life of loss-making institutions that ought to be closed. It is difficult to imagine that an international agency like the IMF could ever have a systematic informational advantage over the financial players, on the spot, regarding the viability of particular financial institutions. It is therefore difficult to imagine the IMF succeeding at last-resort lending. My conclusion is that the IMF should stop lending, period.

Notes

I have received helpful feedback from Larry Wall, Joe Sinkey, Jerry Dwyer, and Roberto Chang. They are absolved from responsibility for the views expressed here and any remaining errors.

1. For a wide sample of the literature available on the Internet, see http://www.stern.nyu.edu/~nroubini/asia/AsiaHomepage.html.

2. Michel Camdessus, "International Financial and Monetary Stability: A Global Public Good?" (remarks at the IMF Research Conference "Key Issues in Reform of the International Monetary and Financial System," Washington, May 28, 1999).

3. Paul Krugman, "Saving Asia: It's Time to Get Radical," *Fortune* 138 no. 5 (September 7, 1998), p. 74ff.

4. On the case for dollarization, see Steve H. Hanke and Kurt Schuler, "A Dollarization Blueprint for Argentina," Cato Institute Foreign Policy Briefing no. 52, March 12, 1999; and Guillermo Calvo, "On Dollarization" (unpublished ms., University of Maryland, April 20, 1999).

5. Friedrich Hayek, *Choice in Currency: A Way to Stop Inflation* (London: Institute of Economic Affairs, 1976).

6. It is a mystery to me why Panama does not allow private note issue, and especially why it did not do so during the 1989 conflict when the U.S. government's embargo of Federal Reserve note shipments to Panama caused a shortage of unworn paper currency in the country.

7. On the efficiency of nonprice competition in currency see Lawrence H. White and Donald J. Boudreaux, "Is Nonprice Competition in Currency Inefficient?" *Journal of Money, Credit, and Banking* 30 (May 1998): 252–60.

8. George A. Selgin and Lawrence H. White, "Credible Commitments in Private and Central Banking" (unpublished ms., University of Georgia, July 1999).

9. Granted, some depositors might think that the offshore affiliates of major U.S. or European banks have some sort of implicit guarantees from the governments of their parent institutions' countries. But offshore bank balance sheets do differ from those of their onshore parents, and look like those of banks from the days before deposit guarantees.

10. For a discussion of modern financial market institutions and contractual mechanisms for promoting credibility and stability, see Randall S. Kroszner, "The Role of Private Regulation in Maintaining Global Financial Stability," *Cato Journal* 18 (Winter 1999): 355–61.

11. Charles W. Calomiris, "The IMF's Imprudent Role as Lender of Last Resort," *Cato Journal* 17 (Winter 1998): 289.

12. George A. Selgin and Lawrence H. White, "How Would the Invisible Hand Handle Money?" *Journal of Economic Literature* 32 (December 1994): 1718–49.

13. See Lawrence H. Summers, "Distinguished Lecture on Economics in Government: Reflections on Managing Global Integration," *Journal of Economic Perspectives* 13 (Spring 1999): 13. Barrie A. Wigmore provides evidence that the 1933 crisis in the U.S. banking system was due to a run on the dollar prompted by (correct) anticipation of a devaluation by the U.S. government, which is to say, was *not* due to an instability of laissez faire. See Wigmore, "Was the Bank Holiday of 1933 Caused by a Run on the Dollar?" *Journal of Economic History* 48 (September 1987): 739–55.

14. See Douglas W. Diamond and Philip H. Dybvig, "Bank Runs, Deposit Insurance, and Liquidity," *Journal of Political Economy* 91 (June 1983): 409–19.

15. If we did live in such a world, the bank itself could readily modify its deposit contract in a mutually agreeable way to eliminate the incentive to run; government deposit guarantees are unnecessary. See Lawrence H. White, *The Theory of Monetary Institutions* (Oxford: Basil Blackwell, 1999), pp. 121–33, for an exposition and critique of the Diamond–Dybvig model. For an application of a Diamond–Dybvig type model to the Asian crisis, see Roberto Chang and Andrés Velasco, "The Asian Liquidity Crisis," NBER Working Paper 6796 (November 1998).

16. Finn E. Kydland and Edward C. Prescott, "Rules Rather than Discretion: The Inconsistency of Optimal Plans," *Journal of Political Economy* 85 (June 1977): 473–91.

17. Rudiger Dornbusch, "The Brazil Problem: V-Shaped Recovery and Beyond" (unpublished ms., April 1999), p. 8, available online at http://web.mit.edu/rudi/www/PDF/wbank-brazil1/PDF.

18. Most credible, but not irrevocable. A government bent on devaluation could undo dollarization, just as governments bent on devaluation undid the gold standard even where gold coins circulated.

19. Stanley Fischer, "On the Need for an International Lender of Last Resort," a slightly revised version of a paper prepared for delivery at the joint meeting of the American Economic Association and the American Finance Association, New York, January 3, 1999. Available online at http://www.imf.org/external/np/speeches/1999/010399.htm. Some of the IMF's supporters mistakenly think that the agency already serves as a lender of last resort. See, for example, Stephan Haggard, "Why We Need the IMF," *IGCC Newsletter* (Spring 1998).

20. Charles W. Calomiris, "How to Invent a New IMF," American Enterprise Institute *On the Issues* paper, May 1999; and Allan H. Meltzer, "What's Wrong with the IMF? What Would Be Better?" in *The Asian Financial Crisis: Origins, Implications, and Solutions*, ed. William C. Hunter, George G. Kaufman, and Thomas H. Krueger (Boston, Mass.: Kluwer Academic Publishers, 1999).

21. Federal Reserve economists V. V. Chari and Patrick Kehoe distinguish two conceptions of the lender-of-last-resort role: "bailout" versus "provider of liquidity." The standard concept is the latter. See Chari and Kehoe, "Asking the Right Questions about the IMF," Federal Reserve Bank of Minneapolis Annual Report (1998). The following discussion draws on White, *The Theory of Monetary Institutions*, pp. 74–77.

22. Marvin Goodfriend and Robert A. King, "Financial Deregulation, Monetary Policy, and Central Banking," in *Restructuring Banking and Financial Services in America*, ed. William S. Haraf and Rose M. Kushmeider (Washington: American Enterprise Institute, 1988); and Chari and Kehoe, "Asking the Right Questions about the IMF."

23. Walter Bagehot, *Lombard Street: A Description of the Money Market* (London: Henry S. King, 1873).

24. Ibid., pp. 57–71.

25. Ibid., pp. 66–68.

26. Allan H. Meltzer, "What's Wrong with the IMF?" p. 255.

27. See Calomiris, "The IMF's Imprudent Role," and Anna J. Schwartz, "Time to Terminate the ESF and the IMF," Cato Institute Foreign Policy Briefing no. 48, August 26, 1998.

28. Stanley Fischer, "On the Need for an International Lender of Last Resort."

29. Richard H. Timberlake, "The Central Banking Role of Clearinghouse Associations," *Journal of Money, Credit, and Banking* 16 (February 1984): 1–15.

30. Gary Gorton, "Clearinghouse and the Origin of Central Banking in the United States," *Journal of Economic History* 45 (June 1995): 277–83.

31. Meltzer, "Asian Problems and the IMF," *Cato Journal* 17 (Winter 1998): 272.

32. Michael D. Bordo and Anna J. Schwartz anticipate this conclusion: "Were today's monetary authorities, including the IMF, to lend at short term at a penalty rate on good collateral that exceeds the value of the loan, they would be following Bagehot's principles. However, in a world of deep capital markets, such as prevails today, there are few good reasons why the private markets cannot perform this role." See Bordo and Schwartz, "Under What Circumstances, Past and Present, Have International Rescues of Countries in Financial Distress Been Successful?" NBER Working Paper 6824, December 1998, p. 48.

33. See Calomiris, "The IMF's Imprudent Role," and Meltzer, "Asian Problems and the IMF."

34. Stephen D. Smith and Larry D. Wall, "Financial Panics, Bank Failures, and the Role of Regulatory Policy," Federal Reserve Bank of Atlanta *Economic Review* (January/February 1992): 1–11.

14. Repairing the Lender-Borrower Relationship in International Finance

Ian Vásquez

> When it becomes necessary for a state to declare itself bankrupt, in the same manner as when it becomes necessary for an individual to do so, a fair, open, and avowed bankruptcy is always the measure which is both least dishonorable to the debtor, and least hurtful to the creditor.
>
> —Adam Smith
> *The Wealth of Nations*

A dysfunctional relationship has developed between lenders and borrowers in international finance. Governments have gotten their countries into trouble with their creditors for hundreds of years, and periodic problems with repaying loans will surely continue to be a feature of global finance well into the future. Yet since the 1980s the resolution of financial problems has often treated insolvency as illiquidity and attempted to shield creditors and debtor governments from economic reality, creating disorderly debt workouts in the process.

It is not clear whether that approach, largely the result of International Monetary Fund (IMF) credit and mediation, has ultimately benefited either debtor states or their creditors. The IMF bailed out private investors in Mexico in 1995 and has bailed them out in Asia and Brazil since 1997, leaving ordinary citizens to pay the bill. Fund officials recognize this problem and propose to expand the IMF's practice of lending to countries that have accumulated arrears with private-sector creditors. The fund has simultaneously instituted a credit line to provide emergency funds before a crisis erupts. But the rationale for this schizophrenic behavior—that such actions are necessary to maintain stability, limit the severity of financial crises, and bail in the private sector—remains dubious. Direct two-party

257

negotiations between lenders and borrowers have proved superior to the three-party approach characterized by IMF-led interventions.

A Consensus for Change

Widespread dissatisfaction with the way the IMF handled the Asian and subsequent financial crises has prompted calls for reform of the IMF and, more ambitiously, of the global financial architecture.[1] Even the fund agrees that important changes need to be made in the way it operates. It has promised, for example, to become more transparent, allowing outside economists, policymakers, and market participants to better evaluate its performance and those of its client countries by publicly releasing letters of intent, country reviews, and other internal documents. It remains to be seen whether the lending bureaucracy will in fact become transparent enough to produce greater accountability.

Even before the current era of massive bailouts, the fund had come under criticism, notably after the 1970s collapse of the Bretton Woods system of fixed exchange rates that the IMF managed. Financial turmoil in the 1990s only increased the criticism and led many economists to recommend that the fund be shut down.[2] Though in principle the fund provides short-term credit on the condition that governments improve their macroeconomic policies and introduce structural reforms, in practice it has granted credit to dozens of governments for decades. Seventy countries have depended on IMF credit for 20 or more years (see Appendices A and B). Once a country receives IMF credit, it is likely to remain dependent on fund aid for most, if not all, of the following years[3] (see Figure 14.1). Such a record does not speak well either of the conditionality or of the temporary nature of IMF loans. The fund denies that its conditionality lacks credibility and that it has made loan addicts of nations with some of the worst economic policies. Many nations have, after all, reformed their economies and moved to the market, especially since the late 1980s. A proper evaluation of the fund's performance in reforming countries requires careful scrutiny of how the agency's money and advice were put to use in those cases.

By its own admission, the fund has not yet resolved two problems with the lender-borrower relationship that became acute in the 1990s: how to become a credible surveillance agency that prevents crises from occurring and how to avoid creating moral hazard.[4] The IMF's

Figure 14.1
IMF CREDIT: PERCENTAGE OF YEARS USED BY NUMBER
OF COUNTRIES

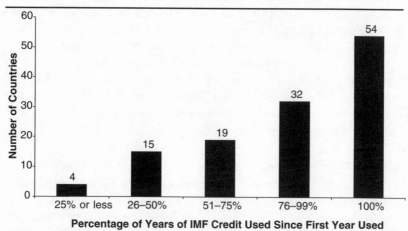

SOURCE: IMF, *International Financial Statistics* (various issues).

NOTE: Does not include Czechoslovakia or countries that first borrowed in 1995 or after.

role as a surveillance agency has been seriously tarnished by the Asian crisis. The fund provided no warning of the impending collapse of currencies and domestic banking systems and in fact lauded the East Asian economies in public documents shortly before the outbreak of the crisis. The financial community was not comforted by the fund's claims that the agency provided warnings to officials in Thailand but kept that information confidential. The episode highlights the inherent conflict in the fund's role as both a credit-rating agency for countries and an agency that attempts to prevent the eruption of financial turmoil. If the IMF detected alarming economic conditions in an emerging economy, the public release of that information would precipitate a crisis; not sounding the alarm, however, would further undermine the IMF's credibility as a surveillance agency. As long as the IMF attempts to play both roles, that systemic conflict will continue to exist.[5]

A prominent feature of recent IMF rescues has been their sheer size; the fund has arranged more than $180 billion in bailout packages since 1997. Economists Michael Bordo and Anna Schwartz observe that past international rescues involved lending small amounts of money to defend fixed exchange rates in return for improved policies, but that "recent bailouts involve handing over relatively large amounts to both foreign lenders and domestic investors *after* devaluation of a pegged exchange rate to avoid their incurring wealth losses."[6] Despite the resulting moral hazard, the IMF has downplayed the problem even as it has proposed initiatives to make the private sector take on greater losses in times of crisis. Because of the "rampant moral hazard" that the IMF creates, the Federal Reserve Bank of Minneapolis, for instance, concludes that "the IMF should cease its lending activities altogether."[7]

A Lender of First Resort?

The IMF, however, has chosen to move in the opposite direction. It has established a mechanism to provide bailout funds designed to prevent financial difficulties *before* countries experience them. The Contingent Credit Line (CCL) program, approved in April 1999, is intended to serve as "a precautionary line of defense" to stave off creditor panics in countries with fundamentally sound economies.[8] But the fund has not shown good judgment in determining what countries would benefit from preventive bailouts. The two times the fund provided such aid—to Russia (July 1998) and to Brazil (November 1998)—the bailouts failed to prevent currency devaluations and financial crises. The funds merely became gifts to speculators and financial institutions, leaving both countries in greater debt.

Even though the CCL establishes specific criteria for access to its resources, it creates major problems that only exacerbate creditor-borrower relationships. The most obvious one is that use of this IMF instrument will signal the markets that authorities believe a country's economy is under stress, thus creating a self-fulfilling prophecy. While proponents of the CCL believe its existence will provide markets with sufficient reassurance to keep it from ever having to be used—much in the way emergency liquidity funds from central banks provide confidence in domestic financial systems—the fund lacks any real ability to instill such confidence since it cannot create unlimited amounts of money as can a traditional lender of last resort. (The case against turning the IMF into an international lender of last resort has been convincingly made elsewhere.)[9] That dynamic appears to have contributed to the failure of preventive funding in Russia and Brazil. Furthermore, not only will moral hazard be aggravated by the CCL's signaling function; the generous bailout function will lessen investor caution even more. Indeed, in creating the CCL, the IMF did not renounce its bailout role in cases in which financial turmoil has already begun.

The CCL is also undermined by two dubious assumptions on which its use is based: that countries with sound economic fundamentals are subject to contagion and that the criteria for using CCL funds can be adequate to prevent misuse of the instrument. According to Jack Boorman of the IMF, the new facility will protect countries from contagion "which hits them not because of actions or policies of their own doing, but because of pressure that develops in capital markets in other countries or because of developments in other parts of the world."[10] Yet it is difficult to find a country that has succumbed to crisis that did not also already have severe domestic economic problems. Thailand, South Korea, and Indonesia maintained pegged exchange rates that were impossible to defend after years of massive malinvestment in their domestic economies became evident. That malinvestment was itself a product of government-directed credit and implicit government guarantees to key sectors of their economies. Russia and Brazil maintained pegged exchange rates and consistently large budget deficits. Systemic crisis has not spread to countries with sound economic fundamentals. Had the CCL existed since 1997, it is not clear which country it would have saved.

It is worrisome enough that the IMF is expanding its lending on the theory that economic turmoil results more from creditor panic rather than from the misguided policies of the countries in trouble. But because gaining access to CCL funds is determined largely by IMF judgment calls, there is no guarantee that the money will not be used to support countries whose economies are fundamentally unsound. For example, for a country to qualify for the CCL, the IMF must positively assess "its progress in adhering to relevant internationally accepted standards." And the country "should have constructive relations with its private creditors." The IMF has furthermore made clear that "in assessing whether an individual criterion is satisfied, the [IMF] would take into account a range of factors, and would exercise judgment as to whether a sufficient 'critical mass' of factors relevant to the criterion is in evidence."[11]

In short, the fund has expanded its self-ascribed mission to prevent crises by creating a bailout facility that increases moral hazard.

Instead of bringing lenders and borrowers together to work on economic problems, the new credit lines create perverse, counterproductive incentives on the part of both governments and investors.

Resolving Crises in the Post–Bretton Woods Era

The international rescue role of the IMF is a relatively new feature in global finance. Only after the collapse of the Bretton Woods system of fixed exchange rates in the early 1970s did the fund adopt the new role of managing the debt problems of poor countries on a global scale. With the outbreak of the Third World debt crisis in 1982, the fund seized upon that mission, which expanded its influence and resources. During that protracted crisis, authorities ruled out direct negotiations between debtor countries and creditors as unrealistic. The largest U.S. money-center banks had made sovereign loans that exceeded their capital. Most banks were eager for the IMF to provide funding, as were Third World countries that wished to avoid default and gain access to easier credit. Economist Charles Goodhart expresses a widely held view of the situation:

> The evidence seems incontrovertible that without the intervention of the IMF, and the support of national central banks, the crisis in, and after, 1982, arising from these events, would have been contagious, far-reaching, and probably disastrous on a massive scale.[12]

Initially, developed countries responded to the possibility of a Third World debt default by treating it as a liquidity problem and providing new loans both directly and through multilateral agencies. As part of the deal, commercial banks were to continue lending. In the early stages, IMF loans did not necessarily require structural adjustment since authorities believed that indebted nations needed time to get their finances in order. Under IMF programs, countries thus raised taxes and tariffs and reduced government expenditures. By 1985, when it had become obvious that deep-rooted problems in the economies of developing countries were preventing them from growing out of their debt, U.S. Secretary of the Treasury James A. Baker announced a new strategy whereby new money from the IMF and commercial banks would be based on market conditionality. In exchange for that money, indebted countries were to liberalize their economies.

By 1987 it became evident that that strategy was not working. Countries did very little in the way of economic reform, although they continued to receive funding. Banks, although they continued to lend, reduced their exposure in the region. Economist Paul Krugman calculated that from 1982 to 1987 the stock of official creditor loans to the Baker plan countries increased from $50 billion to $120 billion, while that of bank loans remained at $250 billion during that time, then fell to $225 billion in 1988.[13] A slow transfer from private debt to public debt occurred in the absence of a resolution of the underlying problems that had caused the debt crisis.

IMF conditionality appeared to provide little incentive to reform. Sebastian Edwards, formerly the World Bank's chief economist for Latin America, referred to the IMF as "participating in a big charade," because fund programs imply that "there is a high probability that the country will attain balance-of-payment viability in the near future. For many countries this is not the case and everybody knows it."[14] Political scientist Karen Remmer earlier noted the same problem:

> The dominant theme to emerge from this analysis of IMF programs is not that of success, however, but of failure. Unsuccessful implementation of IMF recipes has been the norm in Latin America, not the exception. A high proportion of standby programs has failed to push key indicators of government finance and domestic credit even in the right direction. . . . The power of the IMF remains a useful myth for governments seeking a scapegoat to explain difficult economic conditions associated with severe balance of payments disequilibria, but the ability of the IMF to impose programs from the outside is distinctly limited.[15]

Despite the fund's inability to enforce the conditions it attached to its loans, lending continued. Some observers have noted that, despite temporary suspensions of credit, the IMF's "institutional incentives" to lend and its commitment to the "success" of programs undermine the credibility of the agency's conditionality.[16] By financing governments that were not serious about liberalization and structural adjustment, the fund actually delayed reforms in Latin America during the 1980s. Latin America became more indebted; private commercial banks in the United States were able to postpone recognizing losses; and the living standards of Latin Americans fell.[17] As Anna Schwartz commented in her 1988 presidential address to the

Western Economics Association, "The intervention of the official players has prolonged and worsened the debt problem."[18] Economic historian Peter Lindert found that, as a result of IMF intervention, "most [debtor nations] have participated in a three-party stalemate, in which official agencies, private creditors, and debtor countries agree, after repeated struggles and much uncertainty, to reschedule in a way that postpones large net resource flows."[19]

The end of the 1980s and the beginning of the 1990s finally saw the introduction of far-reaching market reforms, a development for which the IMF often takes credit. But that outcome resulted from economic necessity in the wake of the collapse of development planning. As development economist Deepak Lal noted, it is simply not credible "that it was the 'conditionality' of the structural adjustment and stabilization programmes and the money which accompanied them which turned the debt crisis countries (and others), however haltingly, from the plan to the market. . . . The economic liberalisation that has occurred was due to the 'crisis' in governability which past dirigisme had engendered."[20]

In Latin America, the center of the Third World debt crisis, the turning point came in 1987 when Citibank responded to Brazil's debt default by announcing that it was building up loan-loss reserves of $3 billion. That action prompted other money-center banks to do the same, thus weakening not only Brazil's negotiating position with its creditors but also that of other developing country governments that until then had had little incentive to take reform seriously. The failure of IMF programs to resolve the debt crisis, the continuing deterioration of Latin American economies, and the eventual willingness of private commercial banks to begin preparing for losses helped increase voluntary debt-reduction schemes and economic reforms. (The much-lauded Brady plan of 1989, which forced creditor banks to provide debt reductions in exchange for bonds securitized by the U.S. Treasury and international organizations, came after market solutions were well under way. Indeed, the Institute of International Finance charged that the Brady plan led to a slowing of voluntary debt reductions from $18 billion in 1988 to $11.3 billion in 1989. The Brady plan appears to have brought about a pause in the move toward market reforms and market-based debt reduction.)[21]

It is also doubtful that the IMF strategy helped avert an international financial disaster. That is so, even though loans by the nine largest U.S. banks to 40 developing countries (that are not members of the Organization of Petroleum Exporting Countries) represented 222 percent of the banks' capital. Because not all of that debt was in doubt (some major borrowers in Asia had little difficulty making payments), the real problem was due to concentrated lending to Mexico, Argentina, and Brazil, the countries with the largest debts. A few prominent figures in the financial community had by 1983 suggested that a better option than providing IMF aid to developing country governments would be for commercial banks to set aside loan-loss reserves and write down the value of their troubled loans— the solution that banks ultimately opted for at the end of the 1980s.[22] If U.S. banks were indeed threatened by the Third World debt situation, a far more efficient solution would have been to allow them to borrow directly from the U.S Federal Reserve Board at a penalty. Indeed, the central banks of rich nations are designed to serve as lenders of last resort to their commercial banks. For that reason, the Minneapolis Fed recently noted that "the IMF is redundant to prevent worldwide financial crises."[23]

Had the IMF not been involved in the debt crisis of the 1980s, it is probable that the crisis would have been over as early as 1983 or 1984. Indeed, creditors and debtors would have had little choice but to do what they ultimately did at the end of the 1980s to resolve the crisis. Unfortunately, as Lindert and Peter Morton noted in 1987, "The intervention of the Fund and the [World] Bank has impeded the striking of bilateral bargains between debtor governments and the creditor banks."[24] Shortly before being named the number-two person at the IMF, MIT professor Stanley Fischer seemed to express agreement with that assessment: "I believe that the debt crisis would have been over sooner had the official agencies not been involved." Fischer added, however, that he thought that in the absence of official intervention the adjustment crisis would have been deeper.[25] But it is hard to imagine that Latin America would have suffered more had the liberal reforms that were eventually introduced in the late 1980s and early 1990s been implemented seven or eight years earlier.

International Rescues in the 1990s

Official intervention in the 1990s continued to sever the relationship between borrowers and lenders. Investors avoided incurring wealth losses and countries have avoided, or delayed, open default on their foreign debts. The strategy has been hailed as a success for some countries, including Mexico and Korea, but it has been accompanied by large, avoidable costs.

When the Mexican peso fell in 1994 as a result of expansionary fiscal and monetary policy that was inconsistent with its pegged exchange rate, moral hazard was already well established. In 1995 the IMF and the U.S. Treasury decided, for the fourth time in 20 years, to rescue the Mexican government and its investors from the consequences of irresponsible election-year policies. The bailout allowed Mexico to repay in full about $25 billion in dollar-indexed bonds. The investors suffered no risk or losses because they were able to pass the bill on to ordinary Mexicans in the form of greater debt. The redistribution of wealth from the poor to the rich has been a feature of subsequent bailouts.

The IMF-led intervention precluded a less expensive solution that would have left Mexicans better off. In the absence of official funds, Mexico City and its creditors would have had little alternative to dealing directly with each other to renegotiate the country's debt by extending the payback period on bonds and introducing monetary and structural reforms. One financier estimated that such a workout would have immediately created a market in the new notes at around 80 percent of par—a loss equivalent to less than two days' variation on the value of Intel.[26] A successful renegotiation would have instilled confidence in the market, taken pressure off the peso, and led to a speedy recovery.

The official response to the Mexican peso crisis, however, not only initiated a new era of massive bailouts; it also allowed Mexico to avoid key reforms. The petroleum industry, for example, remains a government-owned monopoly. Its privatization could have helped meet Mexico's debt obligations while further liberalizing the economy. Any pressure to liberalize the Mexican economy was relieved by official funds. Alternatively, oil revenues could have been used as collateral to guarantee loans from the private sector. Indeed, the U.S. Treasury negotiated precisely such an arrangement for the aid it made available to Mexico— undercutting its argument that Mexico was unable to arrange financing from the market to solve its crisis. The shaky banking system, which remains troubled to this day, was also saved. Rather than come up with a timely plan to deal with insolvent banks and liberalize the financial sector, the Mexican government purchased about $70 billion of Mexican banks' bad debts and until 1999 maintained regulations that protected the largest banks from foreign competition (the government may still protect domestic banks in other ways).[27] The experience confirmed economist Charles Calomiris's view that "in practice, crisis countries will always find it easy to promise (but never deliver) true banking reform. Instead, they will tax quickly and deeply, pay back their loans to the IMF, replenish the poker chips of their risk-loving conglomerates, and return to business as usual."[28]

In Asia and elsewhere, the record is the same or worse. Moscow has been sustained by IMF aid for years even though it has not complied with IMF conditions. Indonesia has gone from one IMF agreement to another since 1997 without implementing necessary reforms. The bailout of Brazil did not discipline policymakers in Brasilia or avert a currency crisis. In Thailand and Korea reform has been more forthcoming, but progress in implementing bankruptcy procedures and addressing banking-sector problems has been slow. According to *The Economist*, "The speed and strength of recovery in East and South-East Asia . . . reflect that natural propensity of economies to bounce back. . . . What it does not reflect is fundamental, structural reform, in any country in the region."[29] Economist Catherine Mann of the Institute for International Economics summed up the outlook for Korea:

> The bottom line is that Korea has made relatively little progress toward reforms that will create a more market-oriented economy. In fact, institutional reforms, such as to bankruptcy law and to the social safety net, have tended to impact the smaller chaebol [business conglomerates] the most, while leaving the large chaebol unscathed. This may hollow out from the Korean economy the firms that could pose a competitive threat to the biggest chaebol. In this environment, developing an active financial system that allocates credit according to risk and return will be difficult, if not impossible. Indeed, some of the large chaebol are looking to buy banks.
>
> The chaebol would not restructure themselves, the forces of competition from at home and abroad were too weak, so the Korean government's Financial Supervisory Committee presented to each chaebol a detailed plan of divestiture, area of specialization, change in financial leverage, and greater financial transparency. In the end, if these reforms go through, Korea will have fewer firms in each line of business,

and maybe lower leverage and greater transparency. But it is unlikely to have a much more competitive or market-oriented economy.[30]

IMF and G-7 officials have expressed a desire to involve the private sector more in crisis resolution—indeed, investors with money to lose are less patient when dealing with insolvency or illiquidity. But officials continue to justify official intervention on the grounds that bailouts are needed to overcome spillover effects, collective action and free-rider problems, and other apparent market failures. Referring to international financial stability as a global public good, IMF managing director Michel Camdessus stated: "All have an interest in reforms that will improve the system for the global public benefit. And, as is so frequently true for public goods, not many people care for, and even fewer are prepared to pay for, its improvement even if many comment about it."[31] Moreover, financial officials view it as their responsibility to ensure repayment of debts and prevent default. As former Treasury secretary Robert Rubin emphasized, the measures financial officials take "must not undermine the obligation of countries to meet their debts in full and on time."[32]

Yet recent events do not support the case for official intervention. Only after Brazil experienced a currency crisis—two months after the IMF bailout—did the government there take tentative steps to address the country's problems. The 1998 collapse of the Russian ruble and subsequent debt default—which an IMF bailout did not prevent—rattled world markets and likely reduced moral hazard. Successive interest rate cuts by the Federal Reserve and other central banks then helped calm world markets, raising questions about the utility of the IMF in both preventing defaults and dealing with their global effects. That the Brazilian devaluation did not have the colossal consequences that the IMF and the U.S. Treasury predicted was probably in large part due to the effects of the Russian crisis.

Market discipline has also been at work in Korea. As Jeffrey Sachs notes, the IMF responded to the Korean crisis by providing a tranche of credit in late 1997, but "the Korean debacle ended only when Korea ran out of IMF money, forcing the international bank creditors to agree to roll over the debts owed by Korean banks."[33] Even so, the restructuring was "far from ideal" since the newly restructured debt was generously guaranteed by the Korean government at interest rates that were higher than those on the original debts.[34]

Morris Goldstein questions the IMF approach in Korea. According to him, it is not "clear that the first round of rollovers that did take place ... would not have happened anyway in the absence of a promise of accelerated disbursements from the official sector. The argument that creditors are too numerous and dispersed to make such discussions feasible did not seem to apply in this case. If the rescue package for South Korea were smaller ... and disbursements were not accelerated, a larger amount would have had to be rescheduled." Moreover, losses in Korea would not have made Western banks insolvent.[35]

Two-Party Crisis Resolution

The historical record also suggests that collective-action and other problems have often been resolved by creditor-debtor bargains in the forums of banking clubs, lending syndicates, and bondholder committees. Indeed, in the 19th century, the Corporation of Foreign Bondholders, a private entity in Great Britain, was formed to represent bondholders in negotiations with borrower nations. The United States later saw the formation of the Foreign Bondholders Protective Council. When countries had difficulties repaying their debts, bondholder committees would negotiate new terms and conditions with foreign governments—a process relied on during repeated Latin American defaults, for example, from the late 1800s through the 1930s.[36]

The private sector showed that it was fully capable of organizing itself, bargaining directly with debtors, and enforcing new conditions based on the acceptance of some initial losses. Contrary to the conventional perception of that era, gunboat diplomacy was rare, except when creditor governments justified intervention mainly on political rather than economic grounds, as was the case when the French occupied Mexico in the 1860s or the British occupied Egypt in the 1880s. The United States followed that general pattern as well, intervening only in the Caribbean.[37] British foreign secretary Lord Palmerston summed up the European attitude when U.S. states defaulted in the 1840s: "British subjects who buy foreign securities do so at their own risk and must abide the consequences."[38]

History also shows that, although countries have incentives to avoid crises with their lenders, defaults have repeatedly occurred, but they have usually been partial rather than complete, and lending has often resumed soon after the defaults.[39] Default need not be traumatic for lender or borrower. Indeed, economist Rudiger Dornbusch has suggested that had Korea defaulted rather than relied on the IMF in 1997, Koreans today would be in much better shape. Such a move would have stopped the won from plunging, forced investors to take some initial losses, and quickly brought lenders and borrowers together to work out illiquidity and insolvency issues. Instead, the Koreans got the worst of all worlds—a prolonged currency and financial crisis and greater debt.[40]

Without official third-party intervention, a system of real conditionality and reform would evolve. If sovereign bonds were at issue, for instance, bondholder committees could renegotiate debt and the bonds themselves could be traded in the market, taking on a value that reflected people's confidence in the negotiations.[41] While creditors may not prefer entering into such negotiations to receiving bailout money, the absence of official third-party financing gives them little choice. The same is true of private international loans made entirely to the private sector, where creditors may not wish to get involved in reorganization of firms or their liquidation if official funds might be forthcoming. Direct two-party negotiations would reduce incentives to stall progress on reforms—including instituting bankruptcy procedures in countries that do not already have them—since both parties would have much to lose if they failed to act quickly.

The fact that bond contracts require the unanimous consent of bondholders to restructure has led many people to believe that sovereign bond defaults would today be messy and drawn out since a minority of bondholders could stall the process and bring legal action against the country. Yet since the 1980s several successful voluntary sovereign bond restructurings have overcome those problems. Moreover, creditors have limited ability to enforce court decisions on foreign countries beyond attempting to seize foreign assets outside a sovereign's legal territory. The cost of taking legal action may well be higher than that of entering into debt renegotiations.[42]

Were official bailouts less prominent, we might already be seeing more such workouts. One market-based solution would be to include in bond contracts clauses concerning majority voting or workout procedures in the event of a default.[43] No doubt that would raise the cost of borrowing for some countries, but some countries *should* be discouraged in this way from recourse to easy credit. Another market solution that might arise in the absence of official financing during crises is the creation of private standby lines of credit to countries. For a fee, banks have provided such loans—to Argentina, for example—to allow a country to withstand outside shocks. The existence of such insurance may help create greater investor confidence. Since banks would not provide such a service to all countries, the provision of such loans (unlike that of IMF loans) would be a useful signal to the markets about which countries can be expected to have relatively sound economic fundamentals in place.

A market for credit risk insurance and restructuring insurance could also develop in response to market participants' diverse tastes for risk. In times of crisis, not all investors would behave in the same way, thus reducing the severity of financial turmoil. As Mann points out: "In the current situation, the more difficult, drawn out, ad hoc, and therefore costly are the financial disaster workouts, the greater are the incentives for investors to demand and institutions to offer instruments ex ante that will help to generate a market-oriented solution to the workout process. So rather than intervening more frequently, official institutions must stand aside."[44]

Conclusion

Since the collapse of the Bretton Woods system, international financial crises have become more frequent and more severe. Official intervention has been the response to these crises, ostensibly to help the market overcome deficiencies in coordination, information, and insurance and to help prevent crises from expanding and deepening. Yet such interventions, typically led by the IMF, have interfered with direct creditor-debtor bargains that would have provided those so-called public goods. Official intervention also undermines the creation and evolution of market institutions that can do much to stabilize the international financial system.

Third-party intervention has largely favored creditors and thereby created a more fragile global economy. The IMF's reaction to this criticism is to consider "bailing in" the private sector by lending into arrears so as to put more pressure on it to take losses. In the market, measures to bail in the private sector would not be necessary since the private sector would already be bailed in. Official efforts to bail in the private sector, however, may precipitate the financial turmoil they were designed to prevent since lenders would have an incentive to pull out of a country whenever they sensed that international authorities were prepared to force losses on them.

In a world where open default was a real possibility and official intervention was not, the market would naturally require some measure of debt relief. But private creditors need not fear such an outcome. In many cases debt relief can improve the financial standing of both creditor and debtor. As University of Chicago economist Randall Kroszner has observed, "It may indeed be better to forgive than to receive. Asking for less can result in receiving more while also making the distressed country better off."[45] Bankers may have made money during the 1980s debt crisis, but surely they would have made more had there been no "lost decade" of growth— something that could have been prevented by allowing debtors and lenders to recognize effective default and move on from there. Repairing the relationship between creditors and borrowers in international finance requires that official third parties move out of the way.

Appendix A
USE OF IMF CREDIT BY ELIGIBLE COUNTRIES, 1947–99

Country (by region)	First Year Used	Number of Years Used	Percentage of Years Used after Year of First Use
Africa			
Algeria	1989	11	100.00
Benin	1978	22	100.00
Burkina Faso	1978	22	100.00
Burundi	1968	29	90.63
Cameroon	1974	26	100.00
Central African Republic	1974	26	100.00
Chad	1970	30	100.00
Congo, Dem. Republic	1972	28	100.00
Congo, Rep. Of	1977	23	100.00
Equatorial Guinea	1980	20	100.00
Ethiopia	1949	22	43.14
Gabon	1978	20	90.91
Gambia	1977	23	100.00
Ghana	1962	35	92.11
Guinea	1969	31	100.00
Guinea-Bissau	1979	21	100.00
Ivory Coast	1974	26	100.00
Kenya	1974	26	100.00
Lesotho	1977	23	100.00
Liberia	1963	33	89.19
Madagascar	1974	26	100.00
Malawi	1975	25	100.00
Mali	1964	35	97.22
Mauritania	1976	24	100.00
Mauritius	1969	15	48.39
Morocco	1968	24	75.00
Mozambique	1987	13	100.00
Niger	1983	22	100.00
Rwanda	1966	26	76.47
Sao Tome and Principe	1989	11	100.00
Senegal	1975	25	100.00
Sierra Leone	1967	29	87.88
Somalia	1964	26	72.22

(continued next page)

Appendix A
USE OF IMF CREDIT BY ELIGIBLE COUNTRIES, 1947–99 *(continued)*

Country	First Year Used	Number of Years Used	Percentage of Years Used after Year of First Use
South Africa	1976	15	62.50
Sudan	1958	39	92.86
Swaziland	1979	12	57.14
Tanzania	1974	26	100.00
Togo	1976	24	100.00
Tunisia	1964	25	69.44
Uganda	1971	29	100.00
Zambia	1971	29	100.00
Zimbabwe	1981	18	94.74
Asia			
Afghanistan	1964	13	36.11
Bangladesh	1972	28	100.00
Cambodia	1972	28	100.00
China	1981	10	52.63
Fiji	1974	12	46.15
India	1949	44	86.27
Indonesia	1956	29	65.91
Laos	1975	25	100.00
Malaysia	1976	7	29.17
Mongolia	1991	9	100.00
Myanmar	1967	24	72.73
Nepal	1976	24	100.00
Pakistan	1965	35	100.00
Papua New Guinea	1976	24	100.00
Philippines	1955	39	86.67
Solomon Islands	1981	10	52.63
South Korea	1974	17	65.38
Sri Lanka	1961	39	100.00
Thailand	1976	18	75.00
Vietnam	1977	23	100.00
Western Samoa	1975	17	68.00
Europe			
Albania	1992	8	100.00
Armenia	1994	6	100.00
Azerbaijan	1995	5	100.00

(continued)

Appendix A
Use of IMF Credit by Eligible Countries, 1947–99 *(continued)*

Country	First Year Used	Number of Years Used	Percentage of Years Used after Year of First Use
Belarus	1993	7	100.00
Bosnia and Herzegovina	1995	5	100.00
Bulgaria	1991	9	100.00
Croatia	1993	7	100.00
Cyprus	1974	11	42.31
Czech Republic	1993	1	14.29
Czechoslovakia	1990	3	100.00
Estonia	1992	8	100.00
Georgia	1994	6	100.00
Hungary	1982	16	88.89
Kazakhstan	1993	7	100.00
Kyrgyz Republic	1993	7	100.00
Latvia	1992	8	100.00
Lithuania	1992	8	100.00
Macedonia, FYR	1993	7	100.00
Moldova	1993	7	100.00
Poland	1990	5	50.00
Romania	1973	25	92.59
Russia	1992	8	100.00
Slovak Republic	1993	7	100.00
Slovenia	1993	4	57.14
Turkey	1953	40	85.11
Ukraine	1994	6	100.00
Uzbekistan	1995	5	100.00
Yugoslavia	1949	41	93.18
Middle East			
Egypt	1957	40	93.02
Iran	1955	6	13.33
Iraq	1967	2	6.06
Israel	1957	18	41.86
Jordan	1971	22	75.86
Syria	1960	16	40.00
Yemen, Rep. of	1990	5	50.00
Yemen Arab Republic	1983	5	71.43
Yemen People's Dem. Rep.	1974	16	100.00

(continued next page)

Appendix A
USE OF IMF CREDIT BY ELIGIBLE COUNTRIES, 1947–99 *(continued)*

Country	First Year Used	Number of Years Used	Percentage of Years Used after Year of First Use
Western Hemisphere			
Argentina	1957	33	76.74
Barbados	1977	19	82.61
Belize	1983	8	47.06
Bolivia	1959	35	85.37
Brazil	1951	33	67.35
Chile	1957	38	88.37
Colombia	1954	16	34.78
Costa Rica	1961	30	76.92
Dominica	1979	20	95.24
Dominican Republic	1960	36	90.00
Ecuador	1957	29	67.44
El Salvador	1956	23	52.27
Grenada	1975	16	64.00
Guatemala	1962	18	47.37
Guyana	1971	27	93.10
Haiti	1958	39	92.86
Honduras	1957	33	76.74
Jamaica	1973	27	100.00
Mexico	1976	22	91.67
Nicaragua	1957	33	76.74
Panama	1968	28	87.50
Paraguay	1956	5	11.36
Peru	1958	31	73.81
St. Lucia	1980	6	30.00
St. Vincent	1980	6	30.00
Trinidad and Tobago	1988	10	83.33
Uruguay	1962	32	84.21
Venezuela	1989	11	100.00

SOURCE: IMF, *International Financial Statistics* (various issues).
NOTE: This table includes outstanding use of the IMF's credits within the General Resources Account, Structural Adjustment Facility, Enhanced Structural Adjustment Facility, and Trust Fund loans. Data for Yugoslavia to 1992; data for Czechoslovakia to 1993; data for Yemen Arab Republic and Yemen People's Democratic Republic to 1990.

Appendix B
USE OF IMF CREDIT, 1949–99

40 Years or More (4)
Egypt, India, Turkey, Yugoslavia

30 to 39 Years (20)
Costa Rica, Chad, Peru, Guinea, Uruguay, Brazil, Argentina, Honduras, Nicaragua, Liberia, Bolivia, Ghana, Mali, Pakistan, Dominican Republic, Chile, Philippines, Sudan, Haiti, Sri Lanka

20 to 29 Years (46)
Gabon, Dominica, Equatorial Guinea, Guinea-Bissau, Ethiopia, Jordan, Mexico, Benin, Burkina Faso, Niger, El Salvador, Rep. of Congo, Gambia, Lesotho, Vietnam, Myanmar, Morocco, Mauritania, Togo, Nepal, Papua New Guinea, Tunisia, Romania, Malawi, Senegal, Laos, Somalia, Rwanda, Cameroon, Central African Republic, Ivory Coast, Kenya, Madagascar, Tanzania, Guyana, Jamaica, Panama, Dem. Rep. of Congo, Bangladesh, Cambodia, Indonesia, Ecuador, Sierra Leone, Burundi, Uganda, Zambia

10 to 19 Years (25)
China, Solomon Islands, Trinidad and Tobago, Cyprus, Algeria, Sao Tome and Principe, Venezuela, Fiji, Swaziland, Afghanistan, Mozambique, Mauritius, South Africa, Colombia, Syria, Grenada, Hungary, Yemen People's Dem. Rep., South Korea, Western Samoa, Israel, Guatemala, Thailand, Zimbabwe, Barbados

Less than 10 Years (29)
Czech Republic, Iraq, Slovenia, Paraguay, Poland, Republic of Yemen, Yemen Arab Republic, Iran, St. Lucia, St. Vincent, Armenia, Georgia, Ukraine, Malaysia, Belarus, Croatia, Kazakhstan, Kyrgyz Republic, Macedonia, FYR, Moldova, Slovak Republic, Belize, Albania, Estonia, Latvia, Lithuania, Russia, Mongolia, Bulgaria

Notes

1. See, for example, "Report of the International Financial Institution Advisory Commission," submitted to the U.S. Congress and U.S. Department of the Treasury, March 8, 2000, and Council on Foreign Relations, *Safeguarding Prosperity in a Global Financial System: The Future International Financial Architecture* (Washington: Institute for International Economics, 1999).

2. See, for example, Leland B. Yeager, *International Monetary Relations: Theory, History, and Policy* (New York: Harper and Row, 1976); Leland B. Yeager, "How to Avoid International Financial Crises," *Cato Journal* 17, no. 3 (Winter 1998): 257–65; Milton Friedman, "'No' to More Money for the IMF," *Newsweek*, November 14, 1983; Alan Walters, *Do We Need the IMF and the World Bank?* Current Controversies, no. 10 (London: Institute of Economic Affairs, 1994); Rudi Dornbusch, "A Bailout Won't Do the Trick in Korea," *Business Week*, December 8, 1997; Deepak Lal, "Don't Bank on It, Mr. Blair," *The Spectator* (London), September 26, 1998; and Robert J. Barro, "The IMF Doesn't Put Out Fires, It Starts Them," *Business Week*, December 7, 1998.

3. International Monetary Fund, *International Financial Statistics* (Washington: IMF, various issues).

4. The IMF downplays its role in creating moral hazard, citing the fact that market participants have taken great losses in Asia, but that view is not shared by all members of the IMF. See, for example, Onno de Beaufort Wijnholds, "Maintaining an Indispensable Role," *Financial Times*, March 1, 1999; and D. Wessel, "Rubin Says Global Investors Don't Suffer," *Wall Street Journal*, September 19, 1997. The fund's call to put more of the burden on the private sector when financial crises erupt is an implicit recognition of the moral hazard problem.

5. An additional problem is that the fund faces a conflict of interest since in many cases it would be evaluating a country in which it has its own money at stake. Thus, Barro predicted, for example, that "the IMF will come up with a way to keep up the chain-letter game in which it provides Russia, Ukraine, and Indonesia with enough money to keep payments 'current.'" See Barro.

6. Michael D. Bordo and Anna J. Schwartz, "Under What Circumstances, Past and Present, Have International Rescues of Countries in Financial Distress Been Successful?" National Bureau of Economic Research, Working Paper no. 6824, December 1998, p. 43.

7. Federal Reserve Bank of Minneapolis, *1998 Annual Report: Asking the Right Questions about the IMF* (Minneapolis, Minn.: Federal Reserve Bank of Minneapolis, May 1999), pp. 6, 3.

8. International Monetary Fund, "IMF Tightens Defenses against Financial Contagion by Establishing Contingent Credit Lines," Press release no. 99/14, April 25, 1999.

9. See Onno de Beaufort Wijnholds and Arend Kapteyn, "The IMF: Lender of Last Resort or Indispensable Lender?" chapter 12 in this volume; and Anna J. Schwartz, "Time to Terminate the ESF and the IMF," Cato Foreign Policy Briefing no. 48, August 26, 1998.

10. Quoted in "Boorman Discusses IMF's Transparency Initiatives, Explains Rationale for Contingent Credit Line," *IMF Survey*, May 10, 1999, p. 145.

11. International Monetary Fund, "IMF Tightens Defenses."

12. Charles A. E. Goodhart, *The Evolution of Central Banks* (Cambridge, Mass.: MIT Press, 1988), pp. 48–49.

13. Paul Krugman, "LDC Debt Policy," in *American Economic Policy in the 1980s*, ed. Martin Feldstein (Chicago: University of Chicago Press, 1994), p. 700.

14. Sebastian Edwards, "The International Monetary Fund and the Developing Countries: A Critical Evaluation," in *IMF Policy Advice, Market Volatility, Commodity Price Rules and Other Essays*, ed. Karl Brunner and Allan H. Meltzer, Carnegie-Rochester Conference Series on Public Policy (Amsterdam: North Holland, 1989), p. 39.

15. Karen L. Remmer, "The Politics of Economic Stabilization: IMF Standby Programs in Latin America, 1954–1984," *Comparative Politics* 19, no. 1 (October 1986): 21.

16. See Ian Vásquez, "The Record and Relevance of the World Bank and the IMF," in *Delusions of Grandeur: The United Nations and Global Intervention*, ed. Ted Galen Carpenter (Washington: Cato Institute, 1997), p. 243; and Allan H. Meltzer, "What's Wrong with the IMF? What Would Be Better?" in *The Asian Financial Crisis: Origins, Implications, and Solutions*, ed. William C. Hunter, George G. Kaufman, and Thomas H. Krueger (Boston: Kluwer Academic Publishers: 1999), p. 246.

17. Meltzer, p. 246. Rudi Dornbusch noted that "the IMF set itself up to save the system, organizing banks into a lender's cartel and holding the debtor countries up for a classical mugging." Rudiger Dornbusch, *Dollars, Debts, and Deficits* (Cambridge, Mass: MIT Press, 1986), p. 140.

18. Anna J. Schwartz, "International Debts: What's Fact and What's Fiction?" *Economic Inquiry* 27, no. 1 (January 1989): 4.

19. Peter H. Lindert, "Response to Debt Crisis: What Is Different about the 1980s?" in *The International Debt Crisis in Historical Perspective*, ed. Barry Eichengreen and Peter H. Lindert (Cambridge, Mass.: MIT Press, 1990), pp. 250–51.

20. Deepak Lal, "Foreign Aid: An Idea Whose Time Has Gone," *Economic Affairs* 16, no. 4 (Autumn 1996): 12.

21. See Ian Vásquez, "The Brady Plan and Market-Based Solutions to Debt Crises," *Cato Journal* 16, no. 2 (Fall 1996): 233–43.

22. Those suggestions were made by George Champion, former chairman of Chase Manhattan Bank, and William Simon, former secretary of the U.S. Treasury. See William Simon, "Cut Off the International Loan Lushes," *Wall Street Journal*, April 6, 1983.

23. Federal Reserve Bank of Minneapolis, p. 6. Deepak Lal also observed that "the fear that bank failures triggered by Third World defaults could lead to another Great Depression is only reasonable if it is assumed that the national authorities would allow bank failures to affect their national money supplies." Deepak Lal, "The 'Debt Crisis': No Need for IMF Bailout," *Wall Street Journal*, April 27, 1983.

24. Peter H. Lindert and Peter J. Morton, "How Sovereign Debt Has Worked," in *Developing Country Debt and Economic Performance*, ed. Jeffrey D. Sachs (Chicago: University of Chicago Press, 1987), p. 75.

25. Stanley Fischer, "The Mission of the Fund," in *Bretton Woods: Looking to the Future* (Washington: Bretton Woods Commission, 1994), p. C-169.

26. Peter Ackerman (address to the University of California at Los Angeles Center for International Relations, December 1998). See also Peter Ackerman and James A. Dorn, "Dose of Financial Morphine for Mexico," *Financial Times*, February 15, 1995.

27. For a discussion on why there has been no recovery in Mexico's nontraded goods sector, which makes up about 50 percent of the country's gross domestic product, see Anne Krueger and Aaron Tornell, "The Role of Bank Restructuring in Recovering from Crises: Mexico 1995–98," National Bureau of Economic Research Working Paper no. 7042, March 1999.

28. Charles W. Calomiris, "The IMF's Imprudent Role as Lender of Last Resort," *Cato Journal* 17, no. 3 (Winter 1998): 280; see also Charles W. Calomiris, "A Welcome to Foreign Banks Could Energize Mexico," *Wall Street Journal*, July 16, 1999, p. A15.

29. "Asia's Bounce-Back," *The Economist*, August 21, 1999, p. 11. Former World Bank chief economist Joseph Stiglitz notes that, "Close to 40 percent of Thailand's loans are still not performing; Indonesia remains deeply mired in recession. Unemployment rates remain far higher than they were before the crisis, even in East Asia's best-performing country, Korea. IMF boosters suggest that the recession's end is a testament to the effectiveness of the agency's policies. Nonsense. Every recession eventually ends. All the IMF did was make East Asia's recessions deeper, longer, and harder." See Stiglitz, "What I Learned at the World Economic Crisis," *New Republic*, April 17 and 24, 2000, p. 60.

30. Catherine L. Mann, Testimony before the Subcommittee on International Trade and Finance of the Senate Banking, Housing, and Urban Affairs Committee, March 9, 1999. Likewise, the *Economist Intelligence Unit* reported: "The bottom line is that the chaebol virtually are the economy. In 1998 the top seven chaebol accounted for more than half of all South Korean exports. The biggest are too big to fail; they know it, and they know the government knows it too. Indeed, chaebol dominance means they can continue to joust with the government over reforms. These basic truths of the balance of power limit Kim Dae-jung's ability to impose change. In the final analysis, state and business in Seoul remain as intertwined as they have ever been. Their interdependence will and must adapt to a changing world. But a truly free market is a chimera." *Economist Intelligence Unit*, "South Korea: On the Leading Edge of Free-Market Reform?" February 17, 1999.

31. Michel Camdessus, "International Financial and Monetary Stability: A Global Public Good?" (remarks at the IMF research conference "Key Issues in Reform of the International Monetary and Financial System," Washington, May 28, 1999). Under-secretary of the U.S. Treasury for International Affairs Timothy Geithner has also stated that "a more expansive definition of this concept of global public goods seems in order." Timothy Geithner, "The World Bank and the Frontier of Development Challenges" (remarks at Northwestern University, May 14, 1999). See also Charles Wyplosz, "International Financial Instability," in *Global Public Goods: International Cooperation in the 21st Century*, ed. Inge Kaul, Isabelle Grunberg, and Marc A. Stern (New York: Oxford University Press and the United Nations Development Programme, 1999), pp. 152–89.

32. Robert E. Rubin, "Remarks on Reform of the International Financial Architecture to the School of Advanced International Studies" (delivered at Johns Hopkins University School of International Studies, Washington, April 21, 1999).

33. Jeffrey Sachs, "Stop Preaching," *Financial Times*, November 5, 1998.

34. Steven Radelet and Jeffrey Sachs, "What Have We Learned So Far from the Asian Financial Crisis?" January 4, 1999, p. 16, www.hiid.harvard.edu/pub/other/aea122.pdf.

35. Morris Goldstein, *The Asian Financial Crisis: Causes, Cures, and Systemic Implications* (Washington: Institute for International Economics, 1998), p. 43.

36. Barry Eichengreen and Richard Portes, *Crisis? What Crisis? Orderly Workouts for Sovereign Debtors* (London: Centre for Economic Policy Research, 1995), pp. 20–21; Carlos Marichal, *A Century of Debt Crises in Latin America: From Independence to the Great Depression, 1820–1930* (Princeton, N.J.: Princeton University Press, 1989); and

Walker F. Todd, "A History of International Lending," in *Research in Financial Services,* ed. George Kaufman (Greenwich, Conn.: JAI Press, 1991), vol. 3, pp. 201–89.

37. Clifford M. Lewis, "When Countries Go Broke: Debt through the Ages," *National Interest,* no. 6 (Winter 1986–97): 48.

38. Quoted in Harold L. Cole, James Dow, and William B. English, "Default, Settlement, and Signalling: Lending Resumption in a Reputational Model of Sovereign Debt," *International Economic Review* 36, no. 2 (May 1995): 369.

39. Herschel I. Grossman and John B. Van Huyck, "Sovereign Debt as a Contingent Claim: Excusable Default, Repudiation, and Reputation," *American Economic Review* 78, no. 5 (December 1988): 1088.

40. Rudiger Dornbusch (remarks at a Brookings Institution Trade Policy Forum conference on "Governing in a Global Economy," Washington, April 16, 1999).

41. Rory Macmillan, "New Lease of Life for Bondholder Councils," *Financial Times,* August 15, 1995.

42. Marco A. Piñon-Farah, "Private Bond Restructurings: Lessons for the Case of Sovereign Debtors," IMF Working Paper 96/11, February 1996.

43. As Barry Eichengreen asks, "If this is such a good idea, why have the markets not done it already? One answer is that, so long as the markets continue to believe that they will always get 100 cents on the dollar courtesy of the IMF, they are perfectly happy with the status quo." Barry Eichengreen, "Is Greater Private Sector Burden Sharing Impossible?" *Finance and Development* (September 1999): 18.

44. Catherine L. Mann, "Market Mechanisms to Reduce the Need for IMF Bailouts," Institute for International Economics, Policy Brief no. 99-4, Washington, February 1999, p. 3.

45. Randall S. Kroszner, "Less Is More in the New International Architecture," in *The Asian Financial Crisis,* p. 451.

281

Contributors

J. (Onno) de Beaufort Wijnholds has been an executive director of the International Monetary Fund since 1994. He served as deputy executive director of the De Nederlandsche Bank for seven years and as the alternate executive director of the IMF from 1985 to 1987. Shortly after earning his Ph.D. in economics from the University of Amsterdam in 1977, he served as a member of the National Council on Development Cooperation, which is based in the Netherlands. He is the author of several books and various articles on monetary and financial subjects, including *The Need for International Reserves and Credit Facilities* and *A Framework for Monetary Stability.*

Rudiger Dornbusch is the Ford Professor of Economics and International Management at the Massachusetts Institute of Technology Department of Economics. He is associate editor of the *Quarterly Journal of Economics* and research associate at the National Bureau of Economic Research. Dornbusch has written articles in various professional journals and is the author or editor of numerous books, including *Macroeconomics* (with Stanley Fischer); *Dollars, Debts and Deficits; The Macroeconomics of Populism in Latin America* (edited with Sebastian Edwards); *Stabilization, Debt, and Reform: Policy Analysis for Developing Countries;* and *Keys to Prosperity: Free Markets, Sound Money, and a Bit of Luck.* He received a Ph.D. in economics from the University of Chicago in 1971.

Francis J. Gavin is a research fellow at the Miller Center of Public Affairs at the University of Virginia and director of the center's Presidency and Macroeconomic Policy Project. Before joining the center, he was an international security fellow at the Belfer Center for Science and International Affairs at Harvard University and a John M. Olin Postdoctoral Fellow in National Security Affairs at the Center for International Affairs, also at Harvard University. He received his Ph.D. and his M.A. in history from the University of

Pennsylvania and received an M.S. in modern European history from the University of Oxford, United Kingdom. Gavin's articles have been published in *Orbis*, the *Annals of the Academy of Political and Social Science*, the *Journal of Cold War Studies*, and the *Washington Post*. He is the author of *Gold, Dollars and Power: The Politics of the U.S. Balance of Payments Deficit, 1958–1971*, forthcoming, 2001.

Byeong-Ho Gong is president of the Korea Center for Free Enterprise, which is based in Seoul. In 1985 he became a teaching assistant at Rice University in Texas, a position he held for five years. During the same period he spent more than a year as a visiting researcher at the Korea Research Institute of Human Settlement, Housing and Construction Division and lectured at Korea University. In December 1989 he became director of the Korea Economic Research Institute's Industrial Studies program. Gong received a B.A. in economics from Korea University in Seoul and a Ph.D. in economics from Rice University in Texas.

Andrei Illarionov was appointed as Russian president Vladimir Putin's chief economic adviser in April 2000 and is director of the Institute of Economic Analysis in Moscow. Illarionov has been an assistant professor for international economics at St. Petersburg University, where he received a Ph.D. in 1987. In 1992 he became deputy director of the Center for Economic Reform, the Russian government's think tank. In April 1993 he became chief economic adviser to Prime Minister Viktor Chernomyrdin, a position he resigned in February 1994. Illarionov has written three books and more than 300 articles on Russian economic and social policies.

Arend Kapteyn is assistant to the executive director at the International Monetary Fund. Previously, he was an economist at the Monetary and Economic Policy Department of the Central Bank of the Netherlands, where he dealt mainly with international monetary and financial matters and transition economies. He was also a member of the Secretariat of the G22 Working Group on International Financial Crises.

Martín Krause is vice dean of the Escuela Superior de Economía y Administración de Empresas in Buenos Aires, Argentina, where he

teaches institutional economics and public policy. He is also profes-
sor of economics at the law school of the Universidad de Buenos
Aires and a visiting professor at the Universidad Francisco Marro-
quín in Guatemala. Krause has cowritten, with Alberto Benegas
Lynch, Jr., two books: *Proyectos para una Sociedad Abierta* and *En
Defensa de los Más Necesitados*. In 1993 Krause was awarded the
Eisenhower Exchange Fellowship.

Deepak Lal is the James S. Coleman Professor of International Development Studies at the University of California at Los Angeles, professor emeritus of political economy at University College London, and
an adjunct scholar at the Cato Institute. He was a member of the
Indian Foreign Service (1963–66) and has served as a consultant to
the Indian Planning Commission, the World Bank, the Organization
for Economic Cooperation and Development, various UN agencies,
South Korea, and Sri Lanka. From 1984 to 1987 he was research
administrator at the World Bank. Lal is the author of a number of
books, including *The Poverty of Development Economics, The Hindu
Equilibrium, Against Dirigisme, The Political Economy of Poverty, Equity
and Growth,* and *Unintended Consequences: The Impact of Factor Endowments, Culture, and Politics on Long-Run Economic Performance.*

Tomas Larsson is a Swedish journalist who has been based in Thailand for 10 years. He has written extensively on East and Southeast
Asian economies and politics for *Svenska Dagbladet*, a leading Swedish daily, and *Business Asia*, a newsletter published by The Economist
Intelligence Unit. Larsson has written and edited several books for
Timbro, a research institute in Stockholm, including *Asiens kris är
inte kapitalismens*. Larsson is currently a columnist on the editorial
page of *Finanstidningen*, a financial daily in Stockholm, where he
writes mainly on issues in international trade and finance.

Brink Lindsey is a senior fellow at the Cato Institute and director
of Cato's Center for Trade Policy Studies. He previously worked as
an attorney specializing in international trade regulation. In addition, Lindsey formerly served as director of regulatory studies at the
Cato Institute and as senior editor of *Regulation* magazine. Lindsey, a
contributing editor at *Reason* magazine, is currently working on a

book on globalization. He received an A.B. from Princeton University in 1984 and a J.D. from Harvard Law School in 1987.

William McGurn is a member of the editorial board of and chief editorial writer for the *Wall Street Journal*. He began his career with the *American Spectator* in Bloomington, Indiana. In 1984 he became editorial features editor of the *Wall Street Journal Europe* and later moved to the *Asian Wall Street Journal*. McGurn joined *National Review* in 1989 as its Washington bureau chief. In 1992 he became senior editor for the *Far Eastern Economic Review* in Hong Kong and wrote *Perfidious Albion: The Abandonment of Hong Kong 1997*. McGurn is a member of the Council on Foreign Relations.

Stephen Moore is director of fiscal policy studies at the Cato Institute. Prior to joining Cato, he was a senior economist at the Joint Economic Committee of the U.S. Congress. Moore is a contributing editor of *National Review* and a regular contributor to the *Wall Street Journal*, the *Reader's Digest*, and other publications in which he has written widely on economic growth, immigration, and fiscal policy. He has been featured on CNN's *Business Money Line*, *NBC Nightly News*, PBS's *NewsHour with Jim Lehrer*, the *McLaughlin Group*, and numerous other television programs. Moore is the author of *Still an Open Door? U.S. Immigration Policy and the American Economy*, was a research coordinator for President Reagan's National Commission on Privatization, and served on *Time* magazine's board of economic advisers.

Julian L. Simon (1932–98) taught business administration at the University of Maryland and was a senior fellow at the Cato Institute. His articles on population economics, immigration, natural resources, and economic growth appeared in various professional journals. He was the author or editor of numerous books, including *The Economics of Population Growth, Population and Development in Poor Countries: Selected Essays, The Economic Consequences of Immigration, The Ultimate Resource*, and *The State of Humanity*.

Mario Vargas Llosa is a Peruvian novelist and essayist whose many books include *Conversation in the Cathedral, The Time of the Hero, Aunt*

Julia and the Scriptwriter, The War of the End of the World, and *A Fish in the Water.* In 1990 he was a candidate for the presidency of Peru.

Ian Vásquez is the director of the Cato Institute's Project on Global Economic Liberty. He has written widely on economic development issues in such publications as *Orbis,* the *Wall Street Journal,* and the *Journal of Commerce* and in major newspapers in Latin America. He is the coeditor of *Perpetuating Poverty: The World Bank, the IMF and the Developing World.* Vásquez received his bachelor's degree from Northwestern University and his master's degree from the School of Advanced International Studies at Johns Hopkins University.

Lawrence H. White is professor of economics in the Terry College of Business at the University of Georgia and an adjunct scholar at the Cato Institute. He is also a visiting scholar at the Federal Reserve Bank of Atlanta and a visiting professor at the Queen's School of Management, Queen's University, Belfast. White has written numerous journal articles on alternative monetary regimes, banking history, and the future of money. He is the author of various books, including *The Theory of Monetary Institutions, Free Banking in Britain,* and *Competition and Currency.*

Index

Argentina
  agreements with IMF, 175, 179
  banking crisis (1995), 245
  currency board and convertibility
    law, 179, 185
  external debt service, 185
  fiscal deficit limit proposal, 184
  rejection of national currency, 180–81
Asian financial crises
  assessment of blame, 50
  beginnings of, 129–32
  causes of, 32–33, 117, 125–26
  contagion, 9, 126–27, 246
  contagion precipitated by, 137
  effect in post-Soviet Russia, 194–95
  IMF handling of, 115–17, 151
  lessons of, 127
  new world as outcome of, 155
  sources of, 132–36
  See also Indonesia; Korea, South;
    Malaysia; Thailand
Attali, Jacques, 153
Auerback, Marshall, 146
Authoritarianism
  transformation of democracy to
    (Kaplan), 20

Bagehot, Walter, 249–51
Baker, James A., 262
Ball, George, 213
Banking systems
  in Asian financial crises, 132–33
  bankers' bank, 250–51
  bank runs and insolvency, 246–47
  contagion effects and weakness, 9,
    246
  in currency board environment,
    245–46
  deposit-guarantee system, 247–48
  effect of protectionism in East Asia,
    144–46
  European and U.S., 134
  moral hazard in Asian development
    model, 33

private clearinghouse association
    (CHA) banks, 251–52
  South Korea, 133, 145–46, 151,
    163–65
  Thailand, 129–30
Bankruptcy laws, Asian, 135
Bennett, William, 61
Bhagwati, Jagdish, 137, 141
Blair, Tony, 150
Boloña, Carlos, 179
Bordo, Michael, 259–60
Bork, Robert H., 61
Bourdieu, Pierre, 30
Brady plan, 264
Brazil
  devaluation, 268
  external debt service, 185
  fiscal deficit limit proposal, 184
  IMF agreements with, 174–75, 267
Bretton Woods agreement
  flaws in design of, 8, 215–20, 222
  gold demonetized under, 242
  gold standard under, 222
  problems of, 213–15
Buchanan, Pat, 43–44

Calomiris, Charles, 246, 267
Camdessus, Michel, 152, 154, 268
Capital controls
  arguments against, 137–38, 141
  under Bretton Woods (1950s), 218
  Chilean-type, 236
  in China, 139
  effect of, 142
  function of, 139
  in India, 139
  interwar period, 222
  Malaysia, 138, 140
Capital flows
  conditions discouraging, 140
  criticisms of capital mobility, 137
  demand for controls, 136–39
  distortion of, 143
  into East Asian countries (1990s),
    143–46

289

Cato Institute

Founded in 1977, the Cato Institute is a public policy research foundation dedicated to broadening the parameters of policy debate to allow consideration of more options that are consistent with the traditional American principles of limited government, individual liberty, and peace. To that end, the Institute strives to achieve greater involvement of the intelligent, concerned lay public in questions of policy and the proper role of government.

The Institute is named for *Cato's Letters*, libertarian pamphlets that were widely read in the American Colonies in the early 18th century and played a major role in laying the philosophical foundation for the American Revolution.

Despite the achievement of the nation's Founders, today virtually no aspect of life is free from government encroachment. A pervasive intolerance for individual rights is shown by government's arbitrary intrusions into private economic transactions and its disregard for civil liberties.

To counter that trend, the Cato Institute undertakes an extensive publications program that addresses the complete spectrum of policy issues. Books, monographs, and shorter studies are commissioned to examine the federal budget, Social Security, regulation, military spending, international trade, and myriad other issues. Major policy conferences are held throughout the year, from which papers are published thrice yearly in the *Cato Journal*. The Institute also publishes the quarterly magazine *Regulation*.

In order to maintain its independence, the Cato Institute accepts no government funding. Contributions are received from foundations, corporations, and individuals, and other revenue is generated from the sale of publications. The Institute is a nonprofit, tax-exempt, educational foundation under Section 501(c)3 of the Internal Revenue Code.

CATO INSTITUTE
1000 Massachusetts Ave., N.W.
Washington, D.C. 20001